BOXING IN PHILADELPHIA

BOXING IN PHILADELPHIA

Tales of Struggle and Survival

Gabe Oppenheim

ROWMAN & LITTLEFIELD
Lanham • Boulder • New York • London

Published by Rowman & Littlefield
A wholly owned subsidiary of The Rowman & Littlefield Publishing Group,
Inc.
4501 Forbes Boulevard, Suite 200, Lanham, Maryland 20706
www.rowman.com

16 Carlisle Street, London W1D 3BT, United Kingdom

British Library Cataloguing in Publication Information Available

Library of Congress Cataloging-in-Publication Data

Oppenheim, Gabe, 1987–
Boxing in Philadelphia : tales of struggle and survival / Gabe Oppenheim.
pages cm
Includes bibliographical references and index.
ISBN 978-1-4422-3645-5 (cloth : alk. paper) — ISBN 978-1-4422-3646-2 (ebook)
1. Boxing—Philadelphia—History. I. Title.
GV1125.O77 2015
796.830974811—dc23
2014016017

♾™ The paper used in this publication meets the minimum requirements of
American National Standard for Information Sciences Permanence of Paper
for Printed Library Materials, ANSI/NISO Z39.48-1992.

Printed in the United States of America

For the Ones with Heart

The defeat of one man is the triumph of the other: but we are apt to read this "triumph" as merely temporary and provisional. Only the defeat is permanent.
—Joyce Carol Oates, *On Boxing*

CONTENTS

ACKNOWLEDGMENTS

To Mr. Pat, RIP, who first introduced me to the world of Philly boxing. You weren't perfect, but neither was I, and we never would've met otherwise. To my editor, Christen Karniski, who took on these pages and gave them life.

To all of the Philadelphia fighters, past and present, for deciding I could be trusted: you worked too hard *not* to have some book like this exist, even if this one isn't exactly it. I hope you feel the trust wasn't misplaced.

To Russell Peltz, John DiSanto, Chuck Hasson, and Larry Merchant, for your knowledge and continual assistance. You four know more about the game than could ever fit in a book. And to all the other boxing officials who graciously shared their takes.

To all those at Penn who supported me, especially Jamie-Lynn Josselyn and Eric Karlan, who deserve the encouragement and kindness they so willingly offer others. To Greg Djanikian, for the support of my writing through the CPCW and Peregrine (to be published inside means a lot to me). To Al Filreis, for everything, but especially for that one semester of independent study, when I was entrusted to go off and try writing the Meldrick chapter. To Susan Cohen and Thomas Robinson, who talked to me when it got late. To the English Department of the University of Pennsylvania, for its grants and support.

And to Paul Hendrickson, less for the writing guidance of this project and others, and much more for the companionship and time. Time has always been the gift. What do we think of us now?

To Shira Koss, who believed in this book when it was three pages long. To Wayne Kabak, who believed in it when it was hundreds longer. To Avi Stern and Max Born for giving me a new start, and to Sam Goldberg, who believed in that new start because he believed in me.

To Ryan O'Donnell and Greg Cayea, for being boxing broskis.

Finally, to my family. To Mom and Dad, for your unconditional and irreplaceable love. Anything more I could say would be less. To Jon Oppenheim, for sitting with me to watch a good fight (and many other kind, brotherly acts).

And in memory of my grandfather, Jack Rosenfeld, whose whole life was an amazing testament to the human will to survive and who had within him a fighter's surpassing heart. It was a great blessing and privilege to be able to discuss with him bouts we had both watched, because he showed no less tenacity in life than the men in the ring we both admired. This is my ten count for him.

INTRODUCTION

The man from Philadelphia that night had been a pro for nine years, since the age of eighteen. In that time, the former drug runner had gained fifteen or so pounds to reach the light-heavyweight limit of 175. He had also lost chunks of his flesh to stab wounds and bullet holes, time to trials and charges, and that crucial bit of freedom that comes with an education. It had been a decade since he had dropped out of school.

All fighters lose immeasurable parts of themselves in sweat and pain and joy. Men are physical creatures. We wear down. But one thing Eric Harding had not lost was a fight. He had crawled through the ropes nineteen times and not once had the ref raised his opponent's hand. As long as he kept forcefully willing his hand into the ref's, he wouldn't worry. Not that it had been easy—it had been far from that. After his first fight, he had entered the Philadelphia night with a draw. Less than a month later, he was back in the ring, knocking out his opponent in one round. In his sixteenth fight, they put him against a 34–1 former champion on four days' notice. He was knocked down, as he would be many more times in his career, but he won a split decision. The final judge favored him by just four points.

Now it was June 2000, and in his twentieth fight Harding was facing a former Olympic medalist. The winner would become the world champion's mandatory challenger. Yet the *New York Times* was calling the bout "little anticipated."[1] That is how it was for a boy from his city. But Harding broke the Olympian's jaw and two of his ribs and won.

Less than three months later, as a 30–1 underdog, he gave the champion all he had. In the second round, he threw an overhand left—his power punch as a southpaw. The champion blocked it with his right hand. Harding's bicep tore like paper.

But he persevered through eight more rounds and would've gone all twelve had his trainer let him. Instead, the trainer took the ringside doctor's advice and threw in the towel. Eric Harding couldn't close his fist—and might never have closed it again had he continued. It was considered a technical knockout for the champion, but it almost didn't matter: up to that point, the judges' scorecards were grossly skewed for the champ, even though some ringside writers thought Harding had been winning.

The Philadelphia boy lost motivation after that. He bulked up to forty pounds more than his fighting weight. And in 2002, they paired him again with the lefty Olympian he had crushed and who hadn't lost since. In the fourth, the Olympian knocked him down with a perfect left. He rose on gelatin legs and wobbled around the ring until the bell.

Fifth round: the Olympian caught him with another left, and he plunged into the wide blue canvas like a brick smacking the face of the sea. A pause. He struggled to his feet as the ref counted to eight.

"Can you continue?" the ref asked. "Are you okay?"

"I'm from Philadelphia," he said, to indicate he was ready and willing, moments before being decked again—this time for good.

✿ ✿ ✿

Most boxing writers begin with an apology for the sport or an explanation of why they cannot apologize. I can't really do either. Joseph R. Svinth, a man who compiles boxing fatalities once said, "Me, I am neither for nor against boxing: like Zen, it is."[2]

That's kind of how I came about it, even if it's a little bit too high-minded a sentiment, a little too detached to really describe how I feel (I once asked a female boxing judge what she thought of Joyce Carol Oates's boxing work, figuring she'd be intrigued by the work of another woman deeply interested in boxing, and she said it was too surreal, too bathed in light, like it was floating in air—this was a few years before female combat sports became mainstream).

So boxing existed, and I wrote about it. That happened first. Whatever feelings I had came later. And they were so mixed up in my feelings for the people in the sport and for the stories they had—the stories

I knew I could tell, that I wanted to tell—that it was hard to figure out where my affection for one ended and the other began. I also can't deny that I became addicted to watching the fights on HBO and Showtime on Saturday nights, and that when things were shitty for me or even when they weren't, I felt real satisfaction in seeing an underdog pull one out over a favored fighter. And that I watch all the fights now.

Did it also help that I was a privileged kid from Scarsdale, New York, hanging out in gritty Philly gyms? Yeah, that had its own appeal, and again, who could separate that from the fighting? And did I flatter myself that I was following in the tradition of the masculine writers who had examined boxing—Mailer, Plimpton, Baldwin, Hemingway—even John Keats, who had traveled sixty miles round-trip with his brother to watch a fight in 1818 even though he was dying of tuberculosis?

Yes.

Both of those factors were things I also felt I had to contend with. It's not just that boxers grow suspicious when a clearly out-of-place white college student tries to enter their gym to talk to them; it's that I, too, grow suspicious of myself, not wanting to take advantage of anyone, to exploit people's real lives. You ask yourself what the hell you're doing there a lot, especially when you know all of your friends are hanging out on a leafy campus miles away.

I do honestly believe that there are real ties between boxing and the arts, though. Boxing, like any other sport, *isn't* art. But there's something there.

A 1931 *New York Times* article described how, years past his boxing prime, former light-heavyweight champion of the world Philadelphia Jack O'Brien took up the violin and held a concert with the New York Schools of Music.

> A long time back, when he was outpointing the opposition all over the country, he started wondering about himself. There was, he said, a something that made him do it; a something, indeed, that is called rhythm in the more effete professions. He considered it timing. . . . Finding the violin an agreeable sort of instrument, he started taking lessons. His instructors all agreed that he was very good. Some months ago, Mr. O'Brien read an article by Arthur Cremin, director of the New York Schools of Music, which expounded the same theory of rhythm. [3]

Not every boxer's skill translates to other forms of movement or expression. But the boxer's skill exists, as a set, as its own thing, a discipline and a craft. Boxers have that thing inside of them that they're continually honing. They're rigorous with it, and they speak about it as if it was a living, breathing thing, and they get disappointed when they don't execute it the way they should. They get angry and sad and they drink and they live life on its edges because their devotion is so intense. It's pretty artsy.

I began the project during my first week of college in Philadelphia. Like the overly ambitious, angsty kid I was, I had applied for a school newspaper column before even setting foot on campus the summer before my freshman year. I had gotten it, which seemed great at first, but less so when I realized I had absolutely nothing to write about. How can you tell kids what to think about their school when you've never been there before? So I decided I would do what I had begun doing in high school in Manhattan: walking around areas I knew were a little suspect, looking for interesting things—a kind of journalistic slumming that every journalist has done because every journalist is a kind of gold digger and, ironically, journalistic gold is more easily found in poor places.

It was hot. I remember sweating through the tight green shirt I was wearing and feeling disgusting. I walked down Walnut Street deeper into West Philadelphia, which I wouldn't have necessarily known was so rundown had it not been for the trip my parents had taken with me to Bed Bath and Beyond in the suburbs during move-in. To get there, we had to drive through West Philly, and I honestly had been shocked. Nothing I had ever seen in Harlem compared with the poverty and emptiness and desperation of the place. I don't think I saw a single window. Just boards of wood and people, like zombies, circling the same bits of sidewalk again and again.

So I started walking west. It took me only a few blocks to come upon an old black man sitting on an apartment building stoop and listening to a twenty-year-old transistor radio. He had a shaved, slightly wrinkled head. He had bushy black eyebrows, a mustache, and big, red plastic glasses. From the start, I had him marked. He looked interesting. If I had had to bet, I would've put money that he had a good story or two. Maybe he had been married and his wife had died and now he sat on the stoop and listened to the radio. Or maybe he had been sitting on the

A Police Athletic League boxing exhibition at the Schwartz Playground at Tenth and Jefferson Streets in 1969. Image courtesy of the Special Collections Research Center, Temple University Libraries, Philadelphia, PA.

same stoop for seventy-five years and had watched the neighborhood change. It really didn't matter. I just wanted something. Some substance.

And he gave it to me. He told me he was seventy-six, that he had been a boxing trainer to world champions, that he had had four wives who had died. That he was a recovered alcoholic who now spent his days writing poetry on his stoop and advising neighborhood children.

Of course, I wrote down everything he said and wrote a little column about this interesting man near the campus, and, boy, students would benefit from going beyond their classrooms to learn from the people who actually occupied the neighborhood around the school.

I'm cynical about the piece now. Not only because its moral is trite and maybe not even actionable and to be honest, Mr. Pat wasn't the most learned man and I'm not sure what a college student paying tuition to learn engineering could get from him, but also because Mr. Pat lied a lot to me that day. William Alfred Patterson, or Mr. Pat, as he told me to call him, had indeed been a boxing trainer but not exactly to world champions. Many fighters he had first trained had left him for other trainers and *then* became champs. And he had indeed had many wives, but they hadn't all suddenly expired on him as if he were some sort of poison.

I probably knew that he wasn't telling me everything. Because even though I took him at his word for the column, I went back for more a couple months later and then again months after that. I went to hear more of his boxing stories. To look at his scrapbooks of old articles about his fighters. To check out his mementos, like the jeans he bought when one of his welterweights fought in Milan in the 1970s.

He had lived a full life—forgetting about whether it was a good one or a moral one, it was a full one—he had been places, he had done things, and he had the stories to prove it. And though it took a lot of questioning to get at the truth of those stories, they ultimately stood up, more or less: the omissions were part of the stories. There was a real fabric there. This guy had lived.

And then there were the other people in the stories. The boxers and trainers and managers and mobsters. They had also lived. And the city they had all come up in, a tough place. This was all substance to an eighteen-year-old with very little to draw upon for his own stories. We all need stories to grab onto (but especially those of us who want to tell them).

Later I would graft on my own research about the way the city was a manufacturing center, a place that valued the work a man could do with his hands, and that when the city's industry rose, so did its boxing culture, and when its industry crumbled, so did its boxing culture. Later I'd really try to shape the thing, to make a narrative out of one trainer, one sport, and one city.

But at first, when I walked to Mr. Pat's smoke-filled apartment—he loved his menthol cigarettes—I was just looking for real stuff. Newspaper clips—they were real. Photos of old amateur fighters with their coaches—also real. The pipe Mr. Pat kept near him to swing at intruders and the gun by his bed—scary as hell—but still real. Not exactly what brought me there—a little too real, not enough history there—but still.

I loved when Mr. Pat would tell me about the way a fighter fought and then add, "Oh, did you know that he was also a drummer in a band?" I also liked when he got really quiet and refused to tell me what happened to a specific fighter. It scared me—it meant that once I finally decided there was a book in all these visits, I had to fill in these huge gaps he was leaving me—but the silence also meant things had happened.

Sonny Liston, the heavyweight champion who lived in Philadelphia, who was for a time controlled by its mob, and who lost his title and later fights to Ali that may or may not have been fixed, said: "Someday they're gonna write a blues song just for fighters. It will be for a slow guitar, soft trumpet, and a bell."[4]

After I started writing this book, I made a point of interviewing as many current and former fighters as I could. One hot summer day I visited 1960s lightweight Sweet Pea Adams, who, with a record of 17–5–2, left the game in relatively good shape when he realized he was never going to reach the top (and also because his management had, against his will, injected him in his left ass cheek with a "booster" in order to better his performance, which he felt ashamed about). He had a black Honeywell fan humming on the floor. Just past the coffee table, which was covered in envelopes and small glass candy jars, was a wooden cabinet on which he had set out at least five boxing trophies and two photographs. In his dining room he had hung an oil painting of himself in his boxing trunks, with no shirt, and his hands wrapped. Sweet Pea tried to make it sound as if he had made peace with his career. "Sometimes you lose, but you win," he said. "I didn't make it in the ring, but I made it in life." He looked sharp in a gray shirt with blue vertical stripes, plastic aviator glasses, and pointy black leather shoes. His arms were still muscled. "Like I said, the best man don't always win. But in reality, you do. Because sometime you gain from the loss."

Then tears welled up in his eyes, and he had to stop speaking.

* * *

The forgotten English writer Denzil Batchelor wrote, "I should be content to see no more fights—but very sad indeed to have to foreswear the literature this disgrace and glory of the past has produced."[5]

It's sort of a problem: the goal of the game is to hurt someone, which immediately makes the game worth writing about, though writing about something almost implicitly condones it.

Let's run through arguments quickly. Fighting is brutal and animalistic. It doesn't matter that auto racing might be more dangerous or more often fatal, because the point of auto racing isn't to damage someone else's body. That's just a tragic, occasional result.

But boxers can also raise themselves from terrible circumstances when they fight, and those who criticize the game don't realize how few chances the kids who get into boxing really have. It's not like they can just go to school and pursue math. There's a whole life on the streets that occupies their time out of school and sometimes pulls them away from school. The schools are shitty anyway, and not everyone—especially the really bad kids—can work together on a team. They need that lonely, individual pursuit. There really are some people whom boxing has saved. They'd be dead without it—or in jail.

Even for the kids who don't need boxing to save them, boxing is a way for a kid to make a name for himself. When the odds are high that you will die completely anonymously, as just another person in a blighted area, that means something. The fame impulse is lauded in Lady Gaga. I know Lady Gaga doesn't beat people in a square ring for a living, but the fame impulse is also what drives the fighters. They want to have a name. To be a name. And look at what they're willing to do to get there. In order to make themselves, they're willing to risk losing themselves completely.

Shit.

The eighteenth-century fighter Big Ben Brain's epitaph reads, "Yet bravely I'll dispute the prize, / nor yield, though out of breath, / 'Tis not a fall—I yet shall rise, / and conquer even Death!"

There's also the argument that a culture that values hand combat doesn't turn to guns for violence—it solves things mano a mano. I'm not sure whether that's true. And I'm too young to say, look, back when boxing existed, everyone was more civil and people didn't gun each other down. It might be true, but I wasn't around to see it. But even for me, someone born in 1987, it really does seem like people respected each other more when there wasn't this continual pop-cultural talk about "respect" and "dissing" and when disagreeing with someone, in the worst-case scenario, meant raising your fists for a awhile and then after the dirty business was done, shaking hands and walking off into the sunset, or the bar, together. Maybe that's just a fantasy, and life was never really like that. I don't know, and it's not really the kind of thing you can research. There are too many factors underlying violence in American cities to explain how it got so out of hand and so deadly. But boxers, at the end of fights, always shake each other's hands, and they often hug. You'll never see camaraderie like that anywhere else in sport. Once when I was in college and watched a really tense fight on Showtime on a Saturday night, the underdog won. I was so excited that I called my girlfriend to my side of the room so she could see what I was seeing. She was flabbergasted at the sight of the two fighters embracing. She had not expected that. She had expected something much more brutal.

Another thing I learned writing this book: Boxing *is* much less brutal on TV. It just is. There are graphics and announcers, and even though the microphones over the ring capture the thud of the blows and even though super slo-mo captures the rippling of the skin after a shot lands, it doesn't feel as real or as painful or as permanent as it does in person. Fights in person aren't contained in the box of the TV. There's nothing controlled and polished and produced about them. One time, I was sitting ringside for a fight card in Northeast Philadelphia, and I had to close my laptop on the press table because the fighters' sweat, every time they thwacked each other, was flying off their bodies into my keyboard, and I was afraid it was gonna short the computer.

❊ ❊ ❊

Neighborhood boys spar on Harper Street in 1969, as part of the summer program Youthmobile, which brought equipment and staff to certain blocks over eight weeks. Courtesy of the Special Collections Research Center, Temple University Libraries, Philadelphia, PA.

Three years after I began this book, I suffered a few minor concussions—not from fighting but from stupid accidents. All the same, I was unlucky to suffer months of post-concussion syndrome, and it was awful. I was dizzy. Disoriented. I couldn't read or concentrate on TV. I couldn't carry on conversations or remember what I had just been thinking. I couldn't control my emotions. I screamed for no reason. I grabbed both ends of the collars of my T-shirts and tore at them like Hulk Hogan. I shredded at least ten, and I cried a lot. The point of all this is that no boxer (or NFL player, for that matter)—not even the guy who has seen Muhammad Ali and truly believes he knows the risks he's taking—can understand what it's like to undergo brain damage, however minor. Because in order to imagine that damage, you have to use your brain—which in the event of this injury, you will no longer have. The brain can't imagine what it's like not to have a brain. It just can't.

An argument against fighting.

✻ ✻ ✻

A little bit more about Philadelphia. Like all former industrial American cities—like Detroit and Baltimore and Camden and Newark—it's empty now, a carcass of what it was. Just so many old, broken-down factories, and the people are gone, so no one's paying taxes to fix anything, and it's a fucking mess. Philadelphia isn't the only American city like that, and I don't even know how you would go about determining the worst one of them all (I'm imagining some sort of toughness competition between the very hardest, most deprived residents of all the cities—it's a dystopian American movie waiting to be made by Clint Eastwood). But I was in Philadelphia already, so that made the choice of writing about it obvious, and then I got lucky, because as it turns out, Philadelphia really is the birthplace of boxing in America—and also the birthplace of the modern American city. And it might be the earliest example of one city getting screwed by a wealthier, more prestigious city that it goes on to envy.

Philadelphia was once a far more successful place than New York. That didn't last, and Philadelphia has been pissed ever since. Philadelphia invented the city grid plan, and New York copied it and did it on a larger and now way-more-famous scale.

There's also something great about the collision between the haves and have-nots in Philly in all the Golden Age movies set in Philadelphia, something I think Hollywood sort of knew about, even if it didn't openly express it. Philadelphia's light-heavyweight champ Jack O'Brien was once training in the gym when Anthony J. Drexel Biddle, the most WASPish, upper-crust Philadelphian of the time, walked in with an opera tenor. Now, Biddle was known to have dabbled in boxing as an amateur and taken a real liking to the sport, so the sight of him in the gym wasn't a total surprise. But what happened next was. The *opera tenor* hopped in the ring and went three strong rounds with the Hall of Famer. "It was a vigorous display," reported the *New York Times*, "with both men slamming away as though they were fighting for a championship title."[6]

Biddle is actually the man who made boxing legal in New York long after it had become standard in Philadelphia. In 1920, the Catholic governor of New York, Al Smith, didn't want to sign the bill to legalize boxing in his state because he feared voters would see it as a Catholic ploy aimed at helping fellow Catholics (since many fighters then were Irish and Italian). So he told a state senator to gather one hundred letters of support from Protestant clergymen over a single weekend. The state senator, figuring the job impossible, called up Biddle for help. Biddle mustered more than six hundred Protestant clergymen's telegrams and letters by Monday morning.[7] And so boxing became legal in New York as a result of the work of the most prominent, ritziest man in Philadelphia.

❖ ❖ ❖

In Philadelphia—ironically, the Quaker City and the City of Brotherly Love—fighting was already ingrained in the culture. It began with fighters holding "sparring contests" of four rounds, and then six, for "scientific points."[8] The law banned official decisions based on these points, but gamblers merely circumvented this by agreeing in advance to follow the judgment of a certain newspaper. Chuck Hasson, the great Philly boxing historian, has argued that Philly fighters became such tough, always-grinding warriors because the culture began with short fights in which every second really counted.

What's for certain is that these early fights are where the slick American style of sticking and moving and bobbing and weaving— where *all* the fundamentals of technical fighting—really developed. The great thing about boxing fundamentals is that they're passed down from one generation of trainers to the next—and if you take a look, some of the greatest trainers of all time, and some of the greatest fighters, too, were touched by the teachings and the styles that came out of Philly— like the blues out of the Mississippi Delta—in the early 1900s. Jack Johnson, the controversial first black heavyweight champ, fought more times in Philly than in any other city besides his hometown. Sugar Ray Robinson, perhaps the best boxer ever, fought under his first promotional contract in Philly, appearing there twenty times. Joe Louis, perhaps the greatest heavyweight of all time, was trained by Jack Blackburn, a lightweight who fought out of Philly at the turn of the century.

I mention the trainers because, as important as the fighters were, it was the trainers who built up a body of boxing knowledge and passed it on. You gotta love the idea of these guys who have seen everything, who know every angle, who can watch a fight and see twenty things you missed. They know what they're looking at when they watch a fight; they know what to look for.

But if these guys are like the camp counselors—the guys who have been around and get how the place is run and how to fit in—then the boxers are like the campers who come into camp every year with their own styles and their own ideas and aren't necessarily willing to bend to the camp's rules or to do things the conventional way. There's that continual push-pull between tradition and individuality.

I just love Johnny "Bang-Bang" Alford. He fought from 1959 to 1968 and became known as one of the city's great boxing characters. He read *Julius Caesar* and *Cyrano de Bergerac* and loved messing with his opponents' heads. In October 1961, his manager told a newspaper, "You know how Cyrano always used to improvise a rhyme just before he ran his sword through an opponent? Well, Johnny actually did the same thing one day in the gym. He was boxing Frankie Taylor and all of a sudden he said, 'Your hands are quick, your heart is stout, but now I'm going to knock you out.' And damned if he didn't hit Frankie with a right hand and deck him."[9]

And imagine: Johnny "Bang-Bang" was doing his verse recitation and boxing in a city made of brick that was crumbling all around him, that was half on fire, where every day there were more guns and more drugs.

How can you not tell that story?

I took the book's epigraph from Joyce Carol Oates's *On Boxing* because of one unforgettable phrase: "Only the defeat is permanent." But I tend to agree with the female boxing judge about the book. If you're gonna write about boxing, you need facts and grittiness and maybe even some awkward bad writing. It can't be perfect. It can't be ethereal. It can't be self-contained. It can't be its own art. It has to be bled into by the fighting itself.

But only the defeat *is* permanent in boxing. And I guess the point of the book is to ask, could it really ever be any other way?

Again and again and again and again and again and again and again.

Until you can't ask it anymore because you're fucking tired of it.

This is not a conventional fight story narrative—there are only eight long chapters, each a meditation on a different aspect of this city, its workers and fighters. One is about death because death can't help but intrude continually into the proceedings of this violent town and the

thoughts of all fighters. Several chapters are profiles of individual fighters, because a single fighter's story often reflects his community's. And
finally, because my primary goal was not to write a linear history—
although a dark story emerges in pieces and ultimately comes together
at the end—it was to capture the fighting city's essence, which meant
attacking the subject from different angles, boxing the hell out of it,
sticking and moving. Any boxer will tell you: the unseen punches are
always the hardest to take.

Part One

Victims of Their Own Momentum

I

THE YOUNG

How a Young Boxer of 18 Became Old, Tired and 28
—*New York Times* headline, November 20, 1977

The first time I met Mr. Pat, we spoke outside his apartment building—an old crumbling mansion that had probably been divided first into two houses but now was split into many smaller apartments. I didn't ask to enter his building that first day, and I don't think he would've let me.

But when I returned a month later, he took me up to his one-bedroom apartment. Up the creaky stairs, where the carpet was so thin in places you could see the wood beneath it, past the apartment with the bullhorns over its door, and finally down the hall into a dingy living room with a metal pipe tucked behind the front door (in case of intruders).

Mr. Pat had drawn the window shades, so there was only dim yellow light from a lamp in the room, and he raised the heat as high as it could go. He sat in a small chair by his desk, and I sat on a futon covered in cat hair from Princess, the cat his daughter had left behind when she had moved out. A large old wooden cabinet TV covered a sizable patch of the room—Mr. Pat said it would work fine if it had a voice chip. He smoked—Newports—and he always asked me whether I minded after he had lit up. The sallow brownness of the room and the heat and the cat hair gave the place a forgotten quality as if no one would notice were this room and person to disappear. The place felt pent-up and forgotten already. Even Mr. Pat seemed burdened by its degradation. I used to stare at him from my uncomfortable position on the futon—is there any other?—brushing the cat hair from my pants, my eyes catching small holes in the white Velcro sneakers that he had bought from Publishers Clearinghouse as he clutched a rolled-up magazine in his hand that he called the Persuader and waited for that damn cat. Then Princess would lazily paw into the room, purring, making sure to rub her body against my corduroy pants. She would then step into her water bowl, and Mr. Pat would slam the Persuader against the table to scare her. "If I find out what you're saying," he'd say, "I'ma kick your ass."

On my first visit into this apartment, he took out one of his scrapbooks for me to review. I first opened to a yellowed photo of 240-pound heavyweight "Two Ton" Tony Galento staring down Joe Louis. June 3, 1939. Then a late-'70s article on Alfonso Hayman. He was Mr. Pat's welterweight contender, and he brought a baby bottle to a press conference—a gift for what he called his "crybaby" opponent, Miguel Barreto. And eventually, after a piece on Cassius Clay, a small handwritten note on a steno sheet.

It stood out from the clutter of stained newsprint and cracked photos. It was just cursive on a notepad.

> *To: My girl*
> *Lena Horne*
> *Good Luck*
> *From Jimmy Young*

"Jimmy Young was a fighter," Mr. Pat said. "Lena Horne's my old lady—"

"Jimmy Young," I said, "was he one of your guys?"

"No," Mr. Pat said, his voice now a whisper. "Lena—she died."

"How'd you get this piece of paper?"

"He wrote it. He met her. At one of them fights." A pause. "I introduced him."

And so there was the link: Mr. Pat recalled Jimmy Young when recalling his obese lover, the sterile one who would paint him in the nude and win everyone over and die of cancer after they broke up after Mr. Pat had cheated. That was his Lena Horne, not the famous singer. But Mr. Pat's meekness when I asked him about Jimmy Young the fighter—he was barely audible—seemed unrelated to what had transpired with Lena. "Jimmy Young?" I had questioned, and Mr. Pat had just whispered. There had to be a reason.

* * *

It started when Jimmy Young was a boy.

A gang had stolen a transistor radio from him that he had bought with money earned folding clothing at a Laundromat.[1] This so upset him—he already thought of himself as weak and fat—that he grabbed a butcher knife and a wrench and set off across North Philly searching for the gang. He never found them, and when he returned home, his dad, Bill, told him to take up boxing.

Meanwhile, his first cousin, Bobby "Boogaloo" Watts, had also been bullied—mugged and sucker punched in the back of the head.

Together, the two boys decided to begin training at the Twenty-third Street Police Athletic League gym.

* * *

Jimmy Young turned pro as a heavyweight in 1969, after twenty-one amateur bouts. He was twenty years old. He had a wife and two young girls.

It was in Philadelphia's Blue Horizon, a former Moose lodge on North Broad Street that was nicknamed the "House of Pain." The place had been converted eight years earlier, but a moose head still protruded from the front of the building. Inside the former auditorium, spectators sat on wooden balconies suspended right over the ring—so close you'd think you could touch the fighters inside.[2]

Young's opponent was a guy from Virginia who came to the weigh-in wearing white trunks with rags stapled to them. The commissioner said, "What color trunks are you wearing tonight?" And Jimmy "Ragman" Jones said, "I'm wearing these." The commissioner said, "No you're not. You ain't wearing them here."

Jimmy Young knocked him out in one minute and two seconds.

His second fight was hard. It was a match made by J. Russell Peltz, a young new promoter who wanted to see local guys duke it out. "His second fight was a really good fight," Peltz says today. "A tough kid, Johnny Gause, from another section of the city. Not your ordinary second—well, today it wouldn't be your ordinary second fight. Back then it was." Young won, but his managers decided that intra-Philly fights were dangerous. The word on the street about Philly fighters was that they beat each other so hard and so often in their own city—in the gyms and in official matches—that they never made it onto the national stage. So

Young's managers and trainers moved him and his cousin Boogaloo Watts to the West Coast.

It turned out to be a bad decision.

"It wasn't in our favor," Watts says now. "Because we went into other guys' backyards." The cousins lost a combined three of four on the West Coast. When they got back, Young again faced difficult opposition. He was cast as a last-minute substitute against Roy "Tiger" Williams, six feet five inches and 230 pounds. A man who would win the Pennsylvania State Heavyweight Title within a year. Young lost.

Young won some and lost some, and he needed money. His new manager, Frank Gelb, would take him to Boys Clubs, where he entertained the kids with his skills. He worked on houses and on the docks. He boxed three exhibitions with Muhammad Ali. They weren't the greatest paydays (for one he received $50), but Young "noticed that when [Ali] punched, he punched in combinations. And that he's a relaxed fighter."[3]

These are lessons he would use later.

* * *

Young's next opponent was gaining steam fast, like a runaway train. He was twenty-seven-year-old Earnie Shavers, whose family had been driven from Alabama by the Ku Klux Klan. A fighter who shaved his head long before that was popular, earning the nickname "Acorn" as an alternative to his other title, "The Black Destroyer," Shavers had grown up in Ohio. When he turned pro in 1969, he took a fight about every week, compiling a record of 42–2 to Young's 7–3 during the same time period. He had failed to knock out his opponent only once. Otherwise, he had destroyed everyone. In Canton and Omaha, at first. Then Miami and Vegas. Sixteen guys out in the first round alone. Ten in the second.

But Shavers had caught the eye of Don King, the Cleveland numbers-writer who entered boxing after serving four years in prison for stomping and pistol-whipping a man to death. The previous Christmas, one of Shavers's three copromoters had offered King a stake in the puncher. Later, King bought a third of the fighter's promotional rights for $8,000 in cash.

This little transaction was important. Shavers was one of the first men Don King bought a stake in. Jimmy Young would come later.

* * *

In boxing's weird way, in its peculiar version of a traditional marriage, the match was set: Young–Shavers for February 19, 1973, in the Spectrum, Philly's relatively new 18,000-seat arena at the southern tip of Broad Street. Exactly thirty-two years before Jimmy Young's last full day alive.

The Supremes sang the national anthem. The match was judged by two men and Carol Polis, making her debut as the first female judge ever.

The fight was a disaster for Young. Shavers knocked him down once in the first and twice more in the third, and the ref stopped it one second away from the bell at the end of the round, a particularly Philly-type loss.[4] Polis "was glad it ended the way it did just because it was my first fight," while the *Inquirer* staff distinguished itself with the headline, "Woman Judge Is Untested."[5]

It was the start of 1973, with Jimmy Young beaten, helpless, under the lights of the Spectrum in South Philly, by the shipyards of Roosevelt Park and the U.S. Naval Reservation. Just west of what was called The Neck, where the squatters lived, a boondocks of wooden clapboard shacks and unpaved streets, mud in the front yard, shithouses in the back. And in a photo at Temple University's archives, a barefoot boy with something dark smeared on his face, staring into a distant camera, amid the puddles, with a look that says he wants to leave. That boy, for all intents and purposes, was now Jimmy Young.[6]

After taking two more six rounders in Philly, Young left. He fought in Maryland, London, Caracas. Aside from one draw, he won them all. In one fight, he knocked out the future European champ. In the rest he won decisions, which was more in keeping with his style. For who was Jimmy Young, this "Yank from Philadelphia,"[7] as he became known in England?

He was a man who was about to gain an identity. He was a slick counterpuncher. A throwback to the old-style Philly boxers, the ones of the first four decades of the twentieth century, who treated the game like a science and waited patiently for holes to open in opponents' offenses before punching with precision.

The style lasted until TV cameras invaded the ring and the slums grew poorer and a new gym-war style developed, whereby the victor was he who had shed less blood before the zoomed-in lens, he who had slugged his way out of the now-drug-infested ghetto and into the spotlight. Technique doesn't look cool on TV. But Jimmy Young had given up Philly as a fight-home,[8] and in a way, he had turned his back on the entire fucking era, which never seemed to respect his abilities anyway. So he was an anachronism, and he fought with panache.

He didn't lack grit. He was stylishly gritty. In the ring, he would snarl, opening his mouth and raising his cheeks and narrowing the slits of his eyes. His small ears seemed to recede. It looked like he had just spat on his opponent. The look roared nasty.

Outside the ring, he was smooth as marble, with a tufty but trim near-Afro, toothpick-thin mustache and baby cheeks that shone. When he climbed through the ropes in glittery regalia, he did seem regal, as if he had merited the robes for being so damned suave.

"He was a good boxer," promoter Russell Peltz recalls. "He was not your typical Philly fighter—that's for sure. He was a boxer. A cute guy."

Over a year and a half, Young racked up six wins. Then he challenged Earnie Shavers again, this time in Landover, Maryland. It was ruled a draw, but those who saw it say Young won.[9] The Associated Press termed the decision "unpopular." And Young, on manager Frank Gelb's advice, kept pushing. They accepted about $4,000 to go to Honolulu to fight the third-ranked contender, Ron Lyle. Young won by counterpunching the slugger. A methodical, chess match style. "I planned to fight him just the way I did," he said afterward. "And I was able to." Randy Neumann, a boxer who had out-finessed Young two years earlier, grew impressed with Jimmy's moves. "Lyle was killer," he says today. "Lyle was one badass. Beating him was big stuff."

* * *

Big stuff does not go unnoticed in the boxing world. Promoters, managers, and trainers are always searching for the next rough jewel. And while the search initially benefits the unnoticed fighter, it also tends to confuse him, quickly, into submission. For as soon as word gets out—as soon as a man flies to the island of Oahu and defeats a third-ranked contender—there ensues a chaotic rush to the prize. The spoils go to he who sidles up to the man-boy's ear before the others, he who whispers the right notes in a lilting symphony of seduction.

Frank Gelb, Young's manager, sold his rights to the fighter to a man named Jack Levin who ran an electric supplies store. Jack Levin was really in cahoots with Frank "Blinky" Palermo, a septuagenarian mobster with slants for eyes, tiny ears tucked into slicked black hair, and a double chin.

You wanna know about Blinky Palermo? He was the old-school mobster who spoke with a rasp. The guy who ran boxing in the 1950s. They sarcastically called him "Saint Francis." Back then, before he went to prison for trying to take over the welterweight champ's career, he led a double life. He fixed boxing matches and extorted money on one hand. On the other, he moonlighted as an honest deli manager. The place was Margolis's at Thirty-ninth and Sansom. Peter Dougherty, a man who grew up in the neighborhood, used to stop at the deli for a Tastykake on his way to school. "He looked to me like a criminal," he says now. "He was a slightly scary character."

Slightly scary? One manager who had a run-in with Palermo once received an anonymous telephone call with this message: "It'll be with a pipe wrapped in a paper sack. You'll never know what hit you."

Now it was the early 1970s. Blinky had just gotten out of prison. He hung around the automat in West Philly. He got in touch with the official manager of Jimmy Young, who was in the area. He also got in touch with Don King. The men who would ruin the fighter's career were in place.

* * *

There is a tape. A small microcassette recorded a few years before Jimmy Young died by two guys who had met him at autograph shows and felt bad about his condition, financial and otherwise. Guys who wanted to hear his story and take him out for some food and some beer on them ("I'm not paying for this," Young would say, just to make sure. "I ain't got nothin'!"). So they chatted over breakfast and they asked him whether Don King was his manager in '75. It wasn't just King, he said, looking scared as shit. "No, Blinky Palermo. I told you about him. He died a few years ago. Blinky, the gangster from New York. I hooked up with him. . . . Blinky stole my money. He stole it. That's what Blinky all about. They both did. Both of them. This nigger's bad, man."

* * *

Why did Jimmy Young go "along with the flow of things," as one writer who knew him said? It's a valid question. Did he, at the time, believe Palermo and his promoter-partner Don King would pursue his best interests? Surely, he must've known whom he was dealing with. By

The mobster Frank "Blinky" Palermo gestures at the press after the FBI arrested him and other crooked boxing figures on September 22, 1959. Corbis Images.

the mid-'70s, news of Palermo and King's malfeasance had circulated the gyms like sweat, flicked in drops off one body and spattered onto another. Aside from killing two people, King had already stolen $72,000 from one of Earnie Shavers's purses,[10] and Palermo was out on parole in connection with boxing-related crimes. One wonders what kind of man would have trusted them. He would have had to be criminal himself, one might think, before realizing that the most desperate men seek help where they find it. In 1975, Don King had already amassed a record of big money fights, having single-handedly conned the poor nation of Zaire and its paranoid leader into putting up $10 million for what became the Rumble in the Jungle. And in 1975, Jimmy Young was broke, having never earned enough from the ring to cover expenses for his family, who even today won't tell the story of Young's career without receiving payment first.[11] Young had worked odd jobs: welding, constructing buildings, driving trucks. He was a part-time longshoreman.[12]

"He was very close with his wife, Barbara, and with his children," Gelb would later say about the decisions that led to the management shift.

So there was that, the way a man who fought for a living needed more prominent fights just to feed Barbara, his own "growling stomach,"[13] and, eventually, five children. And of course, there was the hope, ever present in any proud fighter, of a title shot: some meaningful piece of history that would remain his regardless of losses thereafter. Jimmy Young probably did believe Palermo and King could get him that shot. Years later, Young said they promised him "the chance to get in there" with the big names "to get ahead and make some money."[14] Boxers fall hard for the sophistry of their suitors.[15] There's a reason, after all, that Don King was able to send a letter to Madison Square Garden in 1978, telling it to "please contact me for the services of the following fighters" and then to list the heavyweight champ and six of the top ten contenders (including Young). And there's a reason that, after signing with new management, Jimmy Young would say to other fighters, "See? The world doesn't revolve around Philly."[16] It's not that he wasn't intelligent. Young's North Philly background definitely made him streetwise. But the reason he—as have almost all boxers—enthralled in the courtship sprang from his lifestyle.

Boxers come from unstable families. They don't trust in money to be received later. They trust now.

It's why Don King carried thousands of dollars of cash in his jackets, ready to disburse to any upset fighter who realized his purse had been skimmed by hundreds of thousands. He understood the psychological advantage of greenback wads over paper checks.[17]

So Young beat Lyle, and Palermo and King pounced. They didn't just advise. They dictated. Ordered. In Scranton, King forced Young to sign two contracts with differing compensation within five hours. Of course, King enforced the contract that paid Young less, bilking him out of a "measly $500."[18] At one meeting in Philadelphia, Young and his trainer Bob Brown tried to get in a word. "Sit down and shut the fuck up!" Blinky interjected. "You'll do what you're told."

"I mean, you would think that the mob wouldn't have been that big a deal after awhile," recalls Russell Peltz. "But as long as Blinky was around, they really trashed Jimmy Young."

Yet Blinky Palermo and Don King got Jimmy Young his title fight one April night in 1976.

* * *

"Dadadada . . . dadadada . . . dadadadadaaa!" the Monday Night Football theme blares. A bell rings. On ABC, highlights roll of each fighter. The lights dim in the Capital Centre in Landover, Maryland, leaving only the unnatural radiance of high-wattage lamps illuminating the ring. Howard Cosell launches: "THIS EXCLUSIVE ABC SPORTS PRESENTATION IS BROUGHT TO YOU BY CHRYSLA!" The fans scream—12,472 men, women, and children—and Cosell builds— "We're back LIVE!"—and in shuffles the shadowboxing champ: the Greatest, the Louisville Lip, the renegade, the Muslim. The thirty-four-year-old dancer-warrior-jabber-feinter-comebacker-rope-a-doper. The lithe-giant-snapper-dodger-right-hand-leader-talker-walker-stinger-floater-hyper-ducker-slipper-dipper-jungler-rumbler-Manilla-thrilla-Frazier-slayer-Foreman-killer-Wepner-cutter-Norton-loser-King-defi-er-press-relier-caramel-colored-Ali-baby.[19] He climbs into the ring, swarmed by the posse. He wears white trunks with a black stripe. The ref recites instructions. Ali ignores him, pretending to shadowbox. In the other corner, a twenty-seven-year-old challenger from Philadelphia stands waiting. It is not his show, this carnival culmination of a zany, loony, roller-coaster-Barnum-and-Bailey-cavalcade of a week. And if it's all about to end, it seems he was never there from the beginning.

* * *

It took off a week earlier, with caravans rolling from New York and Philly and D.C. Planes whooshing from LA and Chicago. All to see Ali on this yellow-submarine-magic-school-bus tour. You see, Ali had just fought Joe Frazier for the third time the previous year, and the fight had nearly killed him. He returned to the dressing room that night with "the greyness of terminal exhaustion," moving "as if the marrow of his bones had been replaced by mercury."[20]

So now he was telling everyone that he was in the last year of his career. That he was gonna take a few tune-up fights and then he was gonna face Ken Norton and George Foreman, the only two men in the world who might beat him (Norton already had defeated Ali and broken his jaw, and Foreman had pummeled him but played into his rope-a-dope strategy and lost). The truth is, Ali didn't want to face either man. He was scared of both. That was what fueled the champ at this stage of his career. He wasn't facing nobodies as a rest. He was facing nobodies because he felt he needed to—and his handlers were starting to feel the same.

Enter Don King.

He offered Ali $1 million to take on a real nobody: Jean Pierre Coopman, the 206-pound, six-foot Belgian sculptor and portrait artist. Ali was happy to accept. They made the match in Puerto Rico. And to sweeten the deal, they added in a fight on the undercard featuring another nobody Ali would face next: Jimmy Young.

This tour was all about drumming up entertainment to hide the lack of danger.

Fifty miles from San Juan, a voodoo witch in a shack examined Coopman and declared that he'd win. Coopman's band of five hundred Belgians shouted with mad delight, waving a flag of black and yellow.

"What's that animal on that flag?" Ali asked.

"A lion," said the Belgians.

"Looks more like a dragon or some ugly ol' lizard," Ali said.

Ali picked up a bad head cold and a whooping cough, and the Belgians said they had a shot. Then fire struck the El San Juan hotel at noon on the day before the fight, and all the writers and hangers-on ran past the pools toward the ocean. Ever the actor, Ali remained in his fifth-floor suite and showered before walking down the smoky hallway and riding an elevator to the lobby. At five o'clock, Ali and Coopman arrived at the 12,000-seat indoor Roberto Clemente Coliseum for the weigh-in. As usual, Ali chanted, "Hail, the conquering hero comes! Surrounded by a bunch of bums." He then called Coopman "Cooperman" as the Belgian walked onto the scale wearing red and white swim trunks.

Wrote Red Smith: "The Lion of Flanders looks like the tamest, friendliest jungle beast this side of Ringling Brothers."

Also at the weigh-in were two heavyweights matched on the under-card: Jimmy Young and "King" Roman. Roman was also run by the mob and was brought in by Don King specifically so Young could kick the shit out of someone and thereby become a credible opponent for Ali (not that real aficionados would ever accept the legitimacy of such a win). Except on the night that Ali KO'd Coopman, Jimmy Young looked terrible. Mostly it was Roman's fault. He hit Young below the belt and head-butted him, and no opponent could look good against that. But here Young was, given a stiff he was supposed to be able to knock out, and all Young could do was go ten rounds with him and win a decision. Worse, it turned out that Roman had just lost a month before in South Africa, and Young had opened preexisting cuts.

Still, King had made his match and he was going to stick with it. He never did care what the public thought.

Thus, three weeks later, when the Ali–Young fight was officially announced, everyone assumed it to be a continuation of the carnival. Muhammad Ali's version of Joe Louis's "bum-of-the-month club."

"This Young is a joke, like Coopman," promoter Bob Arum told the *New York Times*. Ali wasn't training. He had just revealed a deal for a toy doll in his likeness. Then he had flown to London on a tour to promote his autobiography, *The Greatest*. The crowds in the department stores had shouted his name and grabbed at him. Ali had just eluded them and hopped a plane for Chicago.

On the sixty-seventh floor of Rockefeller Plaza, Don King danced his jive, freewheeling, only-in-America, electroshock publicity bop: "I think it's a wonderful country that you can find fighters like this and pay them so much money," he told a reporter. "Jim Young will make more money than he ever has before." King had wanted to hold the fight in Costa Rica but said he decided on the Capital Centre in Maryland after its head, Abe Pollin, guaranteed Ali's $1.5 million purse. Young was to make between $75,000 and $100,000.

In the coming weeks, writers—back when there were fight writers, men who spent their lives on the trail of exquisite foulness—rolled in from all corners. Randy Neumann was hired by the *New York Post* to cover the fight, since he had once beaten Young. He hopped a ride to Maryland with his buddy and occasional colleague Jerry Lisker, the *Post* beat who'd become editor the next year. Bob Waters came down from Long Island's *Newsday* and Tom Cushman from the *Philadelphia Daily*

News. Dick Young from the *New York Daily News* and Ed Schuyler from the Associated Press. Bill Lyon and Gene Courtney from the *Philadelphia Inquirer* and Dave Anderson from the *New York Times.* They were, in a way similar to the fighters they covered, childlike in their devotion. They'd talk to all the trainers and cornermen, looking for juicy tips about this boxer's weakness or that one's problems out of the ring. They'd spend long nights in hotel bars, downing beers and sharing tales of the prize ring, competing for story of the night. And the next groggy morning, they'd follow the boxers into the sanctuary of the gym (or, in this case, a converted motel ballroom) to watch them pound the bags and spar. Not that Ali was sparring much that week. He boxed his only practice rounds on Monday, four days before the fight, prompting one guy who had paid $4 to watch him to say, "Hey, Ali! I spent part of my unemployment check to see you. Now do something." On Tuesday, Ali was busy flirting with President Ford's eighteen-year-old daughter, Susan, in his hotel suite.

Afterward he told the press: "If you knew Susan like I know Susan. . . ."[21]

Meanwhile, Jimmy Young sparred three rounds in a motel ballroom with Mike Koranicki, another heavyweight from Philly. Young chose Koranicki because he had fast hands and could mimic Ali.[22] A few years back, Young had sparred with Ali, and he had seen firsthand the wisdom in sometimes losing the gym rounds, if only to prepare for the real rounds. Ali had let Roy "Tiger" Williams pound his ass before Zaire, so that The Greatest would be able to withstand George Foreman's bruising. Jimmy Young surely recalled that fight's ending, the surreal eighth round when Ali rose from the ropes as a demonic Lazarus and, as if levitating over the meekness of a shrunken beast, flurried Foreman to the canvas with secret punches—hard, quick, flush shots that only Ali knew he possessed.

That Ali no longer existed—if he ever did, outside the imagination of a post-Nixon America longing for heroes[23]—and Young knew it. "Yeah, I'm way overweight for this one," Ali said in the gym within earshot of Jimmy Young. "I only train hard for those bad niggers. I don't train too hard for these *little* ones."

"This fight ain't no gift," Young responded to reporters. "I earned it. I been strugglin' for years. I always been the opponent.

"And I always won."

Vegas odds were 15–1 against him.

* * *

Young in a stark black robe with black trunks featuring white stripes down the side and "JY" on the left leg. Ali's distended belly bloated, sagging over his white trunks, prompting Cosell to say there are "two rolls of fat where there used to be one." Young tightening the muscles in his face, his black mustache curling sinister, a sneer emerging. The bell.

Round one: With 1:17 left, Ali throws a right, but Young ducks to his own right and evades it. He then uses this newfound duck-crouch to bound off his bent legs and shift his weight up and forward. He releases a straight right hand in the same fluid uncoiling, poking Ali's face with the immediacy of a spring popping through a mattress. "Ali doing no fighting at all," Cosell says on ABC. "Nothing whatsoever. Just keeping the gloves up in front of the face."

Round five: Young nails Ali's body twice and snaps a jab into his pretty face. Ali tries to punch him back but misses. "Slippery kid," Cosell says.

Round eight: As Ali clubs Young's head with two rights, Young insolently returns his own right to Ali's chin. Then he stares down the champion, who will later say he "saw stars" and that his "knees were wobbly."

Round nine: Young jabs hard, and Ali begins to dance around him, floating on tiptoes once more. An argument that time can, even for a moment, stand still. But Young doesn't believe the thirty-four year old, and he waves his arm from side to side as if giving Ali room to do whatever he wants with moves that do not deceive. "Look at Jimmy Young challenging Ali!" Cosell shouts in his halted cadence. "'Dance!' he says to him in that effect." As he hops and bops, Ali extends his left arm to jab but misses. In the very same instant, Young sees an opening and positions his right hand over the top of Ali's left, which can no longer block in the extended position. Young's right hand smothers Ali. "That's a counta-punch!" Cosell whoops. When the bell rings, the crowd claps more loudly than it has all fight, and Jimmy Young raises his arms to them. Observer and participant both wonder where this can lead, thoughts of a new and different future coursing through them.

In his corner, Young's attendants buzz about him. On the back of one cornerman's robes, the letter "N" has peeled off so it reads only

"JIMMY YOU G." One diagonal away, Ali refuses to sit on a stool, a habit he uses to scare opponents, but he cannot remain erect and must lean on the ropes. Young walks to the center of the ring for the start of the tenth wearing a wicked grin. For the first time all night, he begins the round feinting, toying with Ali, ascertaining whether the champ will read into his every twitch. Ali circles Young clockwise. Young has already torqued his entire thorax to his right, crouched and pulled back his right hand, as one would cock a pistol. When Ali hits three o'clock and tries to flick a jab, Young dips between Ali's arms and releases the rubber band his body has become. It snaps hard, cold, and fast, converting potential energy into its brilliant kinetic realization, with all the velocity and power of a rotating 209-pound man. Ali recoils to the corner, throwing (and missing) a weak jab simply to impress upon the judges his continued role as aggressor, which is what he has been, despite an inability to even graze Young's smooth skin. But Young follows Ali and continues bruising ribs with counterpunches.

Between rounds ten and eleven, the action in the ring causes those outside of it to renege on a previously established deal. This seems strange, but then, there is always a connection between a fighter's fights and the life he leads. A fighter must use the same body in both realms, and whatever punishment it absorbs in one will remain in the other. And it's not always physical. So Ken Norton, who has just fought on the Young–Ali undercard and is scheduled to fight Ali later in the year, is barred from sitting in with Howard Cosell on the ABC broadcast to analyze the Young fight. His manager is watching, after all, and he sees that Young has a chance. And he knows that Norton will lose a million in purse money if his fight with Ali is canceled—that is, if Ali somehow loses the title before their scheduled bout. So Norton's manager forbids him from talking to Cosell now, which would force Norton to praise Young and potentially become party to the destruction of his own upcoming payday. Boxing's version of pleading the fifth.

In the eleventh, Ali misses with a right as Young intentionally ducks through the ropes, poking his head out of the ring. It's a strange tactic, and although technically legal, it seems something no fighter should do. But Ali does miss. And his cornerman screams, "He's tired, Ali! He's tired!" And then a shock of a yelp from Ali's brother, Rahman: "You're losing, Muhammad! You're losing!"[24] At the bell, as Ali puffs his way to the corner, the section nearest him boos.

Norton enters the ABC booth now, probably because his manager has realized what Norton's absence implies: a Young victory.

"Are you astonished to see Ali look like this, Kenny?" Cosell asks.

"Yes, I am," Norton says. "He doesn't have his fast hands, the flurries. And Young's a very good counterpuncher."

"Have you ever seen Ali miss so often?"

"No, I haven't."

With fifty seconds left in the twelfth, Ali bodies Young into a corner, but Young slips every punch. He'd make a fine burglar or spy, stepping between every motion-triggered sensor. Above, below, between—whatever the fractions would allow for. At the end of the round, Young ducks through the ropes again, but then Ali returns to his corner and sits on his stool for the first time. Young pulses with eagerness during this intermission. Before the thirteenth even begins, he pops off his stool and waves to the crowd. At the opening bell, Cosell pierces the thing. "He underrated this kid," he starts. "This kid is a Philadelphia fighter." Ali tries to control things now, but Young shoves his upper body through the ropes, and Ali cannot help but punch Young's ass and back. The crowd gets louder. Ali bullies Young into a neutral corner, left-hooking, uppercutting—WHOOSH—Ali's hands dice the air, running up against a mixture of gases but not a solid. Young has already wormed away, slinking to Ali's other side, nailing the champ with a left and then a right. "Now the crowd is really getting excited!" Cosell shouts. Thousands rise to their feet. Louder, louder, louder. Round fourteen, crescendo-frantic-fantastic-Young in the middle of the ring, and Ali facing him there. Man before man. Young steps forward with his left lead foot, his white Adidas high-top pivoting like a ballerina's, and lurches his head and right shoulder forward. He raises his right arm so that the muscular section from shoulder to the elbow becomes horizontal and parallel to the canvas. He dips his left arm and left shoulder and spins his waist counterclockwise like a homerun hitter in full stride. It appears he's shifting his weight for one final blow to knock out Ali. But Ali notices and raises his left hand in front of his face and his right to his right cheek. He jumps backward onto his right foot, doing so with such urgency that his front foot, the left, leaves the ground, creating a dark shadow under its sneaker. When the front foot finally lands (perhaps a millisecond later), it shifts Ali's weight like a pendulum, forcing his head forward again. But Young hasn't punched yet. No, no, no—

Young hasn't punched yet. It was a trick. A feint. To move Ali's head forward, precisely so that Young can now jab him rapidly in the face, whipping Ali's neck and buffeting him to his right. "Do you know how many months this could cost you if Young gets the decision, Jimmy?" asks Cosell. "How many months—and how much money," Norton answers. Young lands two shots to the body. Ali misses two punches. Young holds Ali. Ali leans straight into Young's left. Twelve thousand four hundred and seventy-two spectators trash their vocal chords. Young and Ali hold each other on the ropes. The ref breaks it up. They move to the center of the ring, circling each other in small motions whose primitive appearance belies a world of calculation. Ali jabs his left toward Young's head, yet the look in Young's eyes at this moment betrays glee. He slides his head to the left, away from the jab, and spreads his spry legs wide, lowering his body down into another crouch. Young then bounces like a Super Ball off his poised knees, stabbing a right cross between Ali's extended left arm and unmoving right. This snaps Ali's head to the right, and he grimaces, stumbles, staggers, and flails his left arm.

Ali's in the corner now, his head a sagging, drooping mess, and the bell rings and the crowd rises once more. Norton screams: "DON'T BLOW MY SHOT, MUHAMMAD!"

Round fifteen: Somewhere, an orchestral section of violins plays its highest, loudest notes, seizing the audience by the throat and holding it there. Young ducks between the ropes again, but Ali lands a left hook. Ten seconds left. Young lands a straight right. "Who would you give the fight to?" Cosell asks. "I refuse to answer," Norton says. Ali holds Young, who manages to knock him in the torso. The bell rings, the crowd jumps, fans clap big swooping claps over their heads, and Young raises his arms high and walks to one side of the ring, where he blows kisses to fans. They whistle back. Ali walks to his corner with his head down. In the front row, a white-haired man in a light suit jumps and applauds at the same time. Wearing white button-down shirts and black pants, Young's seconds raise his hands. They slap him on the back. Ali's seconds unravel the tape around his wrists as his 230 pounds sag against the corner post. Young's cornermen raise him in the air, hug him, jump on him—a mosh pit of wild smiles and whooping. "Look at the joy and E-LAY-SHUN in his corner," Cosell says. Across the ring, Drew Bundini Brown, the Ali hanger-on who had earlier pronounced Ali's juices to be sizzling and hot and ready, looks as if he has swallowed a lemon. Cosell describes Ali's trainer, Dundee, as a "sour face." Ali dons his robe and combs his hair. The bell rings, heralding the announcement. "Ladies and gentleman, here's the decision. Judge Larry Barrett has it 70–68, Ali."[25] Some of the crowd boos, and others clap and pump fists. "Referee Tom Kelly has it 72–65, Ali." Boos cascade from the rafters on down. Ali's seconds raise their hands as if testifying to God. Jimmy Young whips his left glove to his forehead, jerks his head back, and opens his eyes and mouth like a man gasping for air. A wire photographer snaps a shot, freezing Young's choking forever as the bout's definitive image—one of the few things people will later recall about Young, if they recall him at all. It doesn't matter—two of three judges have already handed the bout to his opponent, and that's enough—but the emcee finishes anyway. "Judge Terry Moore has it 71–64.

"Ali."[26]

* * *

If Young's rise to the title fight progressed fluidly upward from the Shavers knockout to his survival against Joe Roman's low blows, his career thereafter broke to pieces in a disjointed, godly way. Disjointed because the goal for which Young had been toiling became obscured by the unreliability of the entire game. Direction lost. And godly because one couldn't understand the order underpinning the mess though one fervently hoped it existed.

This is what they later said.

The crowd: They did not cheer when Ali left the ring.

Jimmy Young, who was "smiling and bubbly"[27] in the dressing room immediately after the fight, inflated by the newfound attention without realizing its evanescence: "I figured I'd win by a split decision. And when I heard the numbers announced, at first, I really thought it would be a split decision."

Muhammad Ali: "I thought I won. But I would like to say that I underestimated Jimmy Young, that I didn't know Jimmy Young was so awkward, that he was as hard to hit, that he was as fast.

"He hit me with two right hands and I saw stars. . . . Jimmy Young will be the next heavyweight champion."

Angelo Dundee, Ali's trainer: "It was probably the worst fight of his career."

DAILY ☒ NEWS

FINAL ★★★★

LARGEST
CIRCULATION
OF ANY PAPER
IN AMERICA

NEW YORK'S PICTURE NEWSPAPER ®

36

New York, N.Y. 10017, Saturday, May 1, 1976

ALI DECISIONS YOUNG
Crowd Protests Unanimous Verdict

Associated Press Wirephoto
Young has Ali back on his heels and backed into ropes.

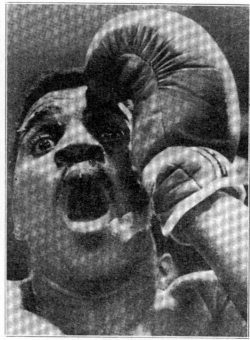

Confident of outcome, handler raises "victor" Young's arm.
UPI Telephoto

He's Open
To Doubt

UPI Telephoto
Unbelieving Jimmy Young stands with his mouth
agape as the decision is announced after his championship bout with Muhammad Ali in Landover,
Md., last night. Jimmy went the full route with an
obviously overconfident, overweight and under-
trained Ali and—it seemed to many—ran the champ
into the ground. Ali won by decision. It was unanimous with the judges, but drew boos from the fans.
Story p. 26; other pics p. 1 and centerfold

The back page of the *New York Daily News* the day after Jimmy Young's fight with
Ali. Courtesy of the *New York Daily News*

Dr. Ferdie Pacheco, Ali's ringside doctor: "He was getting tired a lot sooner than usual. His reflexes were only 25 to 30 percent of what they should be."

Eddie Schuyler of the AP and Dick Young of the *New York Daily News* had Young winning on their scorecards. Schuyler had it 69–66. Dave Anderson of the *Times* had it 68–67 for Young (8–7 in rounds), adding: "It's even understandable that Judge Larry Barrett had Ali ahead 70–68 in points and 7–5 in rounds with three rounds even. It was that kind of fight. No knockdowns. . . . The only explanation for the arithmetic of those [other] two officials is that Terry Moore and Tom Kelly were influenced, perhaps subconsciously, by Ali's reputation rather than his performance."

Years later, Tom Cushman of the *Philadelphia Daily News*: "By the fourth or fifth round, it was obvious that he was not intimidated, and he was a very clever fighter, and Ali at that point didn't have the lightning skills he had earlier in his career, and Young wasn't a paralyzing puncher, but he used the ropes really well and he fought off of them well. He seemed to me like he was a tad quicker. You know, it would have been a very close decision either way, but I really felt that he probably would have won had he been fighting against someone else."

Years later, Randy Neumann, retired heavyweight turned writer: "Young, I thought, would give him a tumble, and I thought he won that fight. That bullshit about sticking his head out of the ring—that's hardly a foul. I find it funny how people interpret the rules. Who said shoving's a foul? So he stuck his head out of the ring? Is that a foul?"

Years later, Joe Frazier, Young's occasional sparring partner and a former heavyweight champ: "I thought Jimmy won that fight. But we wasn't the judges."

The fighters weren't the judges. They never are.

o o o

After the Ali fight, Young knocked out two guys within four rounds and defeated Ron Lyle again—the same Ron Lyle who had twice knocked down George Foreman. Foreman, the twenty-eight-year-old former champ who had lost to Ali in Zaire but had won all of his other forty-six fights, including forty-two by knockout (forty within five rounds), was deemed the perfect opponent for Young. Again, the boxing crowd believed Don King was merely feeding Young to a fighter who he thought could actually make him money.

Michael Katz of the *Times* said, "Few boxing people . . . believe Young [will] give Foreman much trouble."[28] *Inquirer* columnist Bill Lyon said, "It should be a mismatch of the grossest proportions, like a typing duel between Elizabeth Ray and Woodward-Bernstein. George Foreman hits people and they split open like Liberian oil tankers. Jimmy Young hits people and they don't even blink."[29]

Young didn't blink.

"He's got two legs, two arms and one head," Young said of Foreman. "But he don't use it." Young guaranteed "that before the third round, you're going to hear some boos because George Foreman is going to get frustrated and do something dirty."[30]

It took place in eighty degree heat in Puerto Rico. Amazingly, until the seventh round, March 17, 1977, went exactly as Young had predicted. In the first, Young's eyes glinted like razor blades. In black trunks with a white waistband, white stripes, and a white "JY" emblazoned on the left leg, he jabbed, then bulled into Foreman's midsection, then uppercut into his chin. Foreman couldn't figure out how to respond to this move—too quick to be countered and too suffocating to provide room for a response. So Foreman illegally punched the back of Young's neck and shoved him to the floor. As Young had foretold, the crowd began to boo Foreman, and in the third, the ref deducted a point for unnecessary roughness. Before the bout, one writer had called Young's predictions "praying out loud,"[31] but now Foreman reverted to audible self-affirmation, saying, "C'mon, c'mon. I'm the real champ."[32]

It's hard to pinpoint how or why it shifted, but in the seventh, Foreman began smashing Young with all the menace of his previously frustrated intentions. "He's got a look—well, you just wouldn't want to see a man with a look like that on his face in a dark alley," the closed-circuit announcer Bob Sheridan said.[33]

Foreman whipped his left arm as far back as he could—like a windup toy—and let go. It ripped through the atmosphere in a looping arc that crashed into the nerve endings on Jimmy Young's chin. The impact moved down—first to Young's neck, which spasmodically snapped, then to the chest, which heaved, and to the knees, which bent. Young staggered backward on his heels, unable to support an erect posture. He turned his back to Foreman, and the latter gave chase. Foreman threw a left to Young's chest and a right to his ribs, and Young collapsed onto

Foreman's massive frame. Foreman shoved Young off and bashed a left into his jaw.

It continued. A left to the head. A right to the ribs. Gruesome.

Somehow Young turned it around. Credit the Philadelphia in him or the unpredictability of boxing matches. The way men extract things from themselves they didn't know they had. But one way or another, Jimmy Young started landing punches. And the crowd screamed. So did the announcer.

"Jimmy Young with his back against the ropes . . . THROWS A HARD RIGHT HAND OF HIS OWN!"

"JIMMY YOUNG FIGHTS BACK FEROCIOUSLY!"

"JIMMY SCORES A GOOD COMBINATION!"

"A GOOD RIGHT HAND TO THE HEAD OF GEORGE FOREMAN!"

Foreman grabbed Young's waist. The ref separated them. Nineteen seconds remained in the round. Foreman shoved Young into the ropes but had no energy to punch. They gripped each other. Three. Two. "AND JIMMY YOUNG WILL ESCAPE!" The bell rang. Young walked to his corner with his arms raised. The crowd roared. Foreman sat on his stool for the first time all night. And on ABC, Howard Cosell passed judgment on the twenty-eight-year-old from Philadelphia. "If you wanted to know about Jimmy Young's heart," he said, "you found out about it this round."[34]

❋ ❋ ❋

Ring Magazine called it the fight of the year. And the unanimous decision against Foreman allowed Young to demand a rematch with Ali. Not just because he had won but because he had won so very magically, transfixing ten thousand Puerto Ricans who cheered for him as if their fortunes were tied to his that night. It had been Young, first, who mustered the will to survive the seventh round. But as he emerged for the eighth, bouncing on his toes, circling Foreman, and snapping that pretty jab, a symbiosis bloomed. Young triple hooked with the left. Or faked the left and sent the right, slamming into Foreman's slumped head. And the crowd began this muffled cry—three undecipherable syllables initially, chanted rhythmically and repeatedly. "Mmm-mmm-mmm," it sounded. But as Young kept landing punches, more rows picked it up. With force and clarity: "Jim-mmm-Yum." From seat to seat and row to row and section to section. And soon the whole place:

"Jim-my-Young! JIM-MY-YOUNG!" And after Young deflected a Foreman jab, he turned to the crowd and raised his arms high—in the
middle of the round—crystallizing the bond. Young squinted, and he
threw punches faster than Foreman's and from unexpected angles. It all
grew and rose as a violent crescendo, a sweltering night—ninth round,
tenth, eleventh, twelfth. Louder and louder. Eyes like furnaces. A guy
in a white jacket, white shirt, and yellow hat jumping so high he blocked
the view of three rows behind him, tossing his hat in the air. Two
minutes left. "JIM-MY-YOUNG! JIM-MY-YOUNG!" Foreman trapped
in the corner, throwing a right that couldn't reach Young. Young sneaking a left arm around Foreman's extended right and into his open face.
CRUNCH! Brutal, beautiful barbarism. Young bending his left knee
and dipping his left shoulder, twisting his torso clockwise and uncoiling
counterclockwise. Foreman falling forward, landing on the bottom red
rope, his left hand clinging to the top blue one.

"GEORGE GOES DOWN! GEORGE GOES DOWN!"

And in one of the first few rows, a man in a powder blue, short-
sleeved oxford shirt, waving his arms as if liberated from a dictator,
hopping and pumping his fist, his shoulder-length black hair bobbing.

The scorecards: 118–111, 116–112, 115–114. All for Young.

The promoters saw it, wanted to take advantage of the comeback of
Jimmy Young. Hadn't Don King brought in Young to be the opponent
again? So that he could feed a decent name to the rising monster of
George Foreman? Sure, but if King was anything, it was pragmatic.
Young had won, and although he had no loyalty to the man, he had
plenty of loyalty to the winner. Now he could make another match with
Young for even more money.

But first, another story about the mobster Blinky Palermo. A guy
named Ben Thompson wanted to sign Ali to fight Young again and
called Jack Levin—the electrics salesman—to work out the particulars.
It would take place in the 200,000-seat Maracanã Stadium in Rio de
Janeiro in October, with Ali receiving $12 million and Young $2 million.
Levin okayed it, and Thompson flew to Philly to sign the contracts.
They met in a hotel room, and Thompson unloaded from a brown
briefcase a signing bonus of $25,000 in rubber band–wrapped twenties,
fifties, and hundreds. Then a man wearing a pink shirt and a small hat—
Blinky Palermo, though Levin hadn't introduced him to the California
boys—spoke up. Years earlier, Bill Caplan, Thompson's associate, had

in fact seen Blinky at the latter's trial on extortion charges in California. But Caplan had watched from the gallery and only glimpsed Blinky's back—never his front. Now Blinky demanded a $100,000 signing bonus like the one Ali was getting. In truth, Palermo didn't want the bonus. It was just a pretext to cancel the match. But Palermo started yapping, and Caplan said, "Hey! Who *are* you anyway?" And Blinky just looked at him and smirked and said never mind who I am—this is how it's gonna be.

When the meeting ended, Blinky shook hands with Caplan. "Well, Kid," he said, "whatever happens, I want to wish you the best of luck and I hope you do good as a promoter." Then the California kids left the room.

"Hey," Thompson said to Caplan, "you were talking kinda cocky to the guy in the pink shirt."

"Yeah," Caplan said, "he messed up your deal!"

"You don't know who that is?"

"Obviously, I don't."

"Blinky Palermo."

"That was Blinky Palermo! I wish I would've known going in," Caplan said, quivering. "I would've been more polite."

"I can't understand this," Thompson later said. "People in business don't do this."

"This isn't business," Caplan said. "This is boxing."[35]

❊ ❊ ❊

As Jimmy Young's career came to an end—not that he knew it was all slipping away from him, that he would be a vagrant and then a dead man within decades—Ali was still running scared. He still didn't want to face Ken Norton (he didn't have to worry about Foreman, who was so shaken following his loss to Young that he professed to have had a religious epiphany and quit the sport for a decade). So Ali made up shit. He said he was too tired to face Norton and Young, so they needed to box each other to determine a legitimate contender for his belt.

Don King scheduled the fight for November 5, 1977, in a 4,700-seat tennis pavilion outside Caesars Palace in Vegas. ABC was to broadcast (that would be the revenue generator, not ticket sales—a sign of the business's evolution), with Norton getting $1.7 million as the number one–ranked contender and Young $1 million—the second-richest non-championship fight ever. But as it developed, the match took on all the implications of a championship fight.

As in the run-up to such a bout, both Norton and Young won tune-ups in September. They both talked trash about each other's performance: "I wasn't impressed at all," Norton said; "To me, Norton didn't look too good," Young said. On the verge of fame, Young schmoozed with the political elite. It was to a luncheon feting Young that Judge John Sirica rushed after Sirica ordered former Attorney General John Mitchell and Chief of Staff H. R. Haldeman to start serving prison terms for their involvement in Watergate. And on the eve of the fight, the president of the World Boxing Council, Jose Sulaiman, demanded Ali sign a contract agreeing to face the winner of Norton–Young within sixty days or forfeit his title and have that bout retroactively considered a championship. Ali's manager said they'd sign only if Young won, but Ali denied this.

Various Vegas bookkeepers put the odds at 3–2, 7–5, and 9–5—all in favor of Norton. But the talk of the writers, who always had a vague idea of something amiss in Young's camp, was Palermo's machinations—and a possible Vegas backlash. Apparently, the guys in Nevada who had recently begun to solicit fights disliked the idea of an old mobster muscling in on the dough. It was no longer Blinky's show, they wanted to demonstrate. "I must've written a column about Palermo," recalls Tom Callahan, who covered the fight for the *Cincinnati Enquirer*. "But he was there; he was physically there. Everybody I talked to all week, I think this was the common view, that they wanted to show Blinky he didn't run things. In the boxing business, there are two gatherings of people: the media with no stake and all the people in the boxing business. . . . All the offshore guys [the WBC is based in Mexico] who bring in the belt, all the referee types like Davey Pearl, they were all saying all week that Jimmy Young has a big mountain to climb because Blinky didn't have the power anymore. That was like a theme in that fight."

Don King did have the power, surely, but that was the genius of his promotion: he promoted Norton, too, so if Young were to lose due to anti-Blinky sentiment, King would still have control. Just as King had the rights to Foreman *and* Young during their bout, after which the promoter said, "George Foreman will always be my friend, but I must go where the wild goose goes."[36]

"King had the advantage of being on all sides," Callahan tells me today. "If King was involved in a fight, he wouldn't let another team get involved without joining his team."

One of Callahan's good friends is *Philadelphia Daily News* writer Tom Cushman, who actually introduced Callahan to Blinky at the fight. Being the Philly guy there, Cushman took on the role of educator. He told *New York Times* writer Dave Anderson a great deal about Palermo. Two days before the fight, Anderson wrote a column about Palermo's alleged management of Young.

"I've heard the name Blinky Palermo, but I've never met him personally," Young told Anderson for his piece. "When Jack and Ray took over as my managers, I didn't know anything about them. I didn't know if they were crooks or what, but I had to do something. Up until then, I'd never made more than $2,500, and all I can tell you now is that I'm not sorry."

You tell me what those words really mean.

❂ ❂ ❂

This was to be Jimmy Young's last stand. The end of his tragic, Philadelphian career.

The fight was fifteen rounds. And because the two contenders had such different styles—one a counterpuncher, the other a body puncher—the bout cannot be narrated in the small movements that defined Young's work against Foreman. This fight never turned on a single opening, on an opportunity taken or missed. Instead, its heart lay in a subtle stylistic ebb and flow, in an interplay of forces immeasurable and creative.[37] "Young's the kind of opponent whom it is difficult to score," Howard Cosell said before even he realized what was to occur. Young began the night slipping, dipping, and hitting, winning the first two rounds, it seemed, on strategic counters. Every time Norton charged to hit Young's torso, Young finagled away. He then nailed Norton's chin before the latter could face him. At one point, Ali jumped out of his seat when Young landed a big right-left. But as the fight progressed, Norton began rushing Young more aggressively, and when Young tried to clinch his opponent—hug him, really—to smother the punches, the referee separated them.[38] Young was thus unable to use the clinch effectively, as a position from which to punch slyly, as he had done so many times before. Norton pounded hook after hook into Young's ribcage, and Young could not muster strength to dance. After four rounds, Cosell had scored two for Young, one for Norton, and one even. But Norton steadily won the middle rounds, and the crowd sensed it. In the eighth, they once again cried, "JIM-MY YOUNG! JIM-MY YOUNG!" And as if a switch had been flipped, Young's eyes beamed bright, and he flurried Norton into a corner. In the tenth, 11:30 p.m. in Philadelphia, Young noticed Norton's exhaustion, the way his left arm sagged at the waist, leaving him open to a right-hand blow. So Young threw the right without a preceding jab, and Norton turned to jelly, his legs wobbling without direction. If Norton's body blows had slowed Young earlier, they now slowed the puncher himself, who had done all the work while his opponent rested against the ropes. In the eleventh, Young slipped a punch so quickly that Norton wound up hitting only air, flailing and then falling. "JIM-MY! JIM-MY!" Young continued ducking, dodging, and smacking, and one could argue his style set the tone of the tenth through the fourteenth. In the final round, both fighters let go, with Norton rattling Young's ribcage and Young bobbling Norton's head. The final bell rang, and the judges turned in their cards. One *Times* reporter wrote that the "razor-close" fight would come down "to the subjective factor of which style impresses which judge most."[39] At the time, no one watching at home knew that another subjective factor outside the ring might influence the result, which was already very much in question. So damn close. The emcee announced a split decision, and the crowd booed. Judge Art Lurie had it 144–142 for Young, but the other two judges had it 147–143 for Norton, who for a moment didn't react, as if unsure he had heard correctly, and then raised his arms, a towel over his head.

Cosell rushed the ring and asked Young whether he thought he had won.

"Yes, I did," Young said, his expression suddenly lifeless, unblinking eyes over frozen lips. Cosell looked into the fighter's face.

"I don't want to bother you anymore," he said. "You're too disappointed."

❀ ❀ ❀

It was like Cheever had it in "The Swimmer," opening with a group of affluent suburbanites lying by the pool on "one of those midsummer Sundays when everyone sits around saying, 'I *drank* too much last night.'"[40] It didn't matter that it was a Saturday, or that it took place in November. The headaches, the boring of reality's gimlet into a just-waking fighter, were all too literary. The morning after dawned, and it seemed age had rapidly caught up with Jimmy Young, so that by the time he reached the last pool in the county, after swimming through all the neighbors' pools along the way, he no longer possessed that which he had on the first page, and he never would again.

The papers revealed the thinnest margin. The nonvoting referee said he thought Young had won. The three judges had agreed on only five of fifteen rounds. The two judges who scored it against Young had *eleven* total rounds even—"a copout," Dave Anderson wrote, "especially in a fight where there always was enough action for a judge to consider."[41] It must have hurt worse, then, for Young to read Anderson's score—10–5 for Young—or even that of the writers who had a draw, like Leonard Koppett of the *Times*. With a draw, Young's path could have paralleled Norton's, and they might have fought again. But with a split decision, their paths diverged, divided by a line that might've been there always, though Young saw it clearly only now.

It sharpened as rumors spread. "It was a backlash against the mob," promoter Russell Peltz recalls hearing. "Vegas finally stood up, and they went against Young 'cause they knew he was with the mob and they were tired of it. Not tired of it, but in that particular fight, that was the general theory, that they were gonna show the mob that they couldn't just push 'em around and they went the other way, you know."

A fight figure from Los Angeles named Vein Head was overheard, upon leaving the match, to say, "Y'know, Blinky doesn't have the old clout like he used to."[42]

Young understood how his "managers" had led him here and saw the result unfold. The WBC ruled Ali could make one more noncompulsory defense, against Leon Spinks. Spinks won and took the title, but he was offered more money to face Ali again (the big draw!) than to fight Norton, so that's what he did. The WBC stripped Spinks of the title—for avoiding the number-one contender—and retroactively, *Ken Norton became heavyweight champion of the world.* It didn't end. The WBC (possibly under the influence of Don King, who thought Young couldn't attract fans) also forbade Norton from fighting Young again. So Norton fought Larry Holmes—a boxer-puncher also under contract to Don King whom Young thought he could beat—and Holmes took the title in another close split decision. Of course, Don King didn't set up a match between Young and Holmes. Thus a man whose will had already seeped into the drain of a camera, leaving Cosell finally speechless, was cornered by the game to which he had dedicated himself, a game with one goal—the one thing they wouldn't let him have.

Young had watched Spinks beat Ali in the Vegas Hilton. It was February 15, 1978, and he was party to his own retroactive fortune, unable to control its turn. Around him, someone started talking about cocaine, which he had never seen before. Then he began snorting.

Four months later, Blinky matched him with Ossie Ocasio, a mediocre but undefeated Puerto Rican whose career was being "guided" by "Honest" Bill Daly. A former mob associate of Blinky, Daly never let his nickname prevent him from wearing an obvious toupee. The idea now was for Young to lose, so the twenty-year-old Ocasio could move ahead.[43] Years later, Young would say, "I think we knew," then throw his arms in the air and go silent when asked about a fix during an interview. Not that it mattered whether the deal was official. Young entered the ring with cocaine in his system, weighing a jiggly 220 pounds. He had difficulty getting through the ropes. It wasn't a mystery, this change. He told the writers he was there for the "money." And he lost.

The pattern was set for the rest of his career. Young would drug himself into unfeeling submission, lose to an up-and-coming Blinky/King fighter, and then receive the tiniest portion of his due. The Ocasio purse was supposed to be $150,000. Young would later claim Blinky put "thirteen in my pocket after taxes." Or in other terms, $137,000 less than his purse. In the rematch with Ocasio, which Young also lost, he received $20,000. When reporters got wind of Young's low earnings, King claimed the fighter "owes me a lot of money."[44]

What the reporters didn't know was how much Young must have "owed." For the broken man would later claim the following receipts:

- For the $75,000 Ali fight, he took home $16,000.
- For the $250,000 Foreman fight, he took home between $62,000 and $75,000.[45]
- For the $1 million Norton fight, he took home $262,000.

It all came out in a long talk several years ago between Jimmy and two fans. Long after he lost to Michael Dokes, Greg Page, Tony Tubbs, and Tony Tucker—all King fighters who would win a title and then get cheated or use drugs or balloon to 260 pounds or all of the above.[46] Long after he spent $1,300 a week on blow, which kept him awake for six days at a time, and refereed several fights drunk, and publicly urinated on the floor. And after his cousin, the boxer Boogaloo Watts, tried to intervene but was told, "Who is this? This is me. How can you tell somebody what to do with himself?"

It all came out in this long talk between Jimmy and two fans.

After two guys wrote a children's book in 1979 titled *Jimmy Young: Heavyweight Challenger*, which said the Palermo talk was unfounded and that Young could "come back" from his first loss to Ocasio, that "his chance will come, and when it does, you may see a new champion: Jimmy Young!"[47]

After a writer said he seemed uninterested in fighting and he replied, "Can you tell?" After the Great White Hope Gerry Cooney stopped him on cuts. And after George Benton, the North Philly middleweight, took over as his trainer and made him lose thirty pounds and had him win five in a row and earn comeback of the year from *Ring Magazine*. And after that comeback was scuttled when Young drank beer and cognac and smoked marijuana at 4 a.m. with some red-complexioned girl in a parking lot in Southwest Philly before the biggest fight of his return, for Greg Page's USBA title, ruining his chances. After he told the press, "I felt like a drug addict" during the Page fight but attributed it to cold medicine.[48]

After Blinky petitioned the Pennsylvania Athletic Commission to license Blinky as a manager so he could "help the kids at the Montgomery County Boys' Club stay out of trouble."[49] After the Pennsylvania Boxing Hall of Fame inducted Blinky, and Blinky was then linked by an official New Jersey state report to Frank Gelb, the manager who had sold Jimmy. After the report called it "impossible" to believe that Gelb "did not know the sinister background of one of the highest-ranking mobsters in Philadelphia," who were Palermo's associates.[50] And after the Jersey attorney general said Blinky had lines of credit of $5,000 and $10,000 at two casinos in Atlantic City, the city where Gelb had become "the primary boxing impresario." And after Blinky had putatively received "complimentary rooms, meals and drinks worth more than $26,000."[51]

It all came out in this long talk between Jimmy and two fans.

Before Gelb told me he didn't remember the accusations linking him to Palermo and said, "Was he involved in boxing in the '70s? I don't remember. . . . I never knew him to be involved in boxing at the time or at any time."

After Jimmy sparred with Tyson in '84 and was caught with a nice combo; and the next day, Tyson tried the same thing, but Jimmy countered it, and Tyson looked at him like, "What was that?" After Tyson gave him a few thousand bucks ten years later.

After Jimmy traded all his old fight robes to Russell Peltz for money, and his wife separated from him, and he befriended former welterweight champ Meldrick Taylor, who would drive him home from a fight in Atlantic City one night after the two were profiled together in a *Daily News* piece about punch-drunk fighters. After Jimmy appeared for that interview without socks in "filthy sneakers," a "tattered shirt" over a "ratty undershirt," and unzipped blue work pants "stained with grease and dirt." After he told the writer Marcus Hayes he could come back—adding, with a pronounced slur, "I was lying there thinking, this morning, I swear I could do it. Hey, uh, what time is it?"[52] After Hayes responded that Young might not be in condition to fight, and Young sighed and said, "You done burst my bubble."

It all came out in this long talk between Jimmy and two fans.

Before Boogalooo Watts told me "it wasn't so much the punching to me because everybody *didn't* hit Jimmy. Everybody didn't hit him. I think the drugs took over. . . . He just gave up in life."

After the IRS said they'd subpoena his contracts with King, and he said there never were any, that King would just tell him what to do, then give him some money and say, "This is your share."

After he took a fight three months before his fortieth birthday in a gymnasium in St. Joseph, Missouri, for a few thousand because he owed the IRS $50,000.

After friends and family gave him odd jobs around a garage, and Watts had him do small roofing and construction work and lent him some money, and Jimmy sliced his hand cutting metal with shears.

After Jimmy asked Foreman for money at the Golota–Grant fight in Atlantic City, and Foreman said, "E-mail me your address, Jimmy." And he said, "E-mail with what?" After a friend got Earnie Shavers—now religious—to pray for Jimmy, and Shavers said you probably couldn't help the man because he didn't want to leave Philadelphia.

It all came out in this long talk between Jimmy and two fans.

After Jimmy went out to this hoagie place—Harold's in Edison, New Jersey—with former heavyweights Larry Holmes and Ernie Terrell, and they laughed about the old days.

Before a writer from England came and took Jimmy to Popeyes to catch up with the "Yank from Philadelphia." And before Tristram Dixon implored readers to "pray this sweet man can win the toughest battle of all—and stay off the hard drugs."

Before that Sunday, February 20, 2005, when the man "heartbroken by razor-thin losses" died of heart failure after a six-day stay in Hahnemann University Hospital.[53] Age fifty-six. Before the funeral attended by all the heavyweights and the wake with Jimmy in a new suit and flowers sent by the Fraziers. Before the obituaries in London with the headline "So Farewell." Before a friend said, "Nobody—I don't think anybody—had a bad word about Jimmy." And before his son-in-law told me "information don't come free" in response to an interview request.

It all came out in a long talk that day—after too much but before the end—when Jimmy Young ate brunch with two guys named Tom whom he had met at an autograph show. They drove to his North Philly house, a decrepit place on Seybert Street with sheets instead of windows. A blustery day in the cold of winter. And there he was, standing in an orange Hawaiian shirt he had bought in Honolulu while there to fight Ron Lyle. Tom Space couldn't believe he still had the shirt, but it was really all he had, and he turned to Space and said, "Tom, I got nothing. . . . Can you take me out to eat?" So they went to a restaurant, and Jimmy was pretty loud, and they were seated in a corner room, and the chef couldn't make omelets for shit, and Jimmy might have gotten sausage. Then he began speaking, with Tom Jess and Tom Space capturing his words on a microcassette recorder.

"This radio of mine was taken from me June 1963," Young began. He whispered sometimes and roared others, and he drank a few beers, and then the waitress had to quiet him, and a few people even asked for autographs, which they may or may not still have, buried in scrapbooks in their houses. Only once did he laugh, and that was when he told this story about the run-up to a fight when he was promised $100,000, and he knew he'd be cheated of his due so he threatened to pull out and he demanded $20,000 (or $35,000—he kept changing the figure, in his recollection) up front from King, who offered him $5,000; but Young insisted, and King finally gave him $20,000 in cash. Young slurred as he told the story, and it isn't clear which fight he was referring to, whether he actually received less than his purse anyway or whether it even all occurred.

But Jimmy Young said he got "an extra twenty-five to sixty thousand," and he laughed heartily, because that was a day they'll remember: the day when he made the rules.

2

THE WORKERS

I've always looked at boxers as the working class of sport. They deserve more because they put more into it. . . . It's a tragedy. It's a tragedy to the point where sometimes I could almost cry when I see some of the great talents that are just swept aside.
—Jack McKinney, *Philadelphia Daily News* writer

A central fact of life in the region: the whole place is haunted by its own ghosts.
—Steven Conn, *Metropolitan Philadelphia: Living with the Presence of the Past* [1]

Mr. Pat was as historical as Philly figures come. And they always come historical—no one just arrives in Philadelphia—and even if you really have just arrived from somewhere else, the city seeps in, and soon you're as much a part of Philly's fabric as the rest—and it's as much a part of you. That is, if you stay in the neighborhoods.

You could just stay in a hotel off Rittenhouse Square that could be a hotel in any other upscale urban environment, and maybe then you'd be closed off to it. But even Rittenhouse Square, if you spent enough time there, if you rubbed shoulders with the winos, it'd get you. Everything in Philadelphia is long and drawn out—and that's only half bad (and only half good).

But for all that assimilation, Mr. Pat really did have years in Philadelphia on his ledger when I met him. Years working for traveling dog shows and an old-fashioned coke plant—the same coke plant whose oven later exploded and burned his father's face. Years working for a city nursing home and morgue. And years spent in the gyms, watching his fighters grow and succeed and leave him for more advanced trainers, or grow up, succeed, and get arrested, or grow up, succeed, and overdose on drugs.

Hell, Mr. Pat's first trainer himself was a former bare-knuckler, a short, baby gorilla of a man named Mr. Mac, who taught all the old-fashioned tricks of the trade: how to head-butt a man properly so that only the opponent felt the blow, how to thumb a man in the eye.

Mr. Pat's uncle had drowned in the navy, his wild brother Calvin had fought cops (Calvin eventually killed one, Mr. Pat dolefully told me), Mr. Pat's own son had stabbed his ex-father-in-law to death in a fit of raving madness (so raving that when the man came to and realized what he had done, he tried to gouge out his own eyes with razors; this was one thing that still haunted Mr. Pat during our conversations—not only the horrific crime, which he hid from me for three-and-a-half years before discussing it, but the notion of a genetic madness running through the males of his family).

This is what Mr. Pat had witnessed—and as to what he had done, well, he had trained fighters, mistreated countless women, drunk so much he had needed rehab, moved out of South Philly for safety reasons to the area of West Philly immediately west of the University of Pennsylvania, and, throughout it all, fathered several children. His last was the girl he had raised in West Philadelphia, the one who carried his hopes that his sordid life could be redeemed and the one who left him with that damn cat when she moved to New Jersey to become a manager in a fashion company.

And yet, for all that history, personal and municipal, Mr. Pat wasn't even alive when the city had really begun to change, when the economy had reached its turning point and the fight game with it. Sure, Mr. Pat knew the main characters. But it's a funny thing about his life—it led me to an event that preceded his birth by about five years, and Jimmy Young's near-title by one hundred.

The turning point in Philadelphia occurred in 1926. And the great—Philadelphian—irony is that the city truly believed it was then in the prime of its life.

❋ ❋ ❋

Sesquicentennial Stadium, where Dempsey–Tunney I was held before a then-record 120,557 spectators. The first photo seems to have been taken the day of the fight, beforehand, and the second, once the stadium was filled for the bout. Courtesy of PhillyHistory.org, a project of the Philadelphia Department of Records.

There had been bank failures and a loan scandal and stock brokerage closings and postwar unemployment. But it was 1926. That meant it had been 150 years since the nation was founded in Philadelphia. For the 100th anniversary, in 1876, the city had thrown one hell of a party—the Centennial Exposition. Ten million people had gone to see this 1,400-

horsepower engine that could that power 800 other machines.[2] So, on its 150th birthday, Philly thought it could do it all again—why the hell not, right? I mean, industry was still a big deal. Machines with big engines were the future. Manufacturing would never die.

Even during the prep work, the lies were revealed. First the budget was cut, then the exhibits failed to open, and then it started raining. It rained practically every day in 1926. No one showed up, and the project lost $5 million.

But, miraculously, two attractions drew people. The first was a re-creation of Market Street as it existed in 1776, when it was named "High Street." This exhibit was run by the Colonial Dames women's committee, which basically created a colonial village to resemble the one they dreamed of—even though the one they dreamed of had never really existed (kind of ironic that now, when Philly was on the verge of disaster, it couldn't even really remember the past and was confronted with the idea that maybe there never had been such a good time).

The other big success was a heavyweight championship fight featuring Jack Dempsey, who was basically the human equivalent of the 1,400-horsepower machine Philly longed for. Philly snagged the fight because New York had tried to force Dempsey to face a really talented black contender, which he was afraid to do, and Philly was willing to let him fight the opponent he *did* want—a former Marine named Gene Tunney, who was well-read and whose technical skill was often mocked. The match was set for September 23 in the new stadium they had built in the marshes—Sesquicentennial Stadium. The fight sold 120,757 tickets, and everyone, all of Philly and the world, thought that the Manassa Mauler, as Dempsey was known, the unstoppable machine, would trash the thinking, crafty Marine vet.

"The fight's in the bag, Jack," Dempsey's bodyguard says. "The so-and-so is reading a book."[3]

You think Vegas is hot on fight night? Everyone showed up to this match: the old-money Philly families—the Shibes, Biddles, and Drex-els—and the old-money New Yorkers—the Astors and Vanderbilts. And that wasn't all: FDR, Irving Berlin, Walter Chrysler, and Babe Ruth came. Perhaps the most eye-popping attendee was Samuel Vauclain, president of Baldwin Locomotive Works, a major manufacturer of trains in Philadelphia, who bought 2,500 ringside tickets for $67,000.[4]

That money got him, and his cohort, a view of the future. Gene Tunney took the title, winning all ten rounds (in the rain, naturally) on both judges' scorecards (in those days, there were two judges instead of three). For Dempsey, it was as if "the very features that had signified progress in earlier times had now become impediments," as one historian would write about Philly, which in later years would be saddled with vestigial industry—empty factory lofts, narrow streets, and railroad tracks at every turn.[5] All the shit that had once made it a manufacturing capital had now left it empty and hollow.

Whereas Dempsey's brawling, rush-forward style had overwhelmed Jess Willard in their title bout, his wide moves now left him vulnerable to Tunney's right-hand lead, which shook the champ in the first round, setting the tone for future engagement. In the fourth, Tunney's flicking jab cut Dempsey's right eye, proving the battle one of paradigm rather than power. Tunney had the moves, and Dempsey couldn't compensate in brutality.

Later when Dempsey met up with his wife, who had just come in by train, having missed the bout entirely, and she asked him what happened, all the former champ could offer by way of an explanation for his swollen face and bloody mouth was: "Honey, I forgot to duck."

☼ ☼ ☼

In colonial times, Philadelphia was a vital city.

Or maybe it wasn't. That's the thing about Philly, about the colonial world that was reimagined and restaged for the sesquicentennial festivities. It might never have been real. Sure, Philly had lots of laborers and shopkeepers and merchants in the colonial days. Sure, it was a trade center bordered by two rivers. And sure, its population of 23,700 was even bigger than New York's.

But how long did that last? And how long did it need to in order to count?

Things went south quickly. Philly lost the state capital to Lancaster (later Harrisburg) and the national one to D.C. Baltimore's exports surpassed Philly's in value. After the War of 1812, European merchants made New York their harbor of choice, mostly because it had less ice and didn't reside a hundred miles from the ocean like Philly's. And then New York overtook Philly in population.

Yes, Philly might never have had the past it longed for. But then, it didn't have only bad times either. Philly bounced back—it always does (or seems to promise to). In the nineteenth century, in order to return to prominence, the city had to find an industry that didn't involve shipping. And it did: using coal and steam, Philly built up a city of plants and factories, becoming the world's foremost maker of everything from high-quality iron to dental appliances.

Philly did more than just develop industry, though. It developed an industrial culture—a culture that valued the work a man could do with his hands. Because the thing about Philly's plants was that they weren't massive and impersonal. Didn't employ thousands of people or rely heavily on machines. No, Philly plants were smaller and more refined than those in Boston and Baltimore. They were often owned by artisans and charged with producing detailed, intricate items—items that could be assembled only by a skilled pair of hands.

So this culture was one that didn't look down on machinelike efficiency but didn't see it as the be-all and end-all, either. Philly's was a work culture that valued both productivity *and* skill. Slugging *and* boxing. A guy who could pound away *and* use his technique to be crafty and slick—now *that* was a Philly worker. *And* a Philly fighter.

And just as the factories were getting going, so too was the boxing game. In 1857, Philly heavyweight bare-knuckler Dominick Bradley beat Sam Rankin of Baltimore (that loathed competitor city) in the 157th round for the heavyweight championship and $2,000 in bet winnings. At the same time, on a more local level, bar owners in Philly began erecting rings in the back of their establishments so that drunken patrons could watch a few matches and lay down bets. This is how boxing got its start in the town.

It all came from the factories—and the backs of the bars.

∗ ∗ ∗

The fighting in Philly came from the factories, and even now, the two are bound up in each other.

It's not a conscious thing, but when they speak, fighters talk always of work. They call running "roadwork" and body punches "bodywork." To use a jab is "to work the jab." The professor Carlo Rotella has noted others: fighters "outwork an opponent, impress the judges with a good work rate, display good work habits in the ring."[6]

The fighting came from the factories and, yes, the factories developed and, yes, eventually they left Philly because everyone there was unionized and they couldn't make a buck. But before they left, they created a whole language.

One female prospect once told me a story about Bozy's gym, which is in the basement of a church and known as the dingiest and toughest gym in the city. "It has no heat," she said. "I went there to spar the girl, Audrey. I took off my boxing shoes, and my toes was frozen. I was like, 'What is going on?' They was like, 'You *work*, you'll get some heat.'"

* * *

They were all hard workers in Philly. By 1880, 40 percent of them worked in the clothing and textile industry, 7 percent in machine tools and hardware, 5 percent in shoes and boots, 4 percent in paper and printing, 2 percent in iron and steel, 3 percent in lumber and wood, 2 percent in glass, 2 percent in furniture, 2 percent in chemicals, 2 percent in shipbuilding, and the rest in smaller industries.[7]

So which boxers did the factory workers like? Well, again, it was the fighters who could work but who also had skill. Or if they couldn't find someone with both, they'd take one of each.

During a single period of the early 1900s, fans embraced both Joe Grim—whose claim to fame was getting knocked down by heavyweight champ Jack Johnson sixteen times in one match but never staying down—and Philadelphia Jack O'Brien, the agility of whose mind, one *New Yorker* writer said, "exceeded even that of his footwork, which was the most spectacular of his generation."[8]

O'Brien's local successor, Irish light-heavy Tommy Loughran, also strived to be dexterous and smart and was rewarded by his fans with the nickname "Phantom of Philly." Loughran was one of the first men to shadowbox in front of a mirror, prompting his beaten opponent Georges Carpentier to say, "I never heard of anything like that!" The usually 185-pound Loughran also sparred with tiny 112 pounders in order to acquire their speed and footwork. He never hit them and, through a combination of moving and blocking, tried never to be hit. Thus, Philly's preeminent big man created a style that was as elegant as it was rough.

It wasn't this way in other cities. In Erie, Pennsylvania, General Electric sponsored a boxing team. But out there, fans just wanted to see slugging. They viewed defense and technique as effeminate.

* * *

They fought because they wanted to fight but also because fighting was work. Middleweight George Benton, who fought in the 1950s, was one of thirteen children. Middleweight Bennie Briscoe, who fought in the 1960s and 1970s, was the oldest of fourteen.

They fought because they had come from nothing. Briscoe was born in Augusta, Georgia, in 1943. His family moved north just like Joe Frazier's and Bobby Watts's and many other black fighters'.[9] From 1850 to 1950, Philadelphia's black population grew from 34,000 to 480,000.

This had all happened before. Before the blacks, poor Europeans had moved to the city and become fighters. First the English, Irish, and Germans. Then the Jews in the '20s, the Italians in the '30s, then the blacks, and then the Hispanics.

One of the black boxers who fought for work was 1950s lightweight Len Matthews. His old trainer Quenzell McCall said of him:

> One day in the gym he asked me for a dime. I asked him, teasingly, if he had found himself a girl. He said, "Of course not. I want to buy a pack of potato chips. Fighters got to eat, don't they?" I was shocked. He admitted he hadn't eaten for a day. And all he was asking for was a pack of potato chips. It was then that Len Matthews became more to me than just another kid who wanted to be a fighter.[10]

In the 1950s, Grays Ferry's Jimmy Soo was an extremely popular half-Irish fighter from the most Irish section of South Philly who retired and took up truck-driving. Four years later, after his wife had twins—a boy and a girl—he had to come out of retirement to pay for his kids' clothing.

Black fighters fought because they were excluded from industry. The Budd Company, Bendix, Cramp's Shipyard, Baldwin Locomotive, the Crown Can Company, and the Quaker Lace Company did not hire blacks.[11] Others hired few blacks, and all 280 of them in the 45,000-employee textile industry were janitors. Even bantamweight Jeff Chandler's dad was forced to work in a segregated area of Frankford Arsenal, just as Sun Shipyards maintained "colored" yards. In this economic environment, black boxers often had to work side jobs to help support themselves and their families (and then had to keep jobs after "retirement"). Sweet Pea Adams was lucky enough to get a job in manufacturing. "I'd get up early in the morning and I'd run around the reservoir two times. And come home and get a cup of coffee and maybe a sand-wich and then I'd go to work."

Adams's job was at Whitman's Candies: he had to place giant slabs of caramel under a flattening machine. Later, he worked for TWA. Wel-terweight Dick Turner repaired refrigerators, then washed windows, and then worked for the city, checking people's water meters in the summer. Forties lightweight Wesley Mouzon worked for three or four years as a clothing salesman, then co-opened a Laundromat in South Philly. Bob Montgomery worked as a brick mason, a carpenter, and a beer salesman. Current prospect Mike Jones used to drive a forklift at night at Home Depot. And the legendary Bennie Briscoe took up mu-nicipal pest control. "We figured he sprinkled some poison around," promoter Russell Peltz once recalled. "Bennie told me he went in there with a baseball bat."[12]

The work isn't always tangential to fighters' careers. Some guys worked so doggedly that their jobs became a part of their boxing iden-tities. Matt Adgie moonlighted as an iceman and was nicknamed the "Wyalusing Fighting Iceman." At a certain point, he decided to focus on his career and drop the job. He started to lose, though, so his trainer determined lifting ice had been the key all along and ordered him to deliver again. Adgie did, and he resumed winning.[13] South Philly light-weight Eddie Giosa, a '40s *triple* left-hooker, used his hands to make communications equipment for warplanes at RCA.[14] And heavyweight Joe Frazier worked in the mid-'60s at Cross Brothers slaughterhouse, where he'd pound beef with combos in a routine later glamorized by Stallone.

*　*　*

This was the time of the American 1920s, as Arthur Miller said, "when it all seemed to be coasting, expanding opportunity everywhere, the dream in full bloom."[15] Philly was the self-proclaimed workshop of the world, "with a billion dollars invested in 266 distinct lines of manu-facturing."[16] And money flowing for city projects, too. Philly built the world's longest suspension bridge, a 1,750-foot, $45 million structure to Jersey. And a $30 million French-designed parkway to match the Champs-Élysées, ending in a huge neoclassical art museum filled with borrowed Renoirs and Van Goghs. The city's Curtis Publishing pro-duced *Ladies Home Journal* and the *Saturday Evening Post*. And the top hats tuned to Stokowski and his Philadelphia Orchestra as RCA recorded and NBC broadcast, though that was old money, high-class business. Down on the street, the city had 164 movie theaters and sixty more for shows. It had 13,000 speakeasies and 300 brothels, with local leaders spending $20 million on bribes. Raids on South Philly bars uncovered "little black books" filled with the figures: police captains getting $250 every so often, detectives $25, patrolmen $5. An investigating city hall detective was said to have extorted $1,500 from a bootlegger. Then the detective went missing.[17] But the party rolled on 'cause it was the Jazz Age, ladies and gentleman, and the blues clubs dripped smoky-wet and no one could stop that syncopatin' beat even if he tried. "THAT IS THE TROUBLE WITH A GOOD DEAL OF OUR RECENT FICTION, OUR RECENT VERSE, OUR RECENT THINKING AND OUR RECENT MUSIC," decried stodgy old professor J. P. Wickersham Crawford at Penn's 1925 winter commencement. "Most of the jazz music, like jazz literature and jazz thinking, is the product of the untrained mind that does not work in any direction, that does not know how to think and cannot support the effort of trying to think."[18]

But he was drowned by the emotion of Bessie Smith's husky vibrato. "I was with you, baaby, when you diduuuuuuuuuuuuun't have a dime," she quavered before crowds at Horan's Madhouse Club. "I was with you, baaaby, when you diduuuuuuuuuuuuuuuun't have a dime. Now since you've got plenteeey money, you have throwed your good gaal doooown."

At the center of it all was Max "Boo Boo" Hoff, "like a giant spider in the middle of a great web with eyes in front and behind," as one district attorney put it.[19] Hoff was the eccentric teetotalist who made millions as the bootlegger/fight promoter responsible for shipping 350,000 gallons of grain liquor to the rest of America—a stream more vast than Chicago's. He cultivated a stable of one hundred fighters whom he'd promote and use as bodyguards. And he'd help ignite a gang war between the rival Duffy and O'Leary clans for control of the city's booze. On the Duffy side, there was twenty-seven-year-old, four-foot-tall Hunchback McLoon, a former Philadelphia Athletics mascot who ran a tavern and managed fighters. One dim morning, three coats popped him with shotguns. The following week, rival Daniel O'Leary was sleeping with his mistress when five men burst in, shot him, and escorted the woman out. But in the hazy, nicotined boxing world, writers remember

Boo Boo Hoff not for such theatrics but for the whiskey he used to send them and for the title bout of '26. Supposedly, Hoff had helped steer Tunney–Dempsey to Philly. And then on either the day before or the afternoon of the fight, Hoff insinuated himself into Tunney's resting room and had Tunney and his manager sign a contract. The exact terms of the contract or its merits or whether Tunney signed wittingly have never been determined, though Hoff later dropped his lawsuit without a settlement. But the suit said Tunney and Gibson had promised Hoff 20 percent of their earnings in exchange for a $20,000 loan. Rumors spread that Gibson had worried the bout would be arranged for Dempsey, so he involved Hoff in order to right the ship. Hoff, wanting to protect his newfound interest, had a ringside doctor ready to proclaim a foul and award Tunney the bout in case he was knocked down—not exactly a vote of confidence in Tunney's abilities. As it turned out, Tunney wouldn't need such help, since Dempsey couldn't knock him down. Maybe the city should've put more faith in the thinking boxer to begin with.

For it was the '20s, and Philly got plenty money and throwed many good gals down. But suddenly, the veneer began to crack that night, a panicked city realizing its $5 million loss on a rearward-looking exposition. A bet gone awry. Maybe it could've been okay, because Philly once made these gorgeous colonial streets and could do so again. But the truth was, all had only *seemed* to be coasting, only a dream bloomed, and nothing was as sturdy as the city had come to believe. And Dempsey lost on a rainy night followed by several more. His bob and weave, crouch and charge no longer progressive, even though it once seemed so against a plodding six-feet, six-and-a-half inch Jess Willard. And the man who would defy common employment, the millionaire mobster Boo Boo Hoff, ending no better than the fighters he promoted, broke and a sleeping pill addict in a West Philly apartment. Dead at forty-eight.

Cramp's Shipyard closed in '29, though it would tauntingly reopen during World War II only to close again. And New York's George Washington Bridge surpassed Philly's suspension wonder in length. And then the Depression, which would prevent the city from investing in new structures and new technologies, and the war, which would draw all resources for another half decade. So "by the late 1940s, Philadelphia was generally considered to be a 'worn-out city,' with 60 percent of its industrial buildings obsolete and 30,000 properties vacant."[20]

❊ ❊ ❊

The city was hurt not only by its infrastructure—small blocks and cramped alleys, railroad tracks and dilapidated buildings, all of which left absolutely no room for new factories—but by the very workers who had labored so hard to make the city what it was. They took pride in their work, and so they unionized and demanded better wages. They were the ones responsible, after all, for the creation of the complex goods Philly provided the world—all the textile products and radio equipment.

Of course, corporate heads tended to disagree. So they moved their companies to the suburbs at first—simply for the better facilities, if not for the less demanding workforce—and then to the south and west, where workers weren't unionized and other states were willing to subsidize their building costs and reduce their taxes.

In these new open areas, the companies pioneered technologies that made whatever goods Philly still did produce obsolete. No one needed Apex's silk hosiery once nylon was introduced, for instance, and its three-plant, 900-worker company closed in 1954.

Not all the companies left Philly. Some of them stuck around, while still maintaining offices across the Eastern Seaboard in those traditional bastions of business that the old guard felt—or hoped—it could always count on. Something strange began to happen, though, as the older companies were one by one bled to death by the inexorable deindustrialization of America's great cities: the leaders of the companies, too, began to die—often from massive cardiac episodes.

The following is a small compendium of brief obituaries, all of heads of major Philly manufacturers.

1929: David Milne, seventy, a senior member of the family firm J. C. Milne and Sons, makers of woolens and shirtings. "Stricken suddenly" by heart disease while on a business trip to New York.

1930: Charles Webb, seventy-two, founder and president of Charles J. Webb & Co., president of the Philadelphia Textile Manufacturers Association. Dead of heart disease.

1937: Robert Hooper Jr., thirty-six, a divorced executive in the New York office of William E. Hooper & Sons, manufacturers of cotton duck. Dead on his apartment floor, wearing pajamas, an apparent suicide by gas poisoning. A note on a handkerchief, lying on the table next to a bottle of liquor and one of sparkling water, written nearly illegibly with the carbon of a burned match head: "As I lived, so do I go." His textile executive father rushed up from Philadelphia upon hearing the news.

1938: Nathan Folwell II, fifty-eight, the vice president in charge of the New York office of Folwell Brothers & Co., the woolen manufacturer founded by his father in 1857.

1939: William Kitchen, sixty-two, a senior partner in the James G. Kitchen wool brokerage, grandson of the original William Kitchen, who built textile mills on Wissahickon Creek. Dead of a heart attack.

1948: Richard Wood, seventy, a partner in George Wood & Sons, a textile merchant firm founded by his father, and a director of the Philadelphia National Bank and the Pennsylvania Railroad Company.

1951: Arthur Kerr, fifty-seven, a textile executive officer of James H. Kerr & Sons. Dead of a heart attack while driving through Virginia.

1952: Harry Butterworth Jr., sixty-two, chairman of H. W. Butterworth & Sons, makers of textile finishing and rayon spinning machinery. Died in his Chestnut Hill home.

1955: Walter Fancourt III, forty-four, president of the W. F. Fancourt Company, which he had taken over a year earlier after the death of his father.

1957: Frederick Scholler, seventy-one, founder and chairman of Scholler Brothers, manufacturer of textile chemicals.

1962: Myron Feinberg, forty-five, president of the Feinberg Textile Corporation, from injuries suffered in a car accident. A few hours later, his father, Charles, seventy, founder of the company. At Myron's house. Possibly of heartbreak.

Fathers and sons, and so it continued. Norman Haac in '63, Maurice Sherr in '64, Edwin Dale in '67. In boxing, they say, "Work the body and the head will fall." Philly's textile industry took one body blow after another, and the heads passed in turn. By 1986, the textile and apparel industries had lost more than 91,000 jobs from their total in 1947, when they accounted for a *quarter* of the city's industrial employment.[21]

When the companies died, the communities were lost. The slap of one man's hand on another's fleshy back—*that* was community. In 1900, the city had fourteen fight clubs. In 1906, the city held three boxing cards a night six nights a week.[22] These thrived because a group of laboring men wanted to watch others labor for leisure. And that's what fell apart when industry did, as middle-class workers lost their standing, forced to flail for a position in the service economy's upper class or to slink with bowed head back to the lower. They couldn't buy tickets, and there wasn't much for them to celebrate anyway.

Without patrons, the clubs had to close. The 5,000-seat Olympic A. C. closed in '21. Its 2,500-seat successor closed in '49. The third of three Broadway A. C.s in '35. The first Cambria—an outdoor venue—in '54. The 2,000-seat indoor Cambria, called The Blood Pit and The College of Hard Knocks, in '63. Also in '54, promoter Jimmy Toppi closed the Metropolitan Opera House *and* his 5,000-seat outdoor stadium at Broad and Packer.

"If one were to choose a dividing point between the past and present," wrote Philly boxing expert Jack Fried (also known as Matt Ring) in 1954, "there could be none more appropriate than the Dempsey–Tunney fight of the sesquicentennial year."[23]

Ah, 1926. That was the turning point, the moment when brains beat brawn, when a nascent service economy began to replace industrial labor in Philadelphia. It is when the companies began to fold and the people with money began moving to the suburbs. Already at such a distance they were unlikely to return to the city for fights. But what Fried didn't anticipate was that technology—namely television—would make such a return totally unnecessary anyway.

* * *

In the mid-1950s, TV networks began airing fights every night of the week. Suddenly, fans didn't need to buy tickets. "Is Boxing on the Ropes?" one *New York Times Magazine* headline asked. "Yes, says a veteran critic of the manly art . . . and he blames it all on TV." The writer traced the decline of inner-city clubs, noting how "utterly ironical" it was "that there should be more interest in boxing than ever before in history while there is a shrinkage in sites."[24]

In 1956, novelist Charles Einstein spent four pages in *Harper's* expounding the popular new boxing idiom: "Nothing else comes over television so bad so good."

"In free translation," Einstein wrote, "the good part is that boxing is a superb medium for the television camera, not only for its compact nicety of physical dimension, with all of the action occurring within a twenty-foot square, but for the known concentrate of audience—in this case, beer-drinking, cigar-smoking, razor-wielding males—so dear to a sponsor's heart. The bad part is that television had decimated boxing as a business and ruined it as a sport."[25]

Ruined, indeed, for the camera and its sponsors preferred the reckless violence of unrefined sluggers to the quick-witted technique of disciplined boxers. The easily followed single punch to the tricky, hard-to-follow combination of many. And decimated as a business because money now flowed to national companies like Gillette instead of to local clubs that bred fighters.

The sport, in making deals with national companies, inadvertently drained itself, and Einstein chose a brilliant, symbolic story to sum up the rise of TV: the Giardello–Graham fight. Joey Giardello was a South Philly Italian middleweight whom Mr. Pat had helped train at the Passyunk gym. He had gone to New York to fight Billy Graham on national TV, and he had won a split decision. Or so the TV had announced. But after the broadcast had ended, the chairman of the New York Athletic Commission had changed a judge's scorecard, reversing the decision and awarding the bout to Graham. The bookies had then been forced to pay all bettors, for the next morning's papers claimed Graham had won even though TV had shown otherwise. "I should have known," sobbed one bookie before Einstein. "My father always told me. Never take a bet on anything that can talk."

It was the only time, Einstein said, he had ever seen a bookie cry.

* * *

The deindustrialization of Philadelphia completely changed its neighborhoods. The first ring around the core of the city—the "streetcar suburbs," as they were called, for their newfound accessibility in the early twentieth century after the advent of the electric tram—was vacated by whites, who moved to "automobile suburbs" farther out from Philly on the Main Line. Poorer blacks, most of whom had just migrated to the city from the South, made the empty inner ring their new home.

Once they did, the powers that be essentially decided to let the area rot. Strawberry Mansion, a neighborhood in North Philly, is a prime example. John Coltrane and rival fighters "Sugar" Hart and left-hooker Charley Scott[26] lived there in old row houses that had once been grand and beautiful but were now peeling and unstable. Residents wanted to upgrade the area but couldn't, since the manufacturers wouldn't offer them jobs, and federal corporations wouldn't give them mortgages. This latter injustice was spurred by a 1937 map-report drawn by a Roosevelt New Deal agency, which created guidelines for lenders. Areas in Philadelphia with Jews or white ethnics were graded "D" and painted red on the map, indicating they didn't deserve loans because they represented "a lower grade population." That was South and West Philly. North Philly contained the "detrimental influences" of a "heavy concentration of Negro." Also "D." This included Strawberry Mansion.

Strawberry Mansion decayed. Welterweight Scott walked up and down his block asking people to loan him $65 for rent. Gangs of the unemployed roved streets. The area became toxically violent. In 1973, nine-year-old Ronald Hollis was wounded from gang war crossfire on a Strawberry Mansion corner, right near his house. In retribution, a seventeen-year-old was killed two days later. When blacks tried to avoid the violence and moved to older white areas, they were denied. In Woodlawn in 1985, which housed second-generation Irish, Italians, and Poles, a black couple had their window broken by a hurled soda bottle, their presence publicly protested, and, finally, their house burned.

❉ ❉ ❉

The economy was in shambles, and suddenly Philadelphia found its races warring with each other.

The white-black divide reached even the boxing world, which usually respected any man who could fight.

In the sweltering summer of 1964, rioting erupted along Columbia Avenue in North Philly's ghetto after a black couple refused to move their car, which was blocking traffic at an intersection. The consensus white response was that "blame could not even be placed on both races, since the riot was all-Negro and it was unprovoked by any incident that could conceivably be considered a civil rights violation."[27] Meanwhile, at least one black fighter joined the riot, as that block of Columbia Avenue was also home to a Police Athletic League gym.

Welterweight Gypsy Joe Harris said, "I finally couldn't help it when I see these three men tryin' to load a refrigerator into a car. I split my sides laughin', 'cause they don't even know how to steal right. The cops came and hauled them away, and while they were bein' taken this chick jumps up on top of the refrigerator and starts screamin', 'Black men unite!' I said to myself, baby, I'm gonna unite all right, and then Gypsy started diggin' in himself. It wasn't anything worth much. Just small things."[28] Like so much of Gypsy's life, his recollection was as true as it was colorful. In response to NAACP head Cecil Moore's plea of "quit looting," a woman had indeed mounted a fridge and screamed, "Black man, do you hear me? Cecil has nothing to tell you. I'm a black woman. Let them take me."

The white fighters were represented by the Veteran Boxers Association of Philadelphia, named Ring 1 for being the country's first such group. The VBA held its annual banquet at South Philly's famed Italian joint Palumbo's every Mother's Day. In a 1966 VBA magazine, the group clearly defined its constituency in an editorial that ostensibly argued against federal oversight for boxing but actually said much more. "Barry Goldwater," it began, "threw a bright spotlight on the fantastic, deadly encroachment on our American Way of Life, the Free Enterprise System, by Washington bureaucrats, dedicated to the welfare-socialistic ideology.

"One out of every six employed persons in these United States is working for the Federal Government, and all of us are paying the exorbitant taxes that, with other government receipts, account for 35% of our National Income. . . . And what has all this to do with Boxing, you may rightly ask, and the answer is simply this . . . the naming of a Federal Czar would transfer another part of our freedom to the Central Government, and send us faster down the road to socialism."

Page 25 of the VBA magazine featured an ad from the Republican City Committee—the very committee blacks had mobilized against in the previous decade (wrote one Philly scholar of this time: "It is probably the negro vote, as much as any other one single factor, that kept Philadelphia Democratic").[29] The ad touted the committee as "Advocate of Clean Politics" and the Veteran Boxers Association as "Champion of Clean Fighting."

❋ ❋ ❋

In a bad economy, amid race riots, new gangs took hold of the ghetto. The early 1960s marked a period of transition from the relatively innocuous "switchblade" gangs of the '50s to the weapon- and drug-dealing gangs of the '70s. In 1962, for instance, only one person died from gang-related violence in Philadelphia. But during the next decade, the drug and weapons trades flourished along with a violent strain of oppositional black nationalism. And so flourished mostly black gangs: the Moroccos, Twenty-eighth and Oxford, the Valley, the Empires,

Twelfth and Poplar, Twelfth and Wallace, the Mongo Nation, the Fifth Street Gang, and the Nineteenth and Carpenter Street Gang. By 1973, a *New York Times* study reported 100 to 150 gangs in the city with membership of 6,000 to 8,000 ranging in age from ten or eleven to the mid-twenties. From 1962 to 1973, the *Times* reported 245 gang-related deaths, including those of a seven-year-old and a nine-year-old, with an average fatality age around sixteen. By contrast, the South Bronx was thought to have "only" 100 gangs, prompting Philadelphia authorities to say their city had become more violent than any other. In 1979, cross-fire between two gangs—Wheels of Soul and the Ghetto Riders—in Camden (considered "East Philly" by most) at a Thanksgiving football game, that symbol of American wholesomeness, wounded fourteen and spurred the 3,000 in attendance to dash for safety. By 1980, Philly was said to be a main source of New York's illegal weapons, and Pennsylvania had thousands of dealers who charged $50 per "piece." Then came coke and crack.

One civil group tried to promote the city's image with a new slogan and hired the publicist Elliot Curson, a veteran of Reagan's first political campaign. All he could muster was "Philadelphia isn't as bad as Philadelphians think it is."

* * *

For potential black boxers, ghetto upheaval turned economic and social paradigms on their head. Where once boxing was seen as a primary escape to the good life and a damn cool job at that, it no longer promised lucre (due to the lack of local clubs) or badass credibility. In a service society, skilled hands had no redeeming value. For money, one could deal drugs. To prove strength, one could pop a cap in the back of twelve-year-old Jay Bedford's head as he returned home from church in South Philly.

As early as 1952, Weinberg and Arond noted the tenuousness of ghetto career choices in their landmark study of boxing culture. "It can be inferred tentatively that the social processes among juveniles and adolescents in the lower socioeconomic levels, such as individual and gang fights, the fantasies of 'easy money,' the lack of accessible vocational opportunities, and the general isolation from the middle-class culture, are similar for those who become professional boxers as for those who become delinquents. The difference resides in the role-model the boy picks, whether criminal or boxer."[30] Increasingly, boys were choosing the former simply for lack of alternatives. Mayor Frank Rizzo, the white former police chief,[31] appointed Zack Clayton—a former fighter, the first black to referee a title bout, and Pennsylvania's boxing commissioner—as head of gang control. Clayton enlisted two-time lightweight champ "Bobcat" Montgomery to help. But, as Clayton said, the problem extended beyond any one group: gangs "burst up today and dissolve tomorrow." And so Philadelphia was left chasing ideas, trying to root out a fiercely violent streak in a young and disaffected population.

Growing up in South Philly in the 1960 and 1970s, professor Gerald Early of Washington University observed the disaffection:

> There was a kind of breakdown in African-American street culture. Odd to say that because a lot of people would say that street culture is a breakdown of "normal culture." [But] in the '70s in Philly, a lot of bad things happened. The growth of the Black Mafia and murders that were taking place in the city.[32] A real breakdown in street culture there and in respect for being able to be good with your hands. People may have still had a certain amount of respect for it, but the skill itself didn't seem to be so useful in the streets anymore. I mean, I just can't tell you—the kinda drugs that were coming and the automatic weapons. And it's a fact, and I think this was really the breakdown, so that kinda being good with your hands wasn't able to withstand the [shift]. It didn't seem to have a great use anymore. Having a 9 mm automatic made you the equal of anyone who was good with his hands. And with the drug thing and the tearing down of what was happening, I just think that whole sense of the craft got lost. Just really got lost. The breakdown of kind of a masculine street culture that valued that craft. I guess it got displaced. It's very sad, you know. I grew up in Philly in the '50s and '60s and the loss of that craft is very sad.

❁ ❁ ❁

The few men who still believed in hands turned elsewhere. Baseball had always been around but opened to blacks only after the color barrier fell in 1947. Three year later, the editor of *Ring Magazine* wrote of new heroes, of the way "boys who once looked upon Joe Louis with pride and envy and wanted to emulate him, now are focused on Jackie Robinson and other topnotch ballplayers." As early as 1949, a magazine article on boxing's decline said "basketball is the sport that arouses public interest today."[33] And the trainer of Sugar Ray Robinson—who was perhaps the century's greatest boxer and who began his career in Philly for legendary promoter Herman "Mugsy" Taylor—would say all the fighters are playing basketball, except for the heavyweights, who play linebacker. An example from a recent *Inquirer* article: "When he entered his freshman year of high school, McClain had to choose between boxing and football because he couldn't lift weights in boxing [boxers have to make a certain weight limit by fight time] and was required to lift weights for football.

"Football prevailed."[34]

It was a vicious cycle, as other sports drew the athletes and thus attracted more attention and money, which in turn drew more athletes. In 1945, 13,500 attended the *Philadelphia Inquirer*'s amateur "Diamond Belt" tournament. Six years later, only 4,000 came, and the *Inquirer*'s charity division decided it could no longer afford the show. By the mid-1960s, boxing wasn't good work anymore. Only Cassius Clay elicited intense public interest and dollars. So when Philly heavyweights Leotis Martin and Dave Bailey were matched on the undercard of Clay–Liston in Boston in November 1964, they were promised $750 each. But when the Clay–Liston match was postponed, the two heavyweights faced each other in Philly for $125 and $150, respectively. That same night at the Philadelphia Athletic Club, Bennie Briscoe beat Sugar Wyatt for the second time in his 15–0 career. But he collected 10 percent of the net receipts from the show, which turned out to be a meager $171. He then divided that sum among his manager, trainer, and cornermen. The show's promoter didn't fare any better. Lou Lucchese, a former amateur flyweight, was a manager and promoter from Reading, Pennsylvania, who had grown up in the '20s and '30s idolizing boxers. His friends nicknamed him "Little Tony Canzoneri" due to his resemblance to the famed lightweight champ. He had once claimed to be eighteen years old when he was actually fourteen in order to get into fights. He ran a novelty toy shop with his brother and served as a local justice of the peace, but it was his "life's dream" to promote fights. Two weeks earlier, he had put on his first show at the Philadelphia Athletic Club and lost $1,200. One local writer said Lucchese was "round as a basketball and equally resilient."[35] This time, he thought he'd at least break even after 762 attended. But the club raised his rent from $250 to

$420, and he lost again. "Who am I working for?" he lamented to a reporter, invoice in hand. "I'm trying to do something for the fighters, but things like this make me feel like forgetting the whole thing."

Today, at eighty-seven years old, he tells me in a croaky voice over the phone from Reading that "it was real hard, real hard. *Jesus*." Three years ago, a doctor told Lucchese that he had liver cancer and thirty days to live. But in September 2007, he's "still singing," even with prostate cancer and diabetes and a "bag for the penis" to deal with incontinence. So he admits he's in "bad shape," but he doesn't let it preclude his reminiscing about those 1960s gyms, flooded with willing fighters who couldn't get work because no one was offering any. "Boxing was dead," he says, "not just in Philadelphia but all over." Those who did attend Lucchese's cards were "regular people off the street," many of whom, he says, knew how to sneak in without paying the $4 or $6. He tried giving away tickets to spur interest and he even wrote a letter to a senator requesting help. He partly blames it on the factories closing, dispersing, or disenfranchising his would-be patrons. "I tried the best down there," he says, remembering the time Joe Frazier's manager, Yank Durham, a good friend, promised him he could promote all of Frazier's fights. "No one can have him but you," Durham swore after Lucchese gave Frazier a spot on a card in Pittsburgh in 1966. Then Yank Durham turned around and handed his fighter over to Mugsy Taylor, the other Philly promoter. "He was a pretty smart guy," Lucchese says of Durham now, chuckling.

The other promoter, Mugsy Taylor, was a rough old Jewish mobster, an associate of Bugsy Siegel. He had begun his career in the early 1900s leading a horse-drawn cart through the city with cowbells and fight posters to advertise Jack McGuigan's boxing club. He bought his own club in June 1912 and spent the next sixty years staging wars that men would forever remember, including what he called "the greatest heavyweight fight I ever looked at," Marciano–Walcott of 1952, when Rocky threw the perfect right in the thirteenth round and Jersey Joe recoiled to his left with the most exquisitely pained look, as if he had downed a glass of lemon juice and nails. It was Herman Taylor who helped bring the Tunney–Dempsey fight to Philly and, after it rained during the match, took all the women out afterward to the Jewish section of South Street to buy them new dresses. But by 1967, Mugsy was eighty years old. He staged one last hurrah, drawing 4,689 men and $20,806 to West

Philly's Arena to see eccentric welterweight Gypsy Joe Harris win his twenty-second straight bout. Gypsy was just one man, however, and the commission soon barred him after "discovering" he was blind in one eye (they had probably known all along and looked the other way). Taylor promoted less and less during the next ten years until he died at ninety-three in 1980. Eventually he just started threatening competitors. "I heard from Herman Taylor a couple times," sniggers Lucchese today. "He called me a carpetbagger and all that bullshit. Hehehe." Lucchese stopped promoting in 1972, after his twenty-one-year-old son died in a car accident, and he lost all feeling for the work later in the decade, when his wife died.[36]

Without Lucchese, Philly boxing might have dissolved then, and maybe it would be better if it had, instead of enduring this drawn-out struggle that may yet end the same way. Perhaps it was cruel to pretend the past could be sustained, like when Walter Mondale promised and promised to keep Frankford Arsenal in Philly open, even as employees received relocation notices. And perhaps the city should've let go its terminal culture of hands, should've embraced the change no longer deniable, to survive this new world that focuses on service. But in 1969, none of this mattered to Russell Peltz, a mustachioed twenty-two-year-old kid from the suburbs who had sneaked out of his house seven years earlier as a high school sophomore to buy a ticket to the light-heavyweight fight between local Harold Johnson and Doug Jones. It was a $10 top-price ticket, and promoter Herman Taylor had his signature embossed on the thing. And Peltz brought it home and showed his sister and said, "Look, Herman Taylor's signature right on the ticket!" And Peltz inhaled its heady masculine whiff, as Gypsy Joe did his favorite beverage, whiskey and milk. And when it came time for Peltz to work, he took a newspaper gig with the *Bulletin*. There he befriended boxing writer Jack Fried, and he heard people say how the sport was going, how no one *cared* anymore. So he paid a visit to Herman Taylor at his office in the Shubert Building on Broad between Locust and Walnut. It's a theater there. And Taylor was nice for a little while, because he thought Peltz was still a writer coming to interview him. Then Peltz told him he wanted to promote. And "after that, it was all downhill in his office," Peltz recalls. "And I don't think I ever spoke to Herman Taylor again."

First Peltz asked Lucchese whether he could serve as the latter's matchmaker. Lucchese wanted to do it all himself and said no.[37] So Peltz staged his own show, on September 30, 1969, at the Blue Horizon on North Broad. The card starred Boogaloo Watts and Cyclone Hart and, of course, Bennie Briscoe, who knocked out his opponent in the first round, though all three middleweights lit up the ballroom. Watts danced and Hart left-hooked and Briscoe attacked with relentlessness and resilience. As if from another era, the fans flocked to see the 160-pounders work. Attendance was 1,606 and the gross $6,010—both records for the cozy venue. Peltz had to turn away 300 more for whom he had no room. And in the next year, he'd establish a biweekly program at the Blue before starting Monday Night Fights! at the newly built Spectrum off South Broad next to the old Sesquicentennial Stadium. Peltz wore long narrow suits and high collars and knit his brow repeatedly. They called him the "mod promoter" or the "boy promoter" or "Edwardian." It was the last golden era of Philly fighting, a farewell to a certain city and its way, to tickets embossed with fancy signatures. Blue Horizon tickets were $4. The programs cost thirty-five cents, and some were written by Malcom "Flash" Gordon, a weed-puffing, pony-tail-wearing, bespectacled nerd who mimeographed copies in the bathtub of his Sunnyside, New York, apartment. He was one of the last hard-core fans, and in Philly, he saw a revival—"dazzling matchmaking"—that his own city couldn't muster. "Ninety miles up in New York," he wrote, "a staff of many under a brain of nothing (Teddy 'Asshole' Brenner) with backing of millions, over 5 times the population, and 10 times the amount of fistic talent, sit twiddling their thumbs moaning 'TV will save boxing.'. . . Perhaps they owe it to their bosses to come down to Philadelphia [to] see how successful fights are promoted?"

Not everyone loved Peltz. A number of fighters said he had the fans' interest at heart instead of theirs. And this was true. Peltz did prefer to sic two upcoming Philly prospects on each other even though such matches invariably derailed at least one of the fighters' careers (if not, in a bloody war, both). Two hungry Philly guys made for a brilliant match, and Peltz saw the demand for those matches and supplied them. But what about us? the fighters sometimes crowed. We worked so hard to emerge from this city, and your matches guarantee that only half of us will. Maybe. But Peltz had a response then, and in later years, fans' memories would vindicate it. For what is a Philly fighter, really, if not a man who makes his reputation in his city, a man who never does reach national renown but stages amazing displays ONE NIGHT ONLY before neighbors—displays that elders will forever recall, enticing young'uns with auld lang syne? And how could boys rise to the occasion without apposite foes to extract their manhood?

Peltz provided them and the setting in which it could unfold.

It didn't always run smoothly. At one point, two boxers had to be replaced on a Spectrum card (on "Free Warm-Up Jackets night") after they were charged with murdering a Trenton man. One of the two was arrested on his way to the weigh-in. But the shows attracted the last of the workers who clamored to see Bennie Briscoe—the last worker. Peltz promoted all of his fights (they didn't have a long-term promotional contract, but Briscoe's manager was Peltz's brother-in-law, and as Peltz says, "I didn't expect to be screwed by family"). And thus featured, Briscoe came to represent for Philadelphians everything they loved and hated about their city. Briscoe lived in the dense North Philly ghetto, worked as a municipal rat chaser, and shaved his dome of a head for financial reasons: "You see, my parents have ten sons," he told his fans. "So you can just imagine the bread needed for haircuts. So when we were kids, in order that he got his money's worth, Pop would tell the barber to keep cuttin' until there was nothing left."

Then there was his career. Briscoe never sat on a stool between rounds. He ran four miles even on the mornings of fights. And every time his career began rolling, it hit a bump from which, ever resilient, he'd recover. In 1969, Briscoe was readying for a title fight against junior middleweight champ Freddie Little when he lost a shocker to Joe Shaw. Briscoe came right back in 1970 and beat the hell out of Shaw in the Arena at Forty-fifth and Market, forcing Shaw to quit in his corner after the sixth round. Briscoe won his next seven fights by KO— all in Philly—and seemed poised to fight Carlos Monzon for the middleweight title. But on November 15, 1971, a guy named Gutierrez shot a hard right six inches forward, sending Briscoe flailing into the ropes and onto the floor. In the first round. Briscoe rose at nine and came off the ropes, walking into another right that plunged him facedown to the canvas. His manager sobbed. But Briscoe rose yet again, "like a man who returned from the dead,"[38] and mustered the energy to stand for the rest of the round. He returned to his corner glassy-eyed, one thought alone piercing his haze, as he'd later recall: to "knock that motherfucker's head off." In the second, he bored into Gutierrez like a man ripping through the past, desperate to find that time when he was really something. When he was the man. Gutierrez crumpled at 2:17.

What ultimately endeared Briscoe to locals was his final inability to win the big one. No matter how many times he came back, no matter how many times he tried, even after he fought one guy while ridden with hepatitis, and knocked out another after an emergency appendectomy, Briscoe never quite made it. He fought for the title three times, the last at the age of thirty-four, once he had already passed his peak. But it was his first attempt in '72 that epitomized it all, against the Argentinean Carlos Monzon, with whom he had officially drawn five years earlier, even though many spectators felt he won. In the ninth, he smashed Monzon into the ropes with a right. And Monzon dangled there like a queasy drunk poised to vomit. But for whatever reason, Briscoe couldn't follow with a finisher. By the next round, Monzon had recovered his stability and an eventual victory by decision. "We were one punch away from the world championship," Briscoe's trainer said. "But Bennie just couldn't get it across." So he never won, but as one of his biggest fans said to me at a recent Golden Gloves match, maybe there's something Philly about that. And when Briscoe retired at age thirty-nine, the program summed it up: "He had no soft touches, no easy build-up fights to pad his record. He went out and gave an honest night's work. Any fan who had the pleasure of watching Briscoe in his prime always came away with his money's worth. For twenty years, right to his last fight in 1982, Bennie Briscoe was a fight fan's fighter. What more could anyone possibly ask?"

An honest night's work: that's all Philadelphians wanted, until the man couldn't give anymore. All they could possibly ask for was a replacement, someone to stand before national audiences as Philly's storehouse for optimism in place of the actual thing. Yet it was the mid-'70s, and all champs were foreign except the heavyweights, and Ali trash-talked his way into sixty-five million living rooms on NBC just for a bout with Briton Richard Dunn. It seemed only a heavyweight could take Briscoe's place, and for a time, it seemed Joe Frazier was the perfect candidate. He won the gold in '64 and beat Ali in '71 to retain his title and undefeated record. But Foreman knocked him down six times in two rounds before Ali beat him twice and Foreman knocked him out again, and to this day, the thud of his body hitting the floor reverberates up North Broad, past his gym, Cosell's frantic cry still ringing: "DOWN GOES FRAZIA! DOWN GOES FRAZIA!"

There was another heavyweight who trained in the 23rd Police Athletic League with Briscoe and Frazier. Another workingman who entered the gym after a new gang stole his radio that he bought with money made folding laundry. A part-time stevedore and construction worker, robbed of that which he earned, driven to learn and revive the magic craft of hands, of knuckles calloused to palimpsest, brine-soaked but swift, able to trace punitive ribbons of air. And the style he slickly evolved, slippery-smooth—Philly's best hope, if it would still embrace it—technically pure counterpunching, as thread through needles, hands in holes, a clockwork aesthetic but aesthetic nonetheless. Artisanal, fluid force, a city's paradox, the man's manner, flick, flick, flick— *crisp*—fresh like a dream, but dripping real, black and white, yet colored.

His name was Jimmy Young.

3

THE KID

Men must endure / Their going hence even as their coming hither.
Ripeness is all.
—William Shakespeare, *King Lear*

There was a former child prodigy of a boxer who fought in the generation following Jimmy Young's. He was considered an heir to the Philly legacy and by the mid-'90s had befriended Young, whom he'd drive home from a fight in Atlantic City one night after the two were profiled together in a *Daily News* piece about punch-drunk boxers.

Almost a decade after that newspaper piece was published, I walked over to Mr. Pat's hazy den of an apartment with my computer. Together we watched the fight that defined the prodigy. This was not a fight Mr. Pat had ever seen. It had been an HBO fight in 1990, by which time Mr. Pat was out of the fight game, struggling to stay sober. And yet it was a fight I had to show him—he had led me here, and now I needed him to see the destination, to incorporate it into his own catalog of stories. This was the Philly fight for all those in the generations that had followed his.

"Good fighter," Mr. Pat said after we watched. "He had punched himself out. He just gave up hope—that's all."

And if he drifts back, if today's Philly gym rat drifts back, he can see the fighter again and the opponent who ruined him floating on the canvas of the mind. One is about five feet six inches, with a thin body, high cheekbones, clear horizontal lines across his forehead—as if he were puzzled—and disproportionately small ears. He wears bright red trunks with black and yellow stripes down the side. He takes small steps, staring straight ahead.

The other has flat-topped, buzzed hair, shoulders with deep crevices between thick striations, and round, bulging biceps. His forearms seem as thick as his calves. He wears white Franklin shorts with blue fringes along the waist and red stripes down the side. He is Meldrick "The Kid" Taylor, out of North Philly, and he owns the International Boxing Federation's 140-pound title. He is facing Julio Cesar Chavez, the "Lion of Culiacan, Mexico," and World Boxing Council champ.

Taylor is twenty-three years old, with twenty-four pro victories, no losses, and a draw. Chavez is twenty-seven, with sixty-eight wins—fifty-six by knockout—and no losses. Taylor has what promoters dub "lightning": rapid-fire combos and fancy footwork. Chavez has "thunder": bruising blows to the body and crunching shots to the face.

Here they are inside the Las Vegas Hilton on March 17, 1990, struggling in the clinch at the end of the eleventh round, thirty seconds to the bell. Taylor has landed more punches and earned more points, even though Chavez has goaded him into brawling in the later rounds, breaking bones around Taylor's eye and causing The Kid to bleed from his nose and mouth. Chavez is taking "three to get off one," referee Richard Steele will recall thinking during the eleventh round. "How long can [Taylor] take punches like that?"

This had always been Taylor's weakness: an affinity for the street-style slugfest, the one-on-one, fuck-caution war. "This is my home," Taylor once said about North Philly. Or as writer Bernard Fernandez will later put it, "His greatest strength and perhaps his greatest weakness was he was a Philadelphia fighter."

Taylor had resisted enough to maintain a solid lead, throwing combos and backing away, never setting his training totally aside. On the HBO broadcast, Jim Lampley punctuates it. "As round eleven comes to a close, Julio Cesar Chavez must begin to contemplate the reality that he's got three minutes in which to produce an unlikely knockout or he will see his streak end before thousands of his countrymen." As the bell rings to end the eleventh, Chavez nails Taylor's face with a left hook. Taylor's body goes limp and he staggers to the wrong corner before referee Steele pulls him by the wrist the other way. Until now, Chavez has landed 235 of 634 punches. Taylor has landed nearly twice as many—418 of 1,060.

In the corner, the individual strands of Chavez's short black hair glisten with sweat as his trainer and cutman squirt water in his face and rub his neck with an ice bag. In Spanish, they yell, "You've got to go for this round." Chavez's body shows no wear. One diagonal away, Taylor's cornermen scream the same thing, even though Taylor has seemingly won a majority of rounds already. The cutmen press an ice bag to Taylor's face, squirt a water bottle in his mouth, rub Vaseline on his forehead, and stick Q-tips in his nose. "You need this round!" one guy shouts. Another says, "The fight is hanging on this round here, Mel." And then, "You wanna be champion of the world?" Taylor nods. "You wanna be?"

Chavez's cutmen have grown more intense. They wear red robes with red headbands that have "Julio" embroidered in white. Between previous rounds, they have urged Chavez to win it "por tu familia"—for your family. Now, one fat cornerman digs deeper. "You're stronger than he is," the cornerman says. "You're *more* than he is."

Chavez climbs off the stool. As he leaves his corner, he lowers his head like a bull about to charge. He takes small steps, staring straight ahead. He lowers his left eyebrow, but only for a moment. Perhaps a passive-aggressive come-on, but it's gone too quickly to tell. Taylor rises from his stool. The combination of water and sweat trickles down his glistening black pecs, catching the lights above. Taylor's manager, Lou Duva, shoves a mouth guard over his teeth. Taylor raises his arms stiff and high as if in anticipation of victory. He turns his head just the slightest bit to the crowd. The bell rings.

Back on HBO, commentator Harold Lederman unofficially scores the fight nine rounds to two, 108–101 in points, in favor of Taylor. Later it will be revealed that two of the three official judges also have Taylor ahead after round eleven—one by the score of 107–102 and another by 108–101. But as the two fighters charge each other, they don't know the scores. They know what they've been told—that this round is crucial. And so despite his lead, Meldrick "The Kid" Taylor, with eyes closing and a bloody nose, moves in on 68–0 Julio Cesar Chavez. For forty seconds the two trade close shots before backing off with 2:15 remaining. Fifteen seconds later, Taylor unleashes a rapid combination of lefts and rights out of the clinch, ending with a high, lunging left hook. But Chavez sees it coming and steps back. Taylor's blows hit only the air, and he loses his balance and falls forward. "What a big mistake this kid is making," referee Richard Steele will recall thinking about Taylor's KO attempt. "But he might pull it off."

More circling, more minor exchanges. One minute and twenty seconds left. Taylor's body begins to droop from fatigue. He hangs his hands down by his waist. From his corner comes the cry, "Watch your head!" And just then, it is Taylor who lands a nasty jab to Chavez's nose. "It doesn't appear at this moment that Chavez has the stuff to get it done," Lampley says. "More pawing than punching now at a time when he needs the best." The heavily Mexican crowd chants, "Cha-vez! Cha-vez! Cha-vez!" Fifty seconds to go, and both fighters whale on each other with inside blows. Taylor is now brawling in Chavez's style. He can't repress the street. But then for the next twenty seconds they circle each other, throwing a few jabs, missing on hooks. They both stumble. Twenty-five seconds to go: Chavez lands a big right to Taylor's face and begins swinging wildly. Now provoked, Taylor rushes Chavez into the ropes with a lowered head and both arms flailing. But at nineteen seconds, Chavez sidesteps the charging Taylor, who crashes into the corner, a victim of his own momentum. Taylor is trapped. Chavez hooks with his right and misses. Chavez hooks his left and misses again. But Taylor can't move in the corner. Chavez launches a straight right—and connects to the jaw. Boom. Taylor's head jerks violently to the right, before snapping back just as fast. Taylor crumples. He lands first on the ropes then smacks his head against the corner post. The crowd screams. Fourteen seconds left. Taylor's head rises off the post. He grabs the ropes to his right. He pushes off the ropes with his right hand and the floor with his left. Twelve. His whole body rises. The ref stands over him, counting on his fingers. Ten seconds. Taylor stands clutching the ropes to his left. The ref turns to Taylor's corner, then holds eight long, spindly fingers in front of Taylor's bowed head. The ref raises his left ring finger, extending the standing eight count to a nine count. But Taylor has made it. He is standing. Seven seconds left. "Are you okay?" the ref asks Taylor. A shiny welt bulges under Taylor's right eye, blocking all but a slit of it. Taylor turns to his corner. He says nothing. Six. Five. "You okay?" the ref asks again. No response. Four. The ref throws his arms up, shakes his head side-to-side and waves wildly. Three. The bell rings. The crowd screams. The ref places his hands on Taylor's swollen cheeks. The ref tilts his head to the right and looks into Taylor's sleepy, recessed eyes. "I'm sorry, son," the look says. "I can't let you do this." Suddenly, a spark. Taylor opens his eye slits as wide as he can. "What?" he says, as he shakes his head. The ref tries to remove Taylor's bloodied mouth guard, but Taylor jerks his head away and chomps down. Taylor's manager, Lou Duva, blitzes through the ropes and sticks his pointer in the ref's face. In the crowd, tangles of arms wave and whirl, and whistles pierce the air. The red-robed cornermen hoist Julio Cesar Chavez on their shoulders. He raises his right fist in the air. Then they lower him. Hug him. The robes flash and mingle in a growing red sea. "Cha-vez! Cha-vez! Cha-vez!" the people chant. Chavez blows them kisses. Across the ring, Taylor sits bowed in the corner. Cutmen wipe him with towels, press his bruises with ice. "Had not Steele stopped the fight, it's very likely that Meldrick Taylor may have won the decision," Harold Lederman says on the air. "There's very little question of that, Harold," Lampley answers, "unless they were watching an entirely different fight." Referee Richard Steele, himself a former boxer and Marine Corps teammate of Ken Norton, is immediately asked by an interviewer why he stopped it. "Because, you know, Meldrick had took a lot of good shots," he says. "A lot of hard shots." Did he notice that only a few seconds remained? "I don't care about the time. When I see a man that has enough, I'm stopping the fight." Even in a title bout? "There's no fight worth a man's life." The ring announcer grabs the microphone that descends from the ceiling and declares the official time of the technical knockout: 2:58 of the twelfth round, or two seconds before the end of the fight and what would have been a split-decision victory for Meldrick Taylor who now sits in the corner while Chavez rides high over a wave of flowing red satin.

* * *

"This one fight ruined the kid," Richard Steele says today on the phone from his adopted hometown of Las Vegas. "That's one thing I always wished: that there was something that would have prompted me to stop it earlier. But there wasn't anything because he was winning.

"The kid didn't even need to win that last round. All he needed to do was survive. And they sent him out there like the Philadelphia fighters do and try to win by knockout.

"Yeah, there were some fights I didn't get because of that. Look and listen to this kid today. Makes me know that I did the right thing.

"The people just didn't take care of this kid. And he didn't take care of himself. And it's a black eye on boxing. Here's a gold medal winner ending up as he did. Any other country, there would still be parades, and he would be able to get jobs and represent the country. But they didn't do that. They let the kid ruin himself. . . .

"I know I called the right call, made the right call, and that's it. I lived through it. Praised by half the world. I get 10–2. Ten of the right calls and maybe two of 'you should've let them continue.' That's just people talking from their hearts. They feel sorry for the guy. You can't feel sorry for him. . . .

"You could see it in his eyes, you could see it in his body, how weak he was, how beaten up he was. He couldn't talk. He was bleeding everywhere. Water in the brain had all dried up. He didn't know where he was.

"I just didn't know how much damage he had received. There was no sign, except for his eye, but I'm talking internal damage. . . . You know, that's the most a fighter ever got hurt on my watch. . . . This was one fight, one day, in a kid's life. I was just hoping and praying that he'd be okay to continue his career.

"I thought about that fight for many, many years. Yeah, yeah—questions all the time. . . . It was a devastating event. All of it. The whole fight.

"It was a long time. It was a long time 'cause that fight still goes on. Once you get to the point where you say, 'Hey, I did the right thing. Let it be,' it was several months. When you keep seeing that fight, you say, 'Okay, yeah, okay, it happened just the way I thought it did.' Just keep confirming that what you did was right. You keep getting that, and you can rest with it.

"You get angry at the public; you get angry at the reporters; you get angry at the people who say he was winning. Fights go back and forth. He was winning at some points and losing at others.

"If they're still saying that after all these years, they can't see what really happened. They can't see Lou Duva distracted the kid and draw his attention at the same time I was counting him out. They can't see that Lou Duva told him the wrong thing in the last round. They can't see that Lou Duva stepped on the ring and was disqualified as soon as he stepped on the apron. They don't see that. They don't *want* to see that.

"It's one of those fights I will live with for the rest of my life."

✿ ✿ ✿

After the fight, Steele was assaulted by reporters. Then he and his wife, Gladys, a boxing manager and matchmaker, went to their four-bedroom house. At 10 p.m., they settled into the living room and re-wound the tape of the fight they had just seen. They watched it again and again on the forty-two-inch television. Gladys told Steele he had done the right thing, but that it was hard for her to hear so much criticism. "Would you have had me let the kid go and get hurt?" Steele recalls asking her. "I know," she said. "But you don't deserve all the boos. . . . If you would've let him get knocked out, you wouldn't have been under all that." At about 1 a.m., Steele went to bed, though as usual after a fight, he couldn't sleep. His adrenaline pumped, and he continually replayed the last round ("I hear it all the time," he still says today. "'You need this round! You need this round!'").

The next day, in the morning, either a doctor or boxing commission-er called Steele to tell him about Taylor's hospitalization. Then Steele headed to the Golden Nugget casino, where he worked as a pit boss and was again assaulted with questions.

A day later, the *New York Times* and several other papers ran stories questioning Steele's decision. "Had the referee done the right thing, given Taylor's strong performance up to the knockdown and the likeli-hood of his victory had he survived the final seconds?" the *Times* asked. "Shouldn't the blinking red lights, one of which was in Steele's line of vision, have suggested to the referee that a certain latitude was owed to Taylor? And what about the benefit of the doubt routinely given to wobbly fighters in world title matches?"

Steele and his wife wanted to escape. They looked at rates, and Mexico was relatively cheap, so they booked five days in Cabo San Lucas and Cancún. They hoped the trip would provide a week of rest. But as soon as they landed, "everyone wanted to do everything" with them. On the street, packs of men would rush Steele, saying, "Oh, what a great stoppage!" And as if he were a new toy, they'd show him off to their friends to prove they had met the great ref who helped Chavez. Steele would shake their hands and pose for pictures and sign auto-graphs. He was tired and worn, but this welcome was beautiful, if also unexpected. "It was shocking to me that these people cared so much about this kid," Steele says. He'd return to Cancún on a cruise years later and on another trip he'd stay in Cabo again, and still people re-membered Steele.

Back in the United States, Steele would return to suspicions of a fix, which only grew in March 1991, a year after Chavez–Taylor. This time, Steele was the third man in the ring for another Don King–promoted bout: Mike Tyson versus Donovan "Razor" Ruddock. Tyson was clearly winning when Ruddock came back in the sixth round, landing left hooks and uppercuts and spurring the crowd to chant, "Ra-zor! Ra-zor! Ra-zor!" But in the seventh, after Tyson had landed three straight punches and Ruddock had stumbled to the ropes, Steele ended it without talking to Ruddock. Ruddock immediately shot back "What?" before his entire corner and entourage charged the ring, throwing punches at the opposition.

Several teams insisted Steele not work their fights. "It was out of the question," Steele said, when asked about refereeing the 1994 Chavez–Taylor rematch, adding, "All three of us back together again—that would have really been something." Steele did work Julio Cesar Chavez's first loss, in his ninety-first bout to thirty-two-year-old, 15–1 underdog Frankie Randall. That fight also proved controversial, when Steele deducted two points from Chavez for low blows. In 1995, Steele opened his Las Vegas gym, where he still trains and manages amateurs. A few years ago, ol' Lou Duva came by, asking Steele to work with some of his guys. And around the same time, Steele ran into Meldrick Taylor at some boxing function, and they spoke, but not about the fight or the stoppage. Taylor didn't seem upset, but then, he was so messed up, he could hardly speak. Steele was inducted into the World Boxing Hall of Fame in 2000 and retired from refereeing a few years later to pursue promoting.

After the first Taylor fight, Chavez would never win a belt he hadn't already held and lost. And in his first defeat to that unknown Tennessean Frankie Randall, Chavez proved human after all. "You can't lose a fight because of one fall," he whined, referring to Randall's right in the eleventh round that caught his chin and sent him to the floor. He added, ridiculously, "Out of twelve rounds, Randall won three."[1] Two years later, the new "Golden Boy," Oscar De La Hoya, took Chavez's title for good, and a few days later, Chavez's wife filed suit, claiming her drunken husband had grabbed her by the hair, punched her in the face, and made threats with a kitchen knife.

Chavez would retire several fights too late, in 2005, with 108 wins, six losses, and two draws.

That leaves Meldrick Taylor. He reportedly earned $1 million for the Chavez fight but lost another $10 million in a promotional contract from HBO that was contingent on him winning. After the fight, Taylor was taken to the Las Vegas Medical Center. He had a blowout fracture of his left eye, severe dehydration, vomiting, and had lost two pints of blood. He pissed pure red. The next morning, Taylor tried to leave the hospital to attend a press conference in the Hilton. His managers wanted him to insinuate he had been robbed and call for a rematch. Doctors urged Taylor to stay in the hospital, and he wound up ninety minutes late for the conference.

Taylor's camp filed a protest with the Nevada Athletic Commission, the WBC, and the IBF, stating referee Steele had made a "material error" in not pausing his eight count (because Chavez never stayed in a neutral corner). It didn't go anywhere. Another week later, longtime *Philadelphia Daily News* scribe Stan Hochman visited Taylor at his Philly house. Taylor arrived late for their meeting, claiming his car had been "booted downtown." Taylor also was missing his dog, which he had left unchained, and burned a metal pot trying to make coffee. "My eyes were blurry from the second round on," Taylor told Hochman. "Which is why I fought inside so much. I wanted to move, I wanted to give him lateral movement, but I couldn't take that chance, because I might not see the right hands coming."[2] Then Taylor watched a videotape of the fight on his big screen, replaying it as Steele had done a week earlier. As both would do many times more.

Nothing was the same after that. In August, Taylor fought for the first time after the Chavez bout, winning a ten-round decision over Primo Ramos in Tahoe, Nevada. But the sold-out Caesars crowd disagreed with the verdict and booed, and Taylor, wearing a brace on his left knee, taunted the crowd. In 1991, Taylor won another title, in the welterweight division, against a Bronx kid who fractured and dislocated his left thumb in the fight and was thus unable to block properly. It was a gritty fight for Taylor, who struck with hard, quick body shots despite bleeding from his lip. It was perhaps the last time Taylor's grit transcended his declining physical condition.

Later in the year, Taylor was TKO'd in four rounds by Terry Norris. Before Taylor's next bout, in London against unheralded Crisanto Espana, Lou Duva wore a T-shirt screen-printed with "1984," as if trying to forcefully conjure the skill Taylor displayed that year in winning the featherweight Olympic gold in Los Angeles, as if trying to cast off the residue of Philly's wild-swinging 1990s streets. "I started trying too hard to please the crowd," Taylor said before the match. "I realize now that I'm a fighter from Philadelphia, not a Philadelphia fighter. I can't be part of that tradition if I want to get back to being one of the best."[3] Of course, the tradition had encompassed more than brawling once, but then Meldrick belonged to the gang generation, raised on violence without moderation or discipline. In a world where hands no longer provided jobs and craft no longer offered pride. "He's liable to be a $300 fighter if he doesn't fight like the *real* Meldrick Taylor," Duva threatened, apparently believing the real Meldrick Taylor still possessed the combination of skill and power of the Youngs, the Wolgasts, the O'Briens. "Where's he going to fight—the Blue Horizon?"[4]

He was TKO'd in eight. Trainer Georgie Benton—the slick former middleweight who had helped resurrect Jimmy Young's career a decade earlier—and manager Lou Duva urged Taylor to quit. Taylor quit them instead and found new management.[5]

He also found a skinny, five-feet, six-inch, twenty-three-year-old high school dropout named Tyria Hankins Ekwensi. Everyone said she looked like Robin Givens, and every morning, she'd walk outside her Mount Laurel condo, in nothing but a negligee, ostensibly to check the weather. Ekwensi slinked from one man to another. In North Carolina she had a three-year-old son. Then she moved to Mount Laurel, New Jersey, where a man with whom she had a prior "relationship," according to speculation by authorities, tried to break into her condo. Then she moved to Chadds Ford, Pennsylvania, where she lived with another man who prided himself on wearing gold chains and Reebok Pumps. It was around this time that neighbors started noticing a red Mercedes on the block, one whose license plate read "M. Taylor" and featured a pair of miniature boxing gloves hanging from the rearview mirror. Taylor would visit his new girlfriend and lavish her with gifts, including a Rolex, that would come back to haunt him a few years later. He'd fly her out to Vegas to sit front row for his fights. It was in the City of Sin, at a restaurant, that Ekwensi first walked by the table of Theodore Edmund, a Los Angeles drug kingpin. Edmund introduced himself, gave her his business card, and she gave him her beeper number. During the next fifteen months, they'd use FedEx to distribute and sell more than $27 million in cocaine and heroin. They'd even get engaged, according to Ekwensi's mother. But in August 1992, a SWAT team driving Lexuses, Benzes, and Porsches would surround Ekwensi's two bedroom and bust her, thus ending Taylor's bizarre, costly, and apparently innocent relationship with the vast, dark narcotic underworld.

Back in the gyms, Taylor trained for a comeback and signed with promoter Don King for a rematch with Chavez. "The greatest promoter in the world" and "the epitome of what a promoter should be"[6] is how Taylor described the man linked by rumor to Steele and now linked by contract to his career. King scheduled Taylor to fight on the undercard of Chavez's January 29, 1994, bout against Frankie Randall. It was supposed to be a tune-up night at the Las Vegas MGM Grand, which was hosting its first boxing matches ever; Chavez would dispatch his opponent easily, Taylor would do the same to his, and the national appetite would be whetted for a May showdown between the Mexican folk hero and the Philly Kid. So Don King searched for a nobody to fight Taylor—the kind of small-town guy who had spent his career taking on bums in the back of bars.

Enter Craig Houk, a twenty-nine-year-old welterweight with a receding bowl of blond hair that fell unevenly onto his head as if it had been cut by kindergarten scissors. Houk had spent his whole life from second grade on in Greensburg, Indiana, save for the few years he spent boxing as an amateur in Florida. He had turned pro in 1989, driving through the Midwest to fight in clubs, county fairgrounds, and junior high schools from Bismarck, North Dakota, to Carthage, Missouri, and from Erlanger, Kentucky, to Terre Haute, Indiana. Along the way, he had built a 42–2 record, which was impressive enough to justify Don King's decision to match him against Meldrick Taylor. Of course, that was King's genius, for no journalist had the time or inclination to investigate Houk's record further. King had set up what he dubbed a night of "Super Grand Slam of Boxing" at the MGM Grand. Also on the card was a cruiserweight title fight featuring Thomas "Hit Man" Hearns, a welterweight title fight, a heavyweight fight, and a women's match.

Houk's record might have seemed too good to be true, if only anyone had paid attention. He had beaten a few decent punchers, but mostly guys with records of 1–8, 6–12, 0–2, 0–5, 4–26, 4–7, 0–7, 0–4, 0–3, 0–2, 5–11, 3–6, 1–9, 1–11, 2–15, 3–7, 2–3, 1–8, 2–14, 8–26, 1–14, 2–18, 13–57, 3–19, 3–23, and, most laughably, thirty-six-year-old Simmie Black, whose record at the time of their 1990 bout was 22–126–4.

Craig Houk recalls entering the ring in Vegas "overwhelmed."

"I'm fighting an Olympic gold medalist," he remembers thinking. But then the match actually began, and Houk noticed something wrong with Taylor. "He was just a touch off. Like I don't know if he got it or not. It seems like he got a little bit of what they call boxing syndrome. Just a touch. Not a lot of slurred speech. But just in his body movement. . . . He had so much God-given talent that he could [still] beat me to the punch." In the third round, Taylor beat him to the punch, knocking him out. King's plan was in motion: all Chavez now had to do was beat thirty-two-year-old Frankie Randall, whose 49–2–1 record contained wins against guys with marks of 0–7, 0–9, and 6–16 (that last win coming in the St. Johns Sheraton in Jacksonville, Florida).

Yet Randall wasn't ready to concede. "I've been overlooked and mistook for a long time," he said before the fight, before doing everything that Meldrick Taylor had four years earlier. Wearing that same flattop buzz cut with a thin mustache and thinner eyebrows, Randall bobbed and weaved, jabbed and shuffled. Halfway through the first round, he threw two solid jabs and a right from the top down, using his two-inch height advantage. From then on, Chavez held Randall at every juncture. "No holding!" referee Richard Steele cried again and again. "No holding!" And after the first round, Randall went back to his stool and asked his trainer, "Am I doing alright?" And the trainer said, "Yeah, man. You won that round." And so it continued until the seventh, when the crowd chanted Randall's name again, and he rocked Chavez with three left-right combos. Chavez then pulled back his left arm and, as if it were a spring, uncoiled it into Randall's groin. Randall grimaced and quivered and his teal shorts shook madly. He hobbled to a corner, then doubled over. Referee Steele sent Chavez to the other side of the ring and deducted a point. In the eleventh, Steele would deduct another point for a low blow, and Randall would become the first person ever to knock Chavez down. After the fight, before the decision, Don King sidled over to Chavez and whispered in his ear: "Not this time."[7]

"This time" was the only one Meldrick Taylor ever needed Chavez to win. And the only one Chavez had lost. Taylor's rematch was postponed. The World Boxing Council ordered Randall and Chavez to fight again. In May, on the very night Taylor was to have entered the ring against him, Julio Cesar Chavez recaptured his title. Chavez–Taylor II was finally scheduled for September 17, 1994, the night after Mexican

Independence Day. And if one could pause time like a video on Richard Steele's big screen and then rewind, he might have given Taylor a fighting chance in the rematch. For in that alternate reality, one could scroll all the way back to the beginning, to the gold medal–winning Taylor of 1984, who was seventeen years old, 125 pounds, whose potential was infinite. Or not even so far back, to the Taylor of March 17, 1990, with only twenty seconds to go. Then Taylor would always be rushing Chavez into the ropes, never to reach nineteen seconds and find himself so suddenly ensnared in his own motion. The elusive dream of technology: to find a way to manipulate real time like video.

For a few rounds on that illusive Las Vegas night, time did seem negotiable. Taylor came out looking young and sleek with a newly shaved head and bright red trunks adorned with white fringes. At the opening bell, he darted to the center and shuffled his blue sneakers, bouncing high on the balls of his feet. He jabbed crisp and quick, and when Chavez cornered him with 1:47 left in the first, he ducked a wild left as if he knew it was coming. Seventeen seconds later, Chavez threw a big left in the middle of the ring and Taylor stepped back. Chavez lost his footing and Taylor pounded him with a left-right, sending Chavez into the ropes. In this way, Taylor led early. He even raised his fists, once again, after landing a left-right in the fourth round. It wouldn't last. Referee Mills Lane deducted two points from Taylor for a head butt in the third and a low blow in the sixth, by which point Taylor had to brawl to catch up. Chavez's game, again, but with a more definite result: in the eighth, Chavez rocked Taylor's chin with a left hook. Taylor paused—as if unwilling to succumb to time's unyielding march—tumbled backward, and fell. He would rise and tell referee Mills Lane that he wanted to continue, only to have Chavez pummel him without mercy for nine more seconds. Then Mills Lane ended what had become Taylor's third knockout defeat in the past five fights.

* * *

All you need to know is that Meldrick's life went to shit.

"The Kid" wouldn't enter the ring again for another two years. In either late '95 or early '96, *Daily News* writer Marcus Hayes heard that Meldrick Taylor couldn't get licensed "because he was punchy." Hayes was working on a piece about punch-drunk fighters, including Jimmy Young, so he set up an interview at Patterson's, a vegetarian diner at Fourth and Spring Garden. Taylor was "in spectacular shape," Hayes recalls, "so charming and so alert and just so sharp and totally non-malicious." The interview went smoothly. Taylor pleaded his case: "How are you going to invade in someone's personal occupation and say, 'Because you have this, this, and this wrong with you, you can't fight?'"

Then Taylor started slurring. And then he stole Hayes's notebook and poked him hard in the chest.

"That was less a tragic experience than a terrifying one," Hayes says. "He was very upset after the interview ended because it took him, from my perspective, that whole time to figure out what the interview was about. There was a notebook out (which was only filled with questions), but after the interview, he took the notebook out of my coat pocket and told me I couldn't write the story. And this part was kind of sad. The tape recorder was sitting right beside the notebook and the red light was on the entire time. He didn't realize the conversation was being taped [even though he had consented to it earlier]. He proceeded to follow me around the city for five or ten minutes, tailing me. I didn't know if he was armed or not."

Hayes knew that section of Philly well, since his apartment was nearby, so he pulled his car into a parking lot by the police station and waited for Taylor to drive away, which he did.

"Part of the issue with the condition is that you have violent mood swings. You can be euphoric, morose, violent—it's an injury to your brain. But in the moment, I was very concerned."

Taylor was losing control over his mind, probably at least partly because of the injuries he sustained in the Chavez match. At the same time, though he didn't yet know it, he was losing control over his past. It was March 1996, and Chicago businessman Jose Venzor filed a lawsuit against, among others, Don King, Craig Houk, and the fighter with whom Taylor would always remain linked, Julio Cesar Chavez. The backstory was typical: In 1993, Venzor had supposedly invested in a fight involving Chavez in Chicago. But ten days before the bout, Chavez said he hurt his right hand and wouldn't fight. To make good on the deal, promoter Don King offered up Chavez for another bout in Chicago two years later against Craig Houk, whom he KO'd.

Venzor was now alleging Don King's people had promised Craig Houk an extra $10,000 "to go down" against Chavez. Venzor filed suit alleging his fight had been fixed because Chavez hadn't trained proper-

relationships end with a two-second lie instead of the accretion of many? But for this moment, this two-second window, the tracing of future moments makes perfect, tragic sense. If the fight had continued for two more seconds, Meldrick Taylor would have been the champion. Julio Cesar Chavez would have lost his first fight. And referee Richard Steele would never have been dogged by suspicions that he threw the fight for Don King, Chavez's promoter, with whom he was reportedly buddies. This two-second window was not like a bullet in crossfire or a sinking relationship. It was a singular event that Richard Steele could have changed. Or, from the other angle, that Meldrick Taylor could have changed, if he had only shouted his "What?" after twice being asked: "You okay?"

You almost wonder what Meldrick Taylor did wrong, which gods he forgot to sacrifice to or which cosmic force he neglected to observe. Because Taylor did everything a fighter usually should, yet the laws of nature bent to stymie him. He lost the pivotal fight of his career not because he didn't bring enough, but because he brought *too* much (whoever heard of such a thing?), to the point where he fell in the middle of the round just by whiffing. To the point where Chavez did little but let Taylor corner himself.

The reasons Taylor brawled in the twelfth seem to subvert the very fight culture that spawned him. "I think it might be something of a code of honor for many of the young men—to show you have heart—that someone's not going to take your heart away from you," says Gerald Early, the Washington University professor who grew up in South Philly and wrote the boxing book *The Culture of Bruising*. "That's an expression I heard from guys growing up. . . . There was a code on the street in Philadelphia."

Early is right. Philly boxers often carried their ideas about heart into the ring. Tyrone Everett, a 1970s junior lightweight contender who grew up in North and South Philly, once said a beaten opponent hadn't been able to "do anything" because "he was scared." Why was he scared? "My first right-hand shot to his kidney stole his heart."[10]

Joe Frazier once said, "I don't want to knock my opponent out. I want to hit him, step away, and watch him hurt. I want his heart."[11]

Of course, by attempting to deny Chavez "his heart," Taylor forked over just that—and more. His title, clearly, but also his manhood. Because what makes a man besides his ability to stand independently and live on his own terms? And now Taylor cannot walk without a limp or speak without slurring, let alone control his violent mood swings.

The other, simpler reason Taylor brawled in the twelfth subverts the gym ethos even further: His corner told him to. It doesn't matter why they did so, only that they screamed, "You need this round!" And "the fight is hanging on this round here." After all, Taylor's job was not to question, but to listen and perform—which he did. And lost. In boxing, there can be no order more unnatural than that, no process more tragic. As a combatant trusts his commander in war, a fighter puts his life in his trainer's hands. From the time he leaves the corner until he returns three minutes later, he executes the trainer's strategy. If the trainer advises him to go for a knockout, he'd better do so. And if the trainer tells him to jab and move, he'd better do that. Too often the case, the fighter gets mauled when he does not listen. And sure, in earlier rounds, Taylor had been goaded by Chavez into brawling when his corner had advised him not to. But while Chavez used that tactic earlier—and perhaps succeeded because of Taylor's North Philly roots—it was Taylor's cornermen who clearly decided to exploit his brutal inclination in the twelfth when they barked: "You wanna be champion of the world? You wanna be?"

"He responded like the good soldier," Early says. "They obviously wanted him to end the fight with a bang."

Was Taylor so mindless as to be merely a pawn? The answers can be found in the soldier analogy. No, he was not. In fact, at the time, he was known as a good interview and a brilliant fighter—an articulate guy with a quicksilver creativity in the ring. But then the sophisticated soldier isn't mindless either. He responds as he does not out of mindlessness but out of his training, which conditions him to be a human weapon when he needs to be. These abilities lie dormant in the soldier until his superior taps them. For Taylor, then, the North Philly streets and a certain disposition created in him an inner ferocity. All Lou Duva had to do was call on it at the right moment.

We'll never know how much of Taylor's brawling came from those streets—"the jungle," as one *Sports Illustrated* writer referred to North Philly of the mid-twentieth century—and how much came from "The Kid" himself. One of his three sisters, Wanda Battiste, recalls Taylor "had a lot of fight him in" and was "the type of fighter that would never stop . . . like a Jason in *Friday the 13th*." Which would seem to indicate

Taylor was a born warrior. But there are also the facts of the place—the way it took a small child and forced him to use his hands (or probably worse). Meldrick was the youngest in his family and was named after his twin, Eldrick, who emerged a few minutes earlier. His parents appended the "M" to stand for "mighty." The third brother, Myron, and the three sisters all grew up in Nicetown, another neighborhood of violence and poverty, this one below Germantown. Just recently, a guy argued with his wife there, then blasted her dead on the street with a shotgun.

But the neighborhood below Germantown is also known for its factories. Midvale Steel was located in Nicetown, producing car axles and tires in a plant that looked like a row of oversized military barracks. Link-Belt Engineering was a hulking triangular fortress bounded in the northeast and northwest by two lines of the Philadelphia and Reading Railroad. Its smokestack rose in the middle like a watchtower.

The neighborhood has been back in the news lately as the last of its factories have shut down. Tastykake moved out of its iconic 1922 six-story plant in 2009 in favor of a new facility. The Budd Manufacturing Company, maker of trains, closed for good in 2002.

This is where Meldrick grew up. His father, Ronald, worked at Arno Products and then Service Champ Corporation, where he did packaging and handling. Ronald loved boxing, and when Taylor was six or seven, the father would get down on his knees and pepper the son with weightless punches. "They didn't hurt," Taylor would later recall. "But I wanted to get even, and I used to get so furious and frustrated that I would cry."

When Taylor turned eight, his dad began sending him and Eldrick to the gym to learn how to box to keep them out of jail and off drugs—although Dad wanted his kids to be lawyers and doctors, not fighters.

At ten years old, Taylor scribbled, "I will become champion of the world" in black magic marker on his dresser drawer.

Taylor won the featherweight gold medal at the Olympics in 1984. It was in the semifinals that his hybrid style of street and gym made its mark. He was facing Omar Catari Peraza of Venezuela, a twenty-year-old with a height and reach advantage. On ABC, Howard Cosell raised the question. "You always wonder about Meldrick," he said. "Does he own up too much? Does he look too hard for the knockout? He has such great confidence in his power. You have to fight that way when you come out of Philadelphia. And after all, he trains in Smokin' Joe Frazier's gym." Exactly halfway through the second round, Taylor answered. Peraza bounced twice on the balls of his feet and curled his left glove up and down four times like a cat clawing for an opening. The fifth time, Peraza dropped his glove downward only a few inches before crossing it to Taylor's left cheek. But Taylor dipped to his right and wound back his right arm. Peraza's left reached its full extension, hitting only air and sending him sprawling forward. Taylor unleashed his right flush to Peraza's jaw. Peraza collapsed onto his back. Thus, in less than two seconds, Taylor had demonstrated his ability to foresee a punch, slip it, and counter powerfully. The full package.

"You saw in Meldrick Taylor some of both worlds, of the skill *and* the toughness of the Philadelphia fighter," says Larry Merchant, an HBO analyst for the Chavez fight and a former sports editor at the *Philadelphia Daily News*. "And he was one of those very skillful fighters who couldn't resist getting into battles. I don't know how much that can be accredited to Philadelphia or just to his own temperament. But he had some serious skill. He was a prodigy."

Ultimately, Taylor's fans seem mad about that more than anything else: the loss of a prodigy—the loss of time. Taylor had a 99–4 record as an amateur and was supposed to be "a keeper, a guy who would be a national figure," Merchant says. After the Olympic semifinals, Cosell said, "Congratulations—just a spectacular performance, Meldrick." And Taylor flashed his klieg light grin and with all the boundless energy of a kid, responded: "Yeah, I have off days and I have on days. Yesterday I don't think I had a good performance. I want to make up for that today."

He smiled and continued.

"I want to say hello to everybody back in my hometown of Philadelphia. . . . I'm gonna bring home the gold come this Saturday." Then he got up from his chair and while stepping out of the booth shouted, "Number one!"

Nineteen years after that interview, in 2003, HBO aired a documentary on the Chavez–Taylor fight as a part of its *Legendary Nights* series. HBO held a special screening in a theater on Walnut Street for the Philly boxing community. A few hundred people showed, and afterward, "people were still exercised about it. Still yelling about the fight," Merchant remembers. Today's Meldrick Taylor only comes in at the

Meldrick Taylor's promotional shot taken after he turned pro following his gold medal victory at the 1984 Olympics. AP Photo.

end, after Lou Duva claims he advised Taylor not to fight in the twelfth round, but instead to "dance." A doctor talks about how damaged Taylor has become while his recent fight footage rolls. Then, suddenly sitting face-to-face with the audience is "The Kid." He looks heavier but still youthful. He wears cornrows in his hair, a scruffy beard, and a bright orange T-shirt over a wide frame. He opens his mouth.

"Awtheysaynottoomanykidouttometheywrotebadthingsaboutme-theamanamesaidIwaswashedup," Taylor slurs and mumbles without pause.

"PeoplesayalotthingsaboutmeaboutmycareerI-shouldn'tbefightinganymoreit'snottrueI'mheretoprovemyselfthatI'mstill thesamefighterIwas."

If they're anything like me, the Philly fans that night wanted to believe time had flowed in the other direction, back toward childhood. Because Taylor's gibberish streamed as that of a toddler who delights in the cadence of his words rather than in their meaning. But the crushing reality that the Philly fans faced in 2003, that I faced upon viewing the film years later, is that Taylor's gobbledy-gook contained actual, chosen words, with an intended meaning and an unintended sound. That clash between the damaged man's intent and his physical inability to realize it must've clarified his life frighteningly: Taylor had not reverted to what he was as a youth; he had sped up to what most of us will become as seniors.

"You get punch-drunk, it's not something that happens to you at once," Early says. "It creeps up on you. Five years later, after you leave the ring, it can happen. I guess it's kind of like Alzheimer's, and everyday, a little bit is taken away, you get a little more diminished. And before you know it, there you are. It's insidious."

Early's approach toward the fighter's decline—that it creeps up on him and gradually drains him—seems to contradict what might be termed the fulcrum approach: that every fighter aside from the unblemished few, punch-drunk or not, reaches a turning point that changes everything. But in actuality, the two stances don't contradict, for the turning point is only there in retrospect. Sure, a fighter might know in the immediate aftermath of a brutal loss that he has fought his last good one. As Early himself says, "It takes an exceptional fighter to be able to overcome that." But the fighter buries that self-doubt deep down inside of him and allows only its shadowy outline to appear in his thoughts: "This is only a dip in my continued upward rise. It's just a speed bump." Or as Taylor said after Hawaii officials canceled his bout there in 2000, "Why do they have to pick on me? I'm the illuminated one." One doubts Taylor fully believed he was the illuminated one after being barred from several boxing venues and slurring for a half decade. But a part of him seems to have bought it in an act of self-denial and repression that must have been necessary for a man with a ravaged mind.[12] Indeed, as the fighter begins to dip and slip down that steep slope, the turning-point realization he had buried climbs its way up. But only finally, when it's all over, does the doubt become incontrovertible: Taylor knows he was never the same after fighting Chavez. Jimmy Young knows he lost it all after Norton.

And so the fighter's career turns downward just as it once turned up. Where he might once have been unsure of his ability because of inexperience, he now is equally unsure due to what he has experienced. It's the sad truth about all that training, all the hours spent toiling in a dank gym with beads of sweat dripping: If your momentum propels you to the top of a bell curve (and many, many boxing careers begin and end in a low state of poverty and privation), it will probably drag you back down the other side. For Meldrick Taylor, this process manifested itself in the quality of his opponents. On the downside of his career, Taylor infamously faced Craig Houk and Kenny Kidd, who, even if they weren't throwing fights, were not always who they claimed to be. Anonymous fighters passing through town after town.

No one but Meldrick knows where he stands on the bell curve today. He's got a kid in school who, a teacher tells me, commands such respect on the playground because "all the kids know about who his dad is." In March 2007, Taylor was seen by promoter Don Elbaum training at the Front Street Gym. A guy turned to Elbaum and said, "Don, he wants to fight again." Taylor refuses to be interviewed, and when I tried to speak to his family members, he told them not to participate.

Two seconds. And only then did Taylor shout, "What?" It's a story of near miss that has recurred throughout time.

The first great fight scribe, Pierce Egan, recalled the second bout between Oliver and Painter in 1820: Painter knocked down Oliver with "a tremendous blow upon his temple." Oliver didn't regain consciousness within a half minute, and Painter was named the winner. Just then,

Oliver "rose (as from a trance) from his second's knee, and going up to Painter said, 'I am ready to fight.'

"'No,' said Painter, 'I have won the battle.'"[13]

4

THE DEAD

When a man has lost all happiness, he's not alive. Call him a breathing corpse.
—Sophocles

Do you suppose they would consider putting a statue of me on the steps of the Art Museum after I beat Chavez?
—Meldrick Taylor, March 1990

It was the one topic Mr. Pat refused to address. But he kept alluding to it, some unspeakable family tragedy. He didn't use that word—he just stopped speaking. He'd mention something that had happened, and he'd go silent, and the old, bony man would double over in his chair, and sometimes a tear would emerge from his eyes—it never really descended but just stayed there, like a lens. I'm sure he blinked and they fell, but in the darkness, his eyes always seemed red with a sad glisten. This thing—whatever it was—was the root cause of the pain he felt, the one that made him wonder whether he was going to hell (which he would muse about more often than he realized). It wasn't the downfall of any of his fighters—no, he had cared for them, even the ones who had gone bad, such as Tyrone Everett, who had been shot to death by his girlfriend. That story I could be told. It wasn't that his onetime boss, a mobster named Arnold Giovanetti who managed fighters, had disappeared not long after Tyrone's funeral—his car was found at the airport, and everyone assumed the mob had taken one of their own. That story, too, was repeated.

No, it was a personal family tragedy. And it wasn't Mr. Pat who wound up telling me—he never would have. It was his last ex-wife, Janice, who mentioned it over the phone so casually that it was clear she assumed he had already told me. *Oh, yeah, Tyrone Patterson—well, he tried to gouge out his eyes after he killed his grandfather. . . .*

I looked up the information in the city's public records, and it was true: On February 8, 1979, Tyrone Patterson, Mr. Pat's twenty-five-year-old son with his childhood sweetheart, Frances (from whom he had long since separated), had fatally stabbed his maternal grandfather with a five-inch hunting knife in the back and then the chest. The records yielded more: Just a day earlier, Tyrone had tried to kill himself. In the preceding years, he had been in and out of hospital psychiatric wards. Later, court physicians would diagnose him with severe schizophrenia, involving paranoia and hallucinations. And Tyrone had indeed tried to blind himself with razors in jail when he began to understand what he had done and had been rushed to Wills Eye Hospital. He had also insisted on pleading guilty, though the judge had implored him to consider an insanity plea or some other way out.

"I would be lying, then," Tyrone said. And so they took him away.

When I first brought this story to Mr. Pat, three years after we first met, he shut his front door in my face and told me we'd never speak again. I honestly believed he'd want to unburden himself and share this story—he had been edging up so closely to it for so long. But he didn't look back at me when he left me standing there on Walnut Street, and at that time, I didn't think he'd ever let me back. As it turned out, I was wrong—we would reconcile—and yet, there really wasn't that much time left to see him anyway.

This much I knew then and had for many months, even before Mr. Pat's personal tale had unraveled: There was death on these streets, not only of boxers and managers such as Tyrone Everett and Arnold Giovanetti, but of many other fighters, gang members, ordinary civilians. Death wasn't just another fact of life in this city. It was nearly—in the darkest moments, seemingly absolutely—the primary one.

❂ ❂ ❂

At different times, Philly deteriorated in different ways. In the '60s, there were racial riots. In the '80s, crack overdoses. Neither was the death blow, nor could be, because the city's beauty stemmed from its great vibrancy—the confluence of markets, banks, and courts; opera and jazz and boxing—so the loss of any one couldn't extinguish all. The passing of a single neighborhood wouldn't snuff out 142.6 square miles. It just necrotized one more branch, another extremity, until blood circulated in decreasing circles and finally, not at all, and the whole place rotted. It wasn't uniform. Certain places and traditions went before others, and in fact, a few areas began to revive while others still flailed. Suburbanites moved back into Center City in the late '80s and early '90s even as more and more women turned tricks on West Philly corners. Big pharmaceutical companies ran headquarters in the metropolitan area—Merck, Glaxo, Teva—while longtime local shops closed.[1] But if the chronology wasn't clean, the facts of loss were.

The Spanish once called a boxing knockout a "mini-death." There were so many of these in the city—it was Sophocles's breathing corpse.

* * *

Death was never far from the fight game in Philadelphia from its start. Before fights were legalized, before they were even held illicitly in the backs of barrooms, they were held on boats off the coast. On August 31, 1876, in a ring set up on a barge off the coast of Pennsville, New Jersey, lightweight bare-knuckler "Philadelphia" Jimmy Weeden beat down Billy Walker. Walker later died from his injuries, and Weeden was deemed a criminal and sentenced to a lifetime in Trenton Penitentiary (he died there a year later).[2]

On a Thursday night in March 1897, forty-six-year-old Christian Keilnecker fought thirty-five-year-old Frank Connelly. Keilnecker had been drinking, and Connelly was larger. It took place in a room over a blacksmith shop at Fourth and Oxford. Keilnecker lost. He was later found unconscious in his home, with a closed right eye and a face full of contusions. He was submitted to St. Mary's Hospital. He went delirious and died on the morning of March 20.[3]

On the same morning, Edward Gibbons died at Hahnemann Hospital. He had fought his good friend Samuel Perry the night before, having lost in the third after Perry smashed a glove into the area below his heart. The ref had stopped it, and Perry had returned home, and Gibbons had dressed and stayed at the club, where he began throwing up blood. On the way to the hospital, he sank into a coma.[4]

On December 22, 1900, Edward Sanford died after an amateur bout at the Philadelphia Athletic Club at Broad and Wood. The city's director of public safety banned boxing for nine months.[5]

On September 30, 1903, at the Washington Sporting Club at Fifteenth and Wood in North Philly, Bob Fitzsimmons, whose punch had once killed a sparring partner, knocked out Con Coughlin in the first round. Coughlin died the next day.[6] Two years later, Fitzsimmons, the survivor, the champ, the accidental slayer, would receive this telegraph from his wife: "Am leaving New York forever. Took step week ago. Long contemplated. My attorney's letter should reach Bob to-day. Julia."[7]

January 1908. H. A. Hartnet of Philadelphia was the twenty-three-year-old acting master-at-arms of the berth deck on the U.S. training ship *Cumberland* off the coast of Newport, Rhode Island. One night after dinner, he ordered Manning from the gun deck to help clean the berth deck. Manning did not move quickly so Hartnet shoved him. The two began brawling. The master-at-arms of the gun deck interceded: Clean now, he said, and we'll set up an official fight later. So they cleaned, and the crew set up a ring of rope and the two shipmates donned gloves and three hundred apprentices and officers assembled to watch. In the eighth, Manning socked Hartnet's jaw, and Hartnet fell to the floor, unconscious and bleeding from mouth and nose. He died on January 18 at the Naval Hospital.[8]

April 1910. Across the country, four fighters died in four weeks. In Philly, black lightweight Frank Cole faced Stanley Rodgers on the 19th. Third round: Rodgers nailed Cole in the solar plexus, crumpling his body into that of a crushed spider, sending him falling backward and down, the base of his skull cracking on a wooden plank underpinning the ring. He died the next day.[9]

August 1910. William Brown of San Francisco knocked down William Ford of Philly three times in the Sharkey Athletic Club. Each time, Ford stayed down until nine. Finally, Brown swung his right arm into Ford's jaw, knocking Ford unconscious. At 11:30 p.m., a doctor drove the comatose Ford away, refusing to tell a reporter his destination.[10]

Seventeen days later. Twenty-year-old Frederick Castor faced Frank Sullivan in the Frankford Athletic Club. For five of the six rounds, Castor proved superior. But in the sixth, while trying to KO his opponent, Castor abruptly fell unconscious and died in the hospital the next day.[11]

March 17, 1916. At the Nonpareil Club, thirty-one-year-old Mike Malone punched twenty-three-year-old Andy Crowley in the Adam's apple in the third round, and Crowley died.[12]

March 1930. The intercollegiate boxing semifinals. Inside the Palestra, Penn's middleweight captain Oliver Horne faced Penn State's William Struble. Horne was twenty-two years old and scheduled to graduate from the Wharton School of Business in June. He had rowed crew as a freshman and earned a spot in Lambda Chi Alpha. Struble was a twenty-three-year-old education student slated to begin teaching in the fall. While fighting, Horne suffered a brain hemorrhage. He underwent emergency surgery and caught pneumonia in the hospital. He died at 10:50 p.m. on the 29th with his parents bedside. Penn paid Struble's $1,500 bail for involuntary manslaughter. Struble could not calm his nerves sufficiently to attend the funeral.[13]

As the decades passed, the game got safer—there were better gloves, padded posts, referees more inclined to step in and halt a lopsided beating. There was still danger inside the ring, as there had to be for the game to possess any excitement. What couldn't be regulated were the perils that lurked outside the ring on the streets of Philadelphia.

Eddie Cool was a lightweight counterpuncher from Northeast Philly in the 1930s. He was managed by a local iceman and turned pro at sixteen. He took on all comers, losing eight times in his first thirty-four matches. Gradually he built a creditable record, and on September 9, 1933, he "scored a brilliant victory over Frankie Klick after ten torrid rounds at the Arena," according to boxing historian Chuck Hasson.[14] Cool's win should have set up a big match with either the junior lightweight champ, Kid Chocolate, or the lightweight champ Barney Ross. But two promoters persuaded Cool to fight instead the former junior lightweight champ, Benny Bass. Meanwhile, the current champ Kid Chocolate defended against Frankie Klick, whom Cool had just beaten. And—wouldn't you know it?—Cool wound up losing to Bass, and Frankie Klick took the title from Kid Chocolate. Now, Cool was never abstemious, but this abrupt reversal of fortune triggered his worst impulses, and he allegedly drank for days afterward. A few years later, when Cool lost on the New York stage to Sammy Fuller, he found his way to the local booze halls and eventually passed out in the gutter wearing a cashmere coat. Cool died at the age of thirty-five from liver disease.

Nearly one hundred years later, a Philly welterweight named Gypsy Joe came on the scene. His mom had named him Joe Louis Harris after the great heavyweight champion and "Brown Bomber." Of course, his mom couldn't know what would happen to Joe Louis once his fighting days were over and nothing remained. How the IRS would take his money and he'd collapse from cocaine in '69 and go to a psychiatric hospital for paranoia and after many heart problems and strokes, die young from cardiac arrest in '81, nine years before Gypsy's death from heart failure following lots of heroin and four heart attacks. Even the nickname "Gypsy" seems to presage a long, harsh wandering into night. The boxer acquired the nickname by sleeping with a different woman each night and wearing pointy, tasseled shoes with bells on them into the gym one day.

No writer predicted his fall quite so eerily as *Sports Illustrated*'s Mark Kram, whose June 19, 1967, cover story on Gypsy might be the single best article ever written about a Philly boxer. Notably, to this day, Gypsy remains the only man to have appeared on the cover without being a heavyweight or champion. Kram spent a good portion of the article simply searching for Gypsy, whose nomadic ways frustrated the reporter. So he got the lowdown from one of Gypsy's stablemates, a nineteen-year-old lightweight named Al Massey, who spoke of the respect one garnered as a boxer on the streets of North Philly. "Yet it does not last long," Kram wrote in response. "The slide begins, the end is invariable. Obscurity claims the fighter after the fragrant foxes, hearts empty and hands out, have fled, after the savagery of the gym wars has left him empty." Kram asked about Gypsy in the bars, but the proprietors claimed not to know him, fearing Kram was a cop. Eventually, Kram saw Gypsy walking down a street, eating a candy bar (the fighter was always consuming sweets and his favorite beverage—scotch and milk). Kram and Gypsy walked to the latter's second-floor apartment off Columbia Avenue. Gypsy downed an applesauce and beer. Then Kram asked him whether he had ever heard of Sam Langford, the early-twentieth-century Boston boxer ranked by *Ring Magazine* as one of the ten best heavyweights ever, whose degenerating eyes forced him to retire in 1926 and who was found years later broke and blind in a decrepit Harlem room. "No," Gypsy said, "can't say I have." And so the night went on, with Kram and Gypsy shooting the shit about money and women and the goal: a championship. It ended with them in a club and

Gypsy sliding over the floor in a Temptation Walk, the crowd cooing, "Gypsyyy."

"He is, unfortunately, a Philadelphia fighter," Kram wrote, "a breed that does not stay motivated long. 'The Jungle,' which shoves them into the gym, often lures them away much too soon." A month later, Gypsy's weight, which had steadily increased over many pool hall nights, disqualified him from his slated title match. And then the medical commission barred Gypsy from fighting because he could see from only one eye. Somehow that never came up at medical examinations (Gypsy later claimed to have memorized the whole eye chart; he also claimed that the commission had overlooked his condition until that because he had recently threatened to leave his connected management team).

Suddenly, a young man who had entered the Police Athletic League gym as a kid after a gang chased him for accidentally knocking the leader's ice cream cone onto the floor had no career. Or as he put it, "Boxing was my pursuit of happiness. Now they say I can't do it anymore." Gypsy Joe turned to heroin, buying from the dealers at Tenth and Diamond and spending all his money in the process. He was practically homeless, to the point where promoter Russell Peltz began soliciting donations for him from attendees of the fights. For years, Gypsy's family tried to set him straight, but he sank deeper into depression, and according to his brother, tried to jump off the Ben Franklin Bridge. He died at forty-four after his fourth (probably drug abuse–induced) heart attack.

Kram foresaw the downfall of the man without sight. Saw the parallels to Langford, the perils of the street. The boxing commissioner who suspended Gypsy said, "I can't let him fight. I just can't. I know it's . . . it's like sending him slowly to the gas chamber."[15]

Then there was Tyrone Everett—Ty the Fly—whom Mr. Pat trained at the beginning of his career. A junior lightweight boxer from the gang-riddled, drugged-up streets of Southwest Philly, he was named after the movie star Tyrone Power. And he lived up to the star power of his namesake: Ty was strong, fast, smooth. No one could touch him in the early 1970s.

He was undefeated when they brought the world champion Alfredo Escalera onto Ty's turf in Philly—due to Ty's immense popularity—for a championship match in the Spectrum in 1976. And Ty was brilliant that night. He slid and grooved and pounded Escalera on his way to

Gypsy Joe Harris, the 1960s welterweight banned from fighting for his blindness, poses for an *Inquirer* story in 1989. He had been wandering North Philadelphia, drugging himself, for decades. He'd die the next year. Photo by Jerry Lodriguss.

dominating fifteen rounds. But when the scorecards were announced, Ty the Fly—the man always in control—was in shock: Two of the three judges had scored him the loser, including one from Philly. The packed house began hurling food and bottles into the ring. The Philly judge sneaked away into the night, never to be seen or heard from again. It was judged by *Ring Magazine* as one of the top five robberies of all time. The fix had been in.

Six months later, Ty was killed. His girlfriend shot a bullet through his forehead, perhaps because he had been abusive or because she had caught him in bed with a man. He was gone as quickly as he had pummeled opponents with his unseen punches—and just before his slated rematch with Escalera for the title.[16]

So many fighters were cut down just as they were primed to soar— the ones who coulda been contenders (or remained contenders) if they hadn't been taken so soon. James "Black Gold" Shuler was a North Philly kid—one of ten in his family—called "the smoothest boxer of all" by the *New York Times* after he won a gold in the 1979 World Cup. He was deprived of a chance to win an Olympic medal when the U.S. boycotted the 1980 Games in Moscow. But he turned pro, won the North American middleweight title in his thirteenth fight, and went 22–0 with sixteen knockouts. Then he lost for the first time—to the Hall-of-Famer Thomas Hearns—and a week later he was going north on his new motorcycle, a temporary registration in his pocket, when he collided at an intersection with a tractor trailer rolling east. Dead at the scene. Age twenty-six.[17]

Andre "Thee" Prophet was the undefeated cruiserweight whose big punch was supposed to revive local interest in the sport. The twenty-year-old was riding his motorcycle with an eighteen-year-old girl when they were struck and killed by a hit-and-run driver at Twenty-second and York a bit after 5 a.m.[18]

And then there was Najai "Nitro" Turpin, the twenty-three-year-old from the North Philly housing projects where, as the saying goes, "if you spit, you spittin' in someone else's yard." He never really knew his father, and his mother died from diabetes when he was eighteen. He was then forced to live in a dilapidated house without windows, where he slept in the closet for warmth. He was picked to fight on the NBC reality TV show *The Contender*, which was hosted by Sylvester Stallone. Then Turpin and his girlfriend started having issues. And NBC banned him from fighting until it could air *The Contender*. He shot his left temple with a semiautomatic in a car on Valentine's Day in 2005. Suicide. Stallone, who chose Turpin for the show, called him a guy who "typified the real heart of the city."[19] Turpin had trained in West Philly at the James Shuler Memorial Gym, named after the kid on the bike who was killed twenty years earlier. These things have a way of circling back.

The fear is that they'll be forgotten. John DiSanto, a longtime Philly boxing fan who started a website about Philly boxing history, walked into a graveyard in Collingdale one day, searching for Tyrone Everett's grave. He realized it was unmarked, as were so many other Philly boxers' graves. So in December 2005 he began to collect money for deceased Philly boxers who didn't have gravestones. His first year, DiSanto placed a headstone for Tyrone Everett in Eden Cemetery. A year later, Gypsy Joe finally got a headstone. In 2011, DiSanto erected one for Eddie Cool.

Larry Merchant, the longtime HBO boxing announcer and former editor of the *Philadelphia Daily News* sports section, on death: "I've been covering boxing for HBO for twenty-nine years. We've had two guys who have died. It's always tragic in the biggest sense possible. In the personal sense. I sort of am—I guess have programmed it into myself that this is what they do, these are the risks they take, and it's always, occasionally this is going to happen. As Ali has said on many occasions, he would do it all over again. It's part of boxing and there are a lot of parts of boxing you love, and there are some parts you hate. But you can't have one without the other."

You can't have one without the other: That's what it comes down to. Ernest Becker, the social psychologist, argued in *The Denial of Death* that man's knowledge of his own impending demise coerces him to build his lifestyle as a defense, to attempt "heroics" that will temporarily shield him from his fate. Of course, there's a downside to attempting heroics. There always has been. Pierce Egan, the first true boxing writer, wrote in 1812:

> No men are subject more to the caprice of changes of fortune than the pugilists; victory brings them fame, riches, and patrons, their bruises are not heeded in the smiles of success; and basking in the sun-shine of prosperity, their lives pass on pleasantly till defeat comes and reverses the scene: covered with aches and pains, distressed in mind and body, assailed by poverty, wretchedness, and misery—friends forsake them—their towering fame expired—their characters suspected by losing—and no longer the "plaything of fashion!"—they fly to inebriation for relief, and premature end puts a period to their misfortunes. [20]

Decades after the crime, the detective who brought Mr. Pat's son Tyrone clean clothes after Tyrone committed murder, Sylvester Johnson, became the thirteenth police commissioner in the history of the city. The year was 2002. The hope, as always, was that the violence would end, that the unnaturally early deaths would cease, that the city would find itself on the right side of the story arc, that it would just be able to breathe.

Part Two

New Day Rising

5

THE WORKSITES

Mr. Pat didn't hide all his demons from me—some he readily shared. He told me about his alcoholism (while omitting what brought it on). One night he drunkenly thought he was in a boxing match with a tree and spent hours hitting it like a heavy bag. His nadir came in the early '90s when he was working for the city morgue (a place I tried hard to picture—another worksite). He was sneaking into work each day with a small bottle of moonshine (imported from the South) in his sock. One day during his commute, he drunkenly fell down a flight of underground stairs and onto trolley tracks, from which he was removed in time. It was then that he was forced into rehab.

He also told me about the recovery process—the way he began writing poetry. One poem contained this: "This was the life I chose to live."

That sort of regret was his trademark.

But there was another aspect to his memory that I was drawn to: the recollection of place. Nearly everyone in the Philly boxing world, even the younger fighters, recollected some older bygone gym or arena or neighborhood he or she used to occupy. It wasn't because developers had a habit of tearing down small local gems in favor of large commercial buildings—Philadelphia had no such willing developers. It was more a case of places almost disappearing—crumbling very slowly day by day, until one night, in the darkness, they were just expended, gone. *Poof.*

Others vanished more nefariously.

The names of the places leaked out of Mr. Pat's scrapbook: the Alhambra, the Passyunk Gym (both South Philly staples Mr. Pat spent a lot of time in), the Cambria, Champs. You hear grandiose names such as these—Alhambra, named for the Moorish palace in Spain; Passyunk, named for the street, which was named for the Native American trail (in the Lenape language, "passyunk" means "in the valley")—and you have to find out what happened to them, whether they still exist. I asked Mr. Pat to accompany me on such trips, but he waved me off.

✻ ✻ ✻

Return to the Blue Horizon, still standing on North Broad.

But first, that street flows through place and time, a cultural river like the real thing, cutting through vast, disparate land—the Delaware to the East, the Schuylkill to the West, and a grid in the middle. Two miles in length and one in width—that's how Thomas Holme laid out the city in the seventeenth century. But it was 1854 that opened Broad, unleashed its axis onto the scared, rural pockets, when the state consolidated all of Philadelphia County into one city, which now sprawled beyond the grid into twenty-eight districts, boroughs, and townships. One straight-edged street grafted onto the entropic mess of Passyunk and Moyamensing, large undeveloped chunks of South Philly with Indian names. In the mid-1860s, one could start at the southern tip of Broad at the Delaware and walk up the street through marshes, then vegetable farms, then building lots and railroad tracks, then churches, coal yards, and factories. At the intersection with Locust, one would hit the Academy of Music, then the Academy of Natural Sciences, then the La Pierre hotel, then warehouses, then a military hospital, then railroad depots, more coal yards, foundries, mills and lumber yards, Baldwin's locomotive factory, and then a flouring mill.

Here, past the last mill, one would have entered the Blue Horizon's area of North Broad. Given its distance to Center City in a time before streetcars, this area invited the wealthy as a suburb. The head of Pennsylvania Railroad was said to own a mansion. A coal dealer built another "of architectural grotesqueness" at Broad and Poplar.[1] At Broad and Stiles, there was the Italianate brownstone of Michael Bouvier, Jackie Kennedy's great-granddad. It included a cupola, and out front, trees sprouted from both sides of sidewalk as an oasis and tangled together in what one writer called a "gothic arch"—though in the winter, lush branches withered brittle, until they could barely catch a falling snowflake. Just before Master, one would hit Edwin Forrest's three-floor brownstone walkup, to which the actor adjoined his own theater. And right next door, three more brownstone Italianate mansions.

Time passed.

The Bouvier mansion became LaSalle College, Forrest's house became a school of design, and three adjacent mansions consolidated into a Moose lodge under architect Carl Berger, a longtime lodge treasurer. In 1961, promoter Jimmy Toppi Jr., whose father had owned the Olympia—admission for eighty cents!—and the Metropolitan Opera House and held boxing shows there, bought the five-floor lodge for $85,000 and renamed it after the tune "Beyond the Blue Horizon." The elder Toppi had been one of Philly's biggest promoters for years, but he also managed fighters, and that was an illegal conflict of interest. So from the age of seventeen, his son had acted as the nominal promoter on contracts, with the father merely a contracted second party. After Jr. bought the lodge, a guy named Marty Kramer began to promote there, using $500 a week in seed money from Madison Square Garden, which was looking to develop young talent at small clubs around the country. An adolescent Russell Peltz watched two fights at the Blue Horizon when he was in high school, one of which involved welter Dick Turner. And in '69, when Peltz was out of Temple University, twenty-two, and without money, the Blue was the smallest, least expensive place to start promoting. So Peltz visited Toppi to ask for advice and consent. And even though Peltz was in his twenties, he appeared seventeen to Toppi. And even though Toppi himself had entered the fight racket as a kid, while still a senior at South Philly High, he thought Peltz "was wacko and would never get a license."[2] But Toppi did share an insight, in two distilled lines.

"People will go up a blind alley to see a fight," Toppi told Peltz. "If they want to see it."

Peltz started there, at a time when boxing was dying, in an old lodge. He sold out his first show. "You wouldn't believe the times I've heard the story about how nobody could make the Blue Horizon go," he said that night. "And now the boy promoter is gonna show them how. Hee-hee."[3] Peltz paid $50 to a four-round fighter, $75 to a six rounder, and $250 to $300 to an eight rounder. On normal nights, these costs plus the $650 rent and other fees put him in a $3,000 hole. To break even, he needed at least 750 spectators at an average of $4 a ticket. In the beginning, the people showed. The night of Peltz's third show—which featured Jimmy Young's debut—Peltz made $801.16. But time aggravated the economics. In '84, Peltz staged ten shows on which he *lost* an average of $3,000.

The Blue didn't really make it until the USA Network came along. It was 1986, and Philly was still faltering, though here and there cultural institutions held events full of promise, and in a moment, you could maybe forget the crossfire outside. The Blue was still a local thing: Peltz would sell out only now and then. USA began to air fights on tape delay to its audience of millions, paying $2,000 a show to promoter Dan Duva (the son of Meldrick Taylor's manager, Lou, and Taylor's first promoter), who assembled cards. And one day Dan Duva called Peltz and said, "Listen, we got this show in June. We can't do it. We don't have time. Why don't you do it?" So Peltz put in 31–3 bantamweight Johnny "Dancing Machine" Carter of South Philly against 13–6–2 Juan Veloz. And—wouldn't you know it?—the show was terrific. Veloz won a split decision over Carter, taking two of three judges' cards. The only judge to vote for Carter was Carol Polis, the first-ever woman judge, who thirteen years earlier had worked Earnie Shavers's demolition of Jimmy Young in the Spectrum. A couple months later, Duva said to Peltz, "You wanna do another one?" USA might've been paying $3,000 by then, according to Peltz. So Duva said, "This time, I'm taking $1,000 for myself. You do it." And by the end of '86, Peltz had done three of them. In '87, when USA went live with *Tuesday Night Fights*, it gave Peltz his own deal to conduct the shows. That's when the Blue Horizon started to become known nationally. And then, the second big thing was in '93 when Peltz adopted reserved seating. Before, it had been first come, first served. People would get there at six o'clock and stand at the door. As soon as the doors opened, they'd rush upstairs to get the best seats. The people who had once bought season seats at the Spectrum—all the lawyers and the doctors and the professionals downtown—couldn't take their clients out because by the time they'd arrive at the show, the only seats left would be in the back. So Peltz started experimenting with reserved seats. First a third of the house, then half. And all of a sudden, the white collars returned, able to again take out their clients at $30 a pop for a reserved first-row seat. From 1993–2001, Peltz sold out almost every show. Then he became the coordinator for ESPN2's *Friday Night Fights* and exposed the Blue there. Suddenly, the Blue was big, and a 95 percent white crowd was venturing from the suburbs into the heart of the ghetto to see boxing as it used to be. The long-awaited repatriation, if only for a few nights a year. *Ring Magazine* named it the world's greatest place to watch a fight.

But from the inside, the Blue was crumbling.

Toppi sold it in 1987. In April 1994, Vernoca Michael bought the place for $500,000 with Carol Ray and silent partner Carol Whitaker. They were two women and a man named Carol, and they had absolutely no boxing experience. A local high school principal had merely told Ray the building was for sale and, interested in its architecture, Ray had convinced her friend Michael to help buy it. Ray was a teacher at Simon Gratz High, the school Meldrick Taylor attended in his Nicetown youth. This trio appeared unlikely to revive Philly fighting. Yet Michael wouldn't hear detractors. A black woman unafraid to tell you what she thought, she had graduated high school at fourteen, she says, and enrolled in a special program at MIT and Harvard for precocious students in math and science.[4] She had then studied at the 600-student, historically black Livingstone College in Salisbury, North Carolina. Then she had completed a graduate degree in city planning with a concentration in business and law at Penn in 1972. She had worked in CPA firms in Philly and taught financial management at Temple. She had run a domestic abuse agency. In a way, she was precisely the right person to buy the Blue. Educated, determined, black—with a degree in city planning and looking to help others overcome discrimination, too.

"I'm a product of the '60s," she told me one January day in her office, wearing a blue terry cloth tracksuit over a yellow turtleneck, with black sneakers, hoop earrings, and a silver cross necklace. "I remember my parents telling me what I *could* do."

Michael and Ray bought the building from a Baptist pastor, who supposedly promised that it complied with city regulations. Michael's dad was a Methodist minister, so she had no reason to distrust the guy. In fact, she very much respected old-school clergy for helping to keep kids off the street. Her dad had installed punching bags and equipment in the basement of his Pittsburgh church. But the building *wasn't* compliant with regulations. A month after the purchase, the city's Department of Licenses and Inspection cited the building for fire and electrical rule violations, a permeable roof, and other issues. Later they got in trouble for faulty emergency exits and exposed wiring. A judge who is a fight fan ruled the new owners could keep the Blue open if they made certain fixes, which they did. The state promised to contribute $1 million in matching funds to the cause if the women formed a nonprofit to serve the neighborhood. Michael did so, and she's now a local fixture, having mentored students and sponsored a spelling bee in celebration of the movie *Akeelah and the Bee*. In 2003, the state finally gave the million. The Delaware River Port Authority also provided a $1 million loan. Michael says Mayor Rendell's administration also promised $2 million, but that money never came. In 2003, Mayor Street gave her $140,000. All nice sums but hardly enough to cover the cost of repairs or to maintain a structure left to rot, presumed by the city as retrograde and bygone. "You serious? They still have fights up in there?" a passerby asked, walking in front of the Blue in 2003, when the owners finally received the funding for ghetto revival.[5] Which was barely any funding at all compared to the monies for *South* Broad Street (read: not the ghetto), which in the '90s experienced a building boom and rechristening. It now goes by the name "Avenue of the Arts" and features new theaters for the Wilma company, the Philadelphia Theatre Company, and the local opera. All good for the city, yet disproportionate nonetheless.

In 2001, Peltz left and took with him the $50,000 TV fees he commanded. It had been brewing for a while, and as always, there were two stories. He said he simply couldn't work there anymore because the venue was too small, the parking spaces too few, the catwalks too dangerous for ESPN cameramen, and the drug dealing in the area too unsavory. Plus during an ESPN2 show in June, the men's room had seriously unhygienic plumbing issues. Michael said Peltz didn't respect her and laughed at the idea of her doing boxing business. The truth is probably somewhere in the middle. At the time, the Blue needed a lot of work, and ESPN was only growing larger as the nation's sports entertainment juggernaut. Still, one can also imagine Peltz wanting to do business *his* way after thirty years of promoting.

Peltz moved his first post-Blue promotion to the Park Hyatt (on *South* Broad) and made it black tie optional. He took his second one to the Gershman YMHA at Pine and *South* Broad. He renamed the 1,100-seat venue the Arts Palace and upped ticket prices to $50. Ten of sixteen guys on the card were from out of town. It all felt very different. It was the only time Peltz promoted there.

"The sightlines are great," Peltz says today of the Blue, while chomping a thin slice of pizza in his office. He has a full head of grayish-white hair and few wrinkles, and he looks like a lawyer who was able to retire early. "Listen, you know what? I can't honestly discuss the Blue Horizon because I can't stand the people who own it. So anything I'd say about the Blue Horizon would probably be colored now, other than you know, I know I made the Blue Horizon. . . . I basically ran the place from '69 to 2001."

A month ago, Peltz turned sixty. For as long as I've known him, he has always looked somewhat bemused and somewhat pissed, even if he's not either. His office is a beautiful little house behind the art museum that functions as a museum of its own. The front room: covered in old boxing cards and movie posters, like ones for *The Joe Louis Story* and *Champion* (starring Kirk Douglas). The back room: more posters and Harold Johnson's light-heavyweight championship belt from '62 (this, perhaps, is the object that means most to him here). The basement is filled with tapes and DVDs of fights.

Peltz may seem to be overreacting when he complains about the deterioration of the Blue and its surrounding neighborhood. But he is not a man who speaks without reason. He has experienced this city's dark side firsthand. His office was firebombed several years ago by two boxing-related guys whom everyone fingers in private but no one accuses publicly. The office was robbed in January 1995 by guys he believes to be associated with an ex-fighter from North Philly. Two assailants handcuffed Peltz to his niece, who was working with him at the time, and shoved his assistant Maureen. He had $40,000 in cash in a briefcase on the sofa because there was a fight that night at the Blue and he paid fighters in cash. The briefcase wasn't open, but it also wasn't locked. The thieves were looking for money. He said, "Give it to 'em. Give 'em the money." Maureen gave them a box of tickets containing $750. The thieves left with this box and never even checked the briefcase. Afterward, Peltz stopped paying his fighters in cash.

The Blue Horizon still holds shows about once a month, and so do a few other venues, including the Armory in the northeast and a warehouse in South Philly with all the luster and potential of its neighborhood's sepia past. But in an age of Atlantic City and Vegas and Indian casinos, the city rarely attracts big fights. Bernard "The Executioner" Hopkins staged his sixteenth successful title defense at the Spectrum in

2003. "Philadelphia has to change with the times if it wants more big-time boxing," Don King said about that bout,[6] without specifying what needed to change. Eight years earlier, King had staged a Tyson fight at the Spectrum, but ringside tickets cost up to $500 and the workingmen didn't show. In 1994, Frank Gelb, who had once managed Tyrone Everett and (perhaps unwittingly) sold Jimmy Young's contract to the men who ruined him, promoted a card at the one-year-old Pennsylvania Convention Center in the heart of downtown. The Convention Center had been built on the site of old Reading Railroad Terminal, and it incorporated the steel and glass train shed into the design. They called it "the oldest surviving single-span arched trainshed roof," and the project represented Pennsylvania's largest public development ever. It was Philly's attempt in the '90s to capture lucrative business-tourists and reposition the city as a dynamic blend of innovation and preservation. It was the only way: not to ignore the past through unthinking demolition or bury memories in repaved concrete. Not to tout only the colonial heritage: Independence Hall and the Liberty Bell and nearby Valley Forge. But to restore the past to functionality, to put its years of steel and scarring to use in the present. In the service economy. So four thousand attended his show, and Gelb promised to bring back similar events. But the center didn't become a boxing site, though it did succeed in luring execs and now plans to expand to one million square feet of space.

At the Blue, Vernoca Michael now promotes her own shows, using second-tier city prospects, the guys with better chances of becoming "club fighters" than true contenders. The top fighters tend to ply their trade elsewhere. But the Blue Horizon boys (and now girls) captivate audiences all the same with the kind of small-time personal stories that involve the entire city in their outcome. Take Gennaro Pellegrini Jr., a five-feet, eight-inch cop from the white working-class area of Port Richmond, on the eastern side of the city. They called him "One Punch Gerry" because he had once overtaken a robber on foot and knocked him out cold. He had had eighteen fights in the amateurs and boxed in his free time, but he was spurred to turn pro in April 2004, after being called up for Pennsylvania National Guard duty. His six-year enlistment was actually about to end that month, but under the wartime Stop Loss measure, the military was allowed to extend his commitment—in order to send him to Iraq. That spurred him to try to turn pro before the start of infantry training at Fort Hood, Texas. It was all set for May 21, 2004, a night "surprisingly electric," as Bernard Fernandez of the *Daily News* would later call it. About six hundred relatives and cops and National Guardsmen crowded the ring at the Blue Horizon as a blind boy sang the national anthem and then received a birthday cake for turning eleven. Sitting ringside was police commissioner Sylvester Johnson, the man who had once served a search warrant on a bloodstained house on Hicks Street.

The cops and National Guardsmen in attendance hollered. The bell rang for the first of four rounds. Pellegrini knocked down his opponent, John Andre Harris, whose record was 2–12–2. In the third, he shook Harris again. But though he punched hard, Pellegrini began fading. His opponent had fought sixteen times professionally, and Pellegrini had never. "He was running out of gas," Fernandez recalls, "which was not unexpected since it was his first fight. You could be in good shape every day of his life but not in boxing shape. People were getting a little worried."

"He was losing," recalls Michael. "And I said to myself, I said, 'This man had too much to do in too short a period of time and didn't have really time to concentrate.'"

Pellegrini returned to his corner before the final round, heaving and hyperventilating. "I can't," he told Michael and his trainer Charlie Sgrillo and Joey Eye, the cutman. "I can't."

"Yes, you can," said Michael, whom Pellegrini always called "mom." "Yes, you can. Make it for mom."

"You're supposed to be a fucking soldier," Eye said.[7] "Get out there; do what you have to do."

One minute and forty seconds later, Pellegrini knocked out Harris with a smashing right. The crowd erupted. "He dug down," Fernandez says. "You can't base a whole lot on one fight. [But] he won that fight because he had heart. He willed himself to win."

He was killed in Iraq the following year, and two years after that, I would visit with Sgrillo, his trainer, a former '60s lightweight who runs the Veterans Boxers Association bar in the northeast part of the city. There he grabbed me a Yuengling from the fridge and put a DVD into the player, and we sat sniffling on a muggy summer night before a big flat-screen TV, watching a documentary about a soldier who won it all on his very last punch. Michael, the Blue Horizon owner, hung Pellegrini's camouflage boxing trunks in her office.

Not all the Blue Horizon fighters, however, come from Philly. Another Iraq War vet, Sam Brown, from Kentucky, has become a Blue regular, as has Elad Shmouel, an Israeli light-welterweight nicknamed the "Kosher Pitbull" who once fought there on Passover. Michael finds them through her matchmaker, Don Elbaum, the grizzled elder who claims to have sparred with Willie Pep at sixteen and who promoted Meldrick Taylor in the mid-'90s when no one else would (given how punch-drunk Taylor was becoming, this was controversial).

Elbaum is the man Don King called in the early '70s to break into the business, the man who unwittingly launched the career of Jimmy Young's predator. "DON EL-BAUM!" King shouted into the phone that night, half imploring and half threatening. "DON EL-BAUM!" Elbaum is the guy who made Pellegrini's dream happen, slotting the kid into a last-minute KO before an Iraqi bomb shredded a Humvee's bones. Elbaum is the huckster who promoted Sugar Ray Robinson's last match and, at the press conference, whipped out a pair of gloves. These, he said, were the gloves Sugar used in his first fight. And either Sugar cried then or his wife did, depending on the exact version you hear. But regardless, Elbaum quickly shoved the gloves in a box before anyone could examine them. And when someone finally did, he found either two rights or two lefts (again, the versions differ).[8]

No matter how beloved, Elbaum's new headliners don't make much. Vernoca Michael can't afford to pay more than several thousand—opposed to the tens of thousands Peltz could muster during the USA and ESPN days. Through October 2007, the Blue had attracted about 1,200 for its best card of the year, which featured three undefeated headliners. For its September card, which featured nobodies, 450 showed. And so the Blue remains.

On North Broad between Thompson to the south and Master to the north, two blocks east of Seybert, the street where Jimmy Young lived, and next door to the New Freedom Theatre, housed in Edwin Forrest's old place, the latest incarnation of the black company that once put on *Lackawanna Blues*, a show with one actor and one blues guitarist partly about the way western New York lost its soul when the mills closed. Just south, the stiff concrete umbrella of Sunoco shades old cars. Then Interstate Blood Bank—"All donors $20 now"—where eighty to a hundred donors give a pint every day and wait the mandatory two months until they can give again. Across the street, on Broad's eastern side, is William Penn High School.[9] A school where 82 percent of students receive free or reduced-price lunches.[10] Where a quarter of the 993 students ditch daily. And where seven years ago, Cliff Eubanks painted a mural on the outer wall facing Broad, of burnt reds and deep blues, with a beautiful black girl diving into an open book of gold, calling it "Street of Dreams."

Other sorts of dreams adorn the Blue Horizon's walls.

I walked inside one frigid January day in 2007.

I climbed the steep staircase into the 1,500-seat auditorium. There were rows of folding chairs. Above me were balconies with intricate wooden detailing. Eight-bulb chandeliers hung from the ceiling.

It was early afternoon, and I was alone. Outside, the season's first snow began to fall.

Inside it was silent.

❉ ❉ ❉

So much did not survive. So many of the old factories and arenas crumbled to the dirt.

In 2007, I revisited these places. They were not totally restored. Many were still empty. But the city was a better place than before. It had passed its low point and begun to rise.

The nadir was in January 1992. Ed Rendell—who was district attorney when the city prosecuted Tyrone Patterson in 1979—took office as mayor, pledging to balance the budget, whose deficit promised to grow bigger than the entire budget of Boston. He kind of followed through. The *New York Times* famously called Philly "one of the most stunning turnarounds in recent urban history."[11]

January '92. It's also when Philly held its only major '90s title fight: Meldrick "The Kid" Taylor versus Glenwood Brown at the Civic Center. By January 1992, of course, Meldrick Taylor had already lost to Chavez, had looked slower and sloppier in his subsequent matches, and had admitted to a loss of passion and will. Yet this would be his comeback, his fulcrum, his redoubling of effort before the street dwellers who'd birthed him. "Tonight my dream comes true," he said, in lines written for him by broadcaster HBO. In lines it took him many, many tries to record, as he kept choking on the letters, straining just to enunciate the words.

HBO also produced a short feature on "The Philly Fighter" to air before Taylor's ring entrance. A film crew revisited the old gyms and venues with promoter Russell Peltz. They drove all the way down Broad, to its southern tip, where wrecking crews were dismantling JFK Stadium, that long horseshoe once known as Sesquicentennial, the site of Tunney's triumph over Dempsey. But the demolition guys wouldn't let them shoot. So they hopped back into the truck, and Peltz said, "Just open the fucking door and shoot as we're going out." And then they captured the last moments of the green field, oval track, big lights held up by rusted steel, and a glass skybox overlooking it all. The brick arched entrances and the barren concrete parking lot.

They went to the intersection of Passyunk and Moore in South Philly. The former street is one of several in the city that conform not to a grid but to the outlines of past Indian trails, crisscrossing the perpendiculars in unexpected diagonals. More recently, a gym stood on the corner of Passyunk and Moore, where Joey Giardello and Percy Manning and Bud Anderson trained. And Mr. Pat taught. During its mid-'60s heyday, it was the city's single toughest room below South Street, a second floor haven above a poolroom and bar. But in 1992, one couldn't see its past. Now there was a florist on the corner in a three-floor brick building

They went to Broad and Christian in South Philly, where the third Broadway Athletic Club held fights from '25 to '35 on Thursday nights. It wasn't there anymore. Instead, there was a garage with three light blue doors, each spray painted with a red word: "NEW DAY RISING."

They traveled up Broad to Poplar Street, to North Philly's eighty-three-year-old Metropolitan Opera House. In 1908, Oscar Hammerstein had hired the theater architect William McElfatrick to design the 4,000-seat palace of arches, columns, and balconies. It was to compete with the 3,000-seat Academy of Music farther down Broad. And in November of that year, the two went head-to-head on opening night, as the Academy hosted tenor Enrico Caruso, and Hammerstein put on a 700-member production of *Carmen*. The Academy won at first, filling every seat. But then the curtain went down for intermission, and the socialites hopped carriages north to catch the second half at the Met. An initial success. But five years later the Met was bankrupt, and seven years after that, it ceased showing opera. It later held basketball and boxing and then religious revivals, and it endured now in '92, but not in its virginal delicacy, when it debuted as the city's largest stage. It had faded into the background so that a passerby might mistake it for an elaborate but derelict row house. Its surroundings had lowered and incorporated it like plankton on the rails of the *Titanic*. All the arched structure remained, but dirt clung to the surface.

They continued up to Dauphin and Thirty-third, where George Benton and Bennie Briscoe and Sonny Liston and Harold Johnson and "Crazy Horse" Smith and Charley Scott had trained at the old Champs Gym. That was in the middle of the century, when you could find the champion or top contenders in every division working out there. Now, it was just an empty lot next to a brick building with naked twigs sprouting from the ground.

They went north to the Somerset El station, where there was once the 2,000-seat Cambria, known as the Bloodpit and the Little College of Hard Knocks and Blinky's Club, the last nickname referring to the mobster Blinky Palermo. It was in Kensington, an insular working-class neighborhood of second-generation English, Irish, and Germans, where America's first textile mill had purred and smoked. The Cambria was located next to a cafeteria, though the cognoscenti knew to grab a sandwich next door at Hymie's, the Jewish deli. Promoter Johnny Burns had converted the Cambria from a silent movie theater in 1917. Born on St. Patrick's Day, he was a former flyweight and a liquor seller who always wore a stiff derby, earning the nickname "Mr. Iron Hat." A former manager worked as head usher, and Burns ran the place to please his parish locals. Burns would paste posters inviting neighbors to come see the Jew Tommy Spiegal beat the black "Bobcat" Montgomery. Not that they liked Jews. When Spiegal fought Sarullo, the posters invited them to see the Italian Idol take down the Jew. It was a hierarchy. And lowest were the blacks, who by unspoken rule had to leave the area by dusk or residents might unsheathe pipes. In '66 a black family moved in. The locals rioted for five nights. "Very few people of color went up there," Mr. Pat says.

"I hate that place," he once added. "The lights would go out [in the middle of fights]. I dunno who did it."

As racist as they were, the locals adored their favorite fighters. In the '50s, Irish welterweight Pat Haley faced Johnny Peppe, and in the fourth, Peppe fell to the canvas, where resin adhered to his gloves. When Peppe next hit Haley, the resin stung Haley's eyes. Haley stumbled, and the crowd condemned his poor showing. But then they realized Haley had been blinded, and they went cold and quiet. Haley was taken to the hospital. And the fans remained in the Cambria until the news arrived that their boy would make it. In the interim, one guy offered Burns's wife, Rosie, one of his eyes for Haley.

The Cambria closed in 1963 and became a warehouse. In the early 1990s when the Latinos moved in and a white took a bullet on a corner, locals called for the "spics" to go home.

They went to Forty-fifth and Market, site of the old Arena in West Philly, the city's first major indoor venue. It had opened on Valentine's Day 1920 as the Philadelphia Auditorium and Ice Palace and soon became the 1.4-acre, 7,000-seat venue that fighters headlined after they outgrew the smaller Cambria. It was built by engineer George Pawling, and he held black tie boxing events there in its early years. Later, it held Philadelphia Warriors and 76ers (NBA) games there and Philadelphia Quakers (NHL) games and six-day bicycle races. Marathon dance contests. Rocking chair derbies. Wrestling matches. Circuses. It's where Irving Crane won a title at the '55 billiards championship. A man raced a horse. Sonja Henie skated there in her pro debut, and Elvis sang and Hendrix played. The Roy Rogers Rodeo came every year and even a bullfight. When a cowgirl died during the '46 rodeo, they held her funeral in the Arena. Perhaps the most raucous were the minor league hockey games. The Ramblers attracted a boozy crowd that has been called the forerunner of Flyers crowds. These guys would scream at the players, and after the game the players would run into the stands for payback.

Media magnate Walter Annenberg bought the Arena in the late 1940s, around the time WFIL constructed its headquarters next door, where they shot and broadcast Dick Clark's "American Bandstand" in the mid-'60s. But that wholesome avatar couldn't hide the city's chaos. In 1969 it came to a head when a cop was shot and four kids stabbed during a riot at an R&B concert in the Arena. The great lightweight Al Massey, who trained at the Twenty-third Police Athletic League, drew on the tension in his walkout. Sure, Massey once knocked a guy out in eleven seconds, but he is remembered for the way he entered the Arena ring in the late 1960s. He danced out of the dressing room, through the fans, and when he got to the row of cops, he halted and started shadowboxing. Right before their noses. The crowd went wild.

No one will forget the boxing. The mobster-manager Boo Boo Hoff charged a penny a round here in the 1920s. Yet the locals sneaked in anyway. They figured out how to scoot by ticket takers in the front and sneak in the exit doors on Ludlow Street in the back. They shimmied through the air conditioning ducts on the roof to enter behind the southwest wall clock. They sold parking spaces for a buck in the Provident Mutual Insurance lot across the street and played craps in the men's room. They bought tickets from ushers on the down low.[12]

In 1965, Jimmy Toppi Jr. bought the Arena for $351,000 at auction. Later, crowds on the south side hurled whiskey bottles into the ring when they disliked a decision. And that ring!—it hovered in a cloud of cigar smoke that never dissipated.

The greatest attraction back then was Gypsy Joe Harris. He *was* the swingin' '60s. He took nothing from anyone. Once he went with his buddy Joe Frazier to visit Muhammad Ali. "Who's the shrimp?" Ali said at the door. "Yeah," Gypsy retorted. "Gimme five inches, and I whup your faggot ass good."[13]

The Arena stood empty for years in the late '70s. It was auctioned off in 1977 to a scrap yard owner for $165,000, or nearly $200,000 less than Toppi had paid twelve years earlier. But the scrap guy never got past the $25,000 down payment, and a lumber company paid Toppi only $113,000 for the Arena in 1979. A year later, as boxing matches moved to Atlantic City's rising casinos, new owners bought the place for only $100,000. They called themselves Larmark and renamed the place after Martin Luther King, and it seemed for a moment like a nice tribute. But the truth would turn out to be sadder, more cynical. Larmark would turn out to be a portmanteau of Larry-Mark. Larry would turn out to be more than a local dentist, the head of a cocaine kingdom raking in $60 million a year. Mark would turn out to be Larry's crooked financial adviser, who was in charge of laundering the profits and hiding them from the Feds. Mark would also turn out to be an aspiring promoter and Don King–manqué. But also a terrible businessman. So Larry would grow sick of sinking $5,000 a week into the shitty Arena, which required new plumbing, toilets, sinks, electrical wiring, beer fridges, and air conditioning. Larry would grow sick of Mark's incompetence, especially after his first Arena event, a closed-circuit broadcast of Leonard–Duran, devolved into a window-breaking, door-smashing riot when the satellite dish failed. Larry would grow sick of Mark's newest purchase, a minor league hoops team renamed the "Kings" that attracted a few hundred spectators and cost Larry 25K. Larry would grow sick of Mark's indolent renovators, who spent their days stealing tools and getting high instead of repairing the Arena. Larry would grow sick of the preachers Mark booked, guys who pretended to raise men from the dead by having them walk out of coffins, which audiences subsequently filled with money.[14] So Larry would yell at Mark, and Mark would turn to a man with lots of cash, the ever-predatory Don King. Mark would secretly sell to King his best fighter, a young Philadelphian heavyweight named Timmy Witherspoon who wouldn't know any of this and who would eventually win two titles but lose most of his money to King's blank contracts. But that wouldn't be enough. Just wouldn't be enough money after eighteen straight months of losses. So Larry would order Mark to get rid of the Arena. Get out of this stupid venture in a stupid neighborhood with no hope.

"Give me two more weeks," Mark would plead, before quietly adding, "I'm going to burn it."[15]

The Arena burned at 1 a.m. on October 4, 1981. The roof collapsed and so did parts of the walls. No one ever had a chance to pull an alarm for the sixty-one-year-old structure. The firefighters caught it themselves, en route to another fire elsewhere. Such was Philadelphia in the early '80s: desperate owners torching their own worksites because more value existed in the ash. Four days after the Arena arson, an eight-alarm fire brilliantly consumed a block of textile factories in North Philly. And the night the Arena burned was just one of several with multiple blazes, which the papers always termed "suspicious" until the perp was caught. Indeed, two years later, what remained of the boarded-up Arena burned again. That night, two other four-alarm fires burned within two hours—one at an empty Kensington factory that had also burned once before—and the commissioner himself rode to the scenes to get them under control. This time, though, Larry and Mark had nothing to do with it. A drunk cook had stumbled to the back of the Arena to piss on its bricks. He noticed an open door and flicked his lighted cigarette through it.[16] The fire exploded an electrical transformer, and the flames shot through the sky and glowed for an entire city to see. Four hundred and thirty customers in the area were left without power, and all that remained amid rubble was a marquee announcing "The Arena." Larry and Mark never did receive the $1.25 million in insurance money, getting years of prison instead. And when the reporters asked a local sports announcer for a quote, he said, "Our youth is being burned down in front of our eyes."

The Arena in '92 was an empty lot of weeds and garbage.

The one place HBO did not go for its documentary, though it should have, was Broad and Locust. Years earlier, the corner had held Lew Tendler's Restaurant, the dank den where mobsters, athletes, and writers drank. Tendler was Philly's Jewish lightweight who twice fought Benny Leonard for the title and twice lost. He retired in 1928, saying, "I don't want to wind up without a dime the way so many other fighters have." In 1932, he opened a restaurant next to Horn and Hardart, across from the Academy of Music, the old opera hall. His partner was his best friend, Harry Carlis, but Tendler's kids just called him Uncle Harry. Uncle Harry invested Tendler's money in the Philly restaurant and in steakhouses and donut shops[17] in Atlantic City, on the boardwalk by Steel Pier, and Florida.[18] When prohibition was repealed, the Philly restaurant became immensely popular. Tendler worked there himself until the hours got to his wife.

Tendler's had a unique setup. The front room was called the Sporting Room. The bar was on the right and the booths were on the left. On the floor was a gigantic picture of Tendler in his boxing pose. Years later, Tendler's granddaughter Sharon came for dinner every Sunday night and would yell at entering customers, "You can't walk on my grandfather's picture! You have to walk around."

The bar had the first two big-screen TVs around. All the barflies had nicknames. They were called Oysters, Sugar, Schools, Lippy, Blinky, Fats. A man named Sassy Doc led a group called "The Outfit," which included Jumbo and Little Neck. Sassy hailed from Northeast Philly and was known for setting the Philly record for sports gambling and numbers-writing arrests: thirty-eight. Once the cops bashed in his door with a sledgehammer and found him pouring 1,500 horse-racing bets scrawled on rice paper into a bowl of water. Tendler's bar was packed on fight night. People would bet hundreds of thousands of dollars. As the rounds went on and people got nervous, nobody would move, and nobody would spend money on a drink. This was a problem for the bar. Roy Tendler, Lew's son, had a solution. When the fight would end, and they'd wait for the decision, Roy would shut off the TV. "If I don't see some money on the bar . . ." he'd say, and they would pound bills on the wood, and the fight reappeared like magic.

In back was the main dining room, which they called the Red Room, because the seat cushions were red. It was the kind of place with tiled floors and wooden tables. The walls were covered with photos of stars.

All the different crowds mingled at Tendler's, including the Jew Mob, also known as the Center City Mob and the Sixty-ninth Street Mob.

The Italian mafia came and accepted bets, too. Blinky Palermo once had a showdown with Sugar Ray Robinson at Tendler's. He asked him in front of the restaurant to throw a fight, and though Robinson didn't want to, he really had no choice. So he was going to do it, but in the third, his opponent nailed him and he instinctively threw a left hook back. The opponent fell. Later that night, Blinky sidled over to Sugar at Tendler's.

"It was an accident," Sugar pleaded. "I just happened to catch him with the hook."

"Alright," Blinky said. "Nothing we can do about it now."[19]

The theater crowd came before and after the shows. After the war years, young guys went to Tendler's to meet young girls. Even today, people walk up to Roy Tendler and tell him they met their spouses at his father's restaurant. Lew Tendler himself walked through the place, schmoozing with all the customers. He looked at them as if he knew them, but he often couldn't remember their names, so he called them "Champ." He had a card made up with his favorite sayings, and he handed it out. On one side, Lew beamed a closed-lips grin, with his male-pattern baldness, oversized collar, and polka-dot tie. The other side contained two columns, the one on the left in black and the one on the right in red. "The greatest sin," began the left column. And on the right: "Fear."

The best town	Where you succeed
The best work	What you like
The best play	Work
The greatest need	Common sense
The greatest puzzle	Life
The greatest mystery	Death

The greatest thought   God

The greatest thing, bar none in all   Love
the world

When the theater crowd cleared, the contract bridge players set up their games. Their card talk merged with talk of boxing. That's how the term *uppercut* gained application in bridge to describe a situation where the high but losing trump forces out the higher trump from the declarer's hand.[20]

There was a celebrity crowd of actors, athletes, politicians, and writers. Just as bridge and boxing mixed until one contained elements of the other, so did these men and women soak each other in until a *Daily News* writer who covered music and boxing took up fighting himself (for at least one match, which he won; he soon realized he didn't have the energy for any more). There were other cases. Back in the days of Philly's Republican machine, Alex Gaddess reported on politics for the *Evening Public Ledger*. GOP cronies swarmed him in a place like Tendler's, and eventually his wife, Dot, took up Republican politics herself. "When she walked in to meet Alex," said one friend of a specific date at Tendler's, "she took my breath away."[21] They even used to set up a table in the middle of the place just for the City Hall crowd. The mob and fighters mixed, too, though that was no geographic accident. Tendler's was where Sonny Liston held a 1961 press conference luncheon to announce new management and dispel rumors that he was controlled by Blinky Palermo (he was).

The National Football League was practically invented at Tendler's. From 1947 to 1957, the NFL's four-person executive staff worked out of a three-room dance studio on Walnut Street. Commissioner Bert Bell, an addict of cigarettes, chocolate, and coffee, ate at Tendler's and often brought Tim Mara, the Giants owner, and the Bears' George Halas. He even offered Roy Tendler a job, though Roy declined. "I should've taken it," Roy says today at eighty-four. At one dinner at Tendler's, football as we know it today took shape. Bell insisted an NFL game between the Eagles, which he then owned, and the Brooklyn Dodgers be canceled. It was due to be played the next day in the former Sesquicentennial Stadium, which lacked cover, and the forecast called for rain. The owner of the Dodgers knew the NFL wouldn't take in American society if it played games on "a hit-or-miss basis" so he argued against cancellation. Bell relented, and the show went on. Eventually, fans grew to love the NFL precisely because it played in practically any weather, no matter how inclement.

Celebrities met at Tendler's.

When Ava Gardner visited her cousin in the Marines, she spent time hanging out with Lew Tendler at the restaurant. The Philadelphia Athletics—World Series champions of 1929 and 1930—spent a lot of time in Tendler's, especially catcher Mickey Cochrane (after whom Mickey Mantle was named), outfielder "Bucketfoot" Al Simmons, and first baseman Jimmie Foxx: three of the greatest ever to play.

One baseball player took the partying at Tendler's too seriously. He was a catcher on the St. Louis Browns named "Rollicking" Rollie Helmsley. He would come into town, drink all night, and get three hits the next day. He later joined Alcoholics Anonymous.

During the Minneapolis Lakers' championship years, they would visit Tendler's when they were in town. One time, the lanky bespectacled giant George Mikan ordered meat.

"George, you're not allowed to eat steak," Roy said, knowing Mikan had attended DePaul, a Catholic school.

"Ooooh, I didn't know it was Friday," Mikan cooed.

All the sports writers came: six-feet, four-inch, 200-pound Dan Parker, whom Damon Runyon once called "the most constantly brilliant of all sportswriters"; Pulitzer-winner Red Smith, after whom all sportswriting awards are named; erudite, brawling Jack McKinney, who hosted a national radio show, jumped out of an airplane, collected opera records, and sparred with Sonny Liston; Larry Merchant, the editor who revolutionized sports sections with his midcentury shake-up of the *Daily News*; and Jimmy Cannon, who was considered Damon Runyon's heir and was said to be the first sportswriter to earn $100,000 a year. They formed a cynical panel of critics whom any manager had to impress to steer his fighter into big matches. So before Rocky Marciano's first fight in Philly, his twelfth overall, manager Al Weill said to Jimmy Cannon in front of Tendler's: "The champeen of the world is fighting tonight. Watch and see." Weill knew he had upped the ante, so later that night, he woke Marciano from his prefight nap and urged him to impress the writers. But once the bell rang, Marciano could not evade a punch. He lacked polish, footwork, and lateral movement, and he just stood there absorbing terrible blows, despite opening a cut on his opponent that ended the fight in his favor in the second round. The writers at Tendler's roared over their whiskey that night. This wild swinger was the great white hope?[22] But the place was electrified nearly four years later on the night Marciano challenged local Jersey Joe Walcott for the latter's heavyweight title—in the very stadium where Tunney took Dempsey twenty-six years earlier.

It was on nights like these, in the days when Philly fights still gripped the country, that Tendler's bar pumped heady adrenaline through the booths and out onto Broad, where it coursed through the city and seized you. A frisson raced up your spine, and goosebumps pimpled down your arms, and on the corner, guys spoke without really saying, flooded in bias and anticipation, lacking hard data on heights, weights, and reaches. Men all along the Atlantic would board $25 trains for Philly, and if it wasn't on TV, they'd converge on Tendler's—the locals and the loathed—to try to score free tickets from someone. The *New Yorker* writer A. J. Liebling called this Philly phenomenon "looking for friends to put the lug on."[23] And the night Marciano fought Walcott, Liebling himself took the five o'clock from Penn Station in New York. He arrived in Center City, and being the journalist he was, immediately sought Tendler's. He knew it was the place to be, and in a keen outsider way, he understood why. Tendler, the perennial contender, never the champion, "has remained a Philadelphia idol," Liebling said, "because, I think, he embodies the city's sense of being eternally put upon."[24] Trouble was, Liebling couldn't find the place. And being the journalist he was, he refused to ask directions. He walked awhile, and, tired, he settled for a nearby restaurant named Mike Banana's.

Liebling ate, walked out, and found Tendler's, but it teemed with men all the way to the sidewalk, and he couldn't get inside. Guys struggled to avoid being pushed off the curb under passing taxis. Jersey Joe drove by in a police escort, and the crowd roared. He was knocked out hours later.

Lew Tendler moved from Philadelphia to the Jersey shore in 1960 and leased the Broad Street restaurant to his nephew Pinky. In the summer of 1970 they began shutting it down, "because of the demise of Center City," Tendler's granddaughter Sharon says. "Malls were popping up all over, and people were moving to the suburbs."

In July, Sharon's father, Milton, went to the restaurant to save some of the pictures on the walls. His wife had specifically asked for the family photos and the Sinatra shot. When Milton got there, he checked the freezer room to see whether any food remained. He walked inside, but he didn't prop the door open, and it locked behind him. "This is how I am gonna die," he figured. He sat there and, using who knows what, managed to chisel away the lock and escape. He told the family the story when he got home, and his wife was shocked, because she hadn't even known he was going to be at the restaurant that day. No one would've found him. The family agreed it wasn't Milton Tendler's time to die.

In November, Lew Tendler, the paterfamilias, died of an arterial clot. He was seventy-two. Three years later, Milton had a heart attack and died at forty-four. Tendler's son Phil brought Tendler's boxing gloves and jukebox to a novelty consignment shop. Then Phil died, and his daughter asked for the stuff back, and the shop owner refused.

✻ ✻ ✻

There are nice new townhomes in the lot where the Arena was erected and burned. The rest of the area is rundown projects and KFCs and animal hospitals.

Tendler's is now a nice seafood restaurant that serves the upscale patrons of the nearby theaters, many of which are brand new. This area of South Broad Street—or the Avenue of the Arts, as Ed Rendell re-branded it—is where the nice people go out to see shows and shop. There is a Ritz-Carlton and a Ralph Lauren.

A cab driver once spoke to me about boxing.

"Boxing's not like it used to be," he said. "You got up there that Blue Horizon gym."

"Have you ever been inside?" I asked.

"No, I just dropped people off there. I don't think they had anything in a while."

We were searching for the site of an old gym.

"They probably turned this old gym into an apartment building or condo or stuff," he said. "This area's changing so fast. They're turning old factories into duplexes, bars, and clubs."

6

THE NEW OLD SCENE

It's a shame, though. We ain't got nowhere for the kids to go today. Playstation. Get up! Get out there and do something. Burn up their energy. Those guys that went to the gym, young men that went to the gym and was boxing, never got into a fight in the street. They didn't have to prove nothing. They knew what they can do. Now the kids in the street, they can't fight, so they get guns. Most of 'em are a bunch of cowards. We had a misunderstanding, we used to go in the school-yard. Fight. When it was over, shake hands. And you're friends. . . . I would like to get the kids, young men. I feel sorry for 'em. I really do. Get out of school, what to do? Hang on the corner with a bunch of old guys who are gonna try to get 'em to sell some drugs. Know what I mean? And everybody got a gun. All of 'em got a gun. Then they go to different neighborhoods and shoot 'em up.
—Mr. Pat, November 28, 2006

That was Mr. Pat's idea—bring back the boxing, and the fighting will stop. It jarred me when I first heard it. This idea that one form of violence was preferable—even if it was less dangerous—still seemed twisted. Why make violence part of the answer at all? Why go from guns to fists? Why not work to rid the city of animus altogether?

But of course, the reality on the ground was dirty. The city's poverty and tension—the feeling that something could break out at all times—didn't allow for discussions (or so it seemed, but maybe that's weak of me). And there was that rich history of boxing in the city. In the end, it was too hard to argue against Mr. Pat's idea that this was a fighting town, a tough town. I could've kept trying—it would've been the progressive thing to do. I cringed a little each time someone told me that boxing took rough kids off the street and gave them character and a path. It might've taken them off the streets temporarily, but very few of them would become good enough to make any money off the game, and the rest would be left with just as few skills to compete in the new economy as they had had before. That line was a self-serving excuse to justify the sport—and it's used to justify all intensive youth sports in poor areas. It portrays sport as a way out of bad places (but as the only way), and it stresses the notion that this is all the children can become—athletes. It glorifies athletics as the ultimate profession, while blotting out all others.

But in time, I began reciting the line myself. I stopped reaching for the longest shot, the ideal—that the city would educate its kids, allow them to compete for jobs that would support them and revitalize the tax base. Partly, that was the progressive in me dying in the face of a reality that I—and everyone else—found too messy to sync with ideals.

But partly, it was the romance of the past—the same reason Mr. Pat wanted the boxing culture to return. Sure, he thought the kids needed to be reformed. But that's not why he reminisced about fights, fight nights, bets he had made on fighters. That was nostalgia—that was auld lang syne. And though I hadn't lived it, I had learned enough about those times that I, too, began to want to see something like them again.

So I sought out the new old scene—the places and fixtures where the boxing culture was returning and maybe bits of the economy, too.

✿ ✿ ✿

"ELOHEINU!!" the fans shout. "Eloheiiiiiinu!"

A fan in a green tunic bangs a bongo.

"ELOHEINU!" they chant. "ELOHEIIIIINU!"

From a door behind the seats, the entourage strides into the light. They wear terry tracksuits with Team Thompson embroidered in white and a Hebrew word in silver.

Chai.

"Life."

The boxer leads the pack, Anthony "The Messenger" Thompson, in a white robe. One member of his pack screams, "Oooooohhhhhhh!" Thompson bends to his right and mutters to the first crew member. It looks like, "Go ahead." The guy steps forward to lead the pack.

"Whoaaaaaaa," he screams. Behind him, one of the others carries a wooden seal showing a lion lying down with a lamb. It represents peace, a fan tells me. An allusion to Isaiah 11:6—"The calf and the young lion shall browse together, with a little child to guide them."

As the pack progresses, everyone focuses on Thompson. He looks straight ahead. His eyes are glossy. Sweat pools in the crevice between his clenched neck muscles.

He takes a deep breath and pumps out his chest. His ponytail of shaggy braids bounces behind him. His baby cheeks are covered in scraggly patches of hair. He looks down and notices a cameraman. He leans in, opens his eyes wide, bounces on tips of toes, and roars.

"The heart and soul of Philadelphia has always been boxing," Bob Papa says live on Versus, Comcast's major sports channel, which plans on moving one hundred managers from a Stamford, Connecticut, office to a new Philly skyscraper in 2008, another sign of the revitalization of downtown. "Fight night—coming up next!"

It's January 11, 2007—a Thursday. The city is about to hold the first major match of its first card of the year in an old warehouse—named the New Alhambra—under the highway, near the Delaware River, in the city's southeast corner. A crowd of 1,000 packs the folding chairs (mostly whites) and standing room (mostly blacks). They guzzle Bud Light by the men's room. Blue, yellow, and red spotlights sweep the floor, blurring everything in Kodachrome excitement. This is it. One man versus another. The start of a new year.

* * *

When Russell Peltz first saw the place, he thought it "looked like Dresden after the war."[1] Which meant it was perfect.

Three years had passed since he had left the Blue Horizon, and he wanted to settle down. He had promoted in small places here and there (even in the Blue Horizon one last time), but after trips to Choctaw, Mississippi, and New Haven, Connecticut, he desired a venue he and Philly could call their own. And there was this warehouse.

Thirty years ago, in the twilight of city commerce, the concrete box at the corner of Swanson and Ritner in Southeast Philly was used as a holding pen. Trains pulled in on tracks alongside it and dumped their freight at the loading dock; later, trucks came to pick it up.

In the 1990s, the place was known as Viking Hall and the ECW Arena. The former name came from the primary tenant—the South

Philly Vikings, one of several feathered, sequined, and costumed Mummers Fancy Brigades that competed in a Broad Street parade/pageant each New Year's Day. They built floats and choreographed dances in the white rectangle under I-95. They rented it out for parties and held benefits there, like the one in 2002 for a baby with a brain tumor. On Saturday nights, they held midnight bingo to raise money for props. Then came the wrestlers. In 1993, a new Philly outfit dubbed Eastern Championship Wrestling pioneered a less-rehearsed, more hard-core style of fake fighting and made the old warehouse its 1,000-seat home. Locals flocked to see grown men pretend to beat each other and, as was often the case, actually beat each other. The wrestlers would leave the ring, grab barbed wire or glass, and use that as a mace or slicer. The fans clamored for it, chanting, "You fucked up!" when a man went down, tailgating in the parking lot, and buying household appliances on "bring your own weapon nights."

The venue was disgusting then. One wrestler once said, "The bathrooms were absolutely brutal. I can't even describe how disgusting it really was." The air conditioning and heating never worked (the temperature inside supposedly reached 130 degrees in the summer of 1994). "The place—everybody used the same word—it was a shit hole," says Roger Artigiani, the building's current lessee. "It was in bad, bad condition. But no one cared."

In 2001, just as Russell Peltz was severing ties with the Blue Horizon, Eastern Championship Wrestling filed for bankruptcy. Meanwhile, Roger Artigiani needed to escape Rochester, New York, after going through a bad divorce. His plan was to move to Vegas, and beyond that, he didn't know. En route to Vegas, he stopped in Philly to meet up with a friend who was a partner in the Center City law firm Stein and Silverman, which now owned the warehouse arena. It was dormant, Artigiani recalls, "left in shambles . . . like a train wreck"—precisely the type of fixer-upper he had once flipped for a living.

"Let me see what I can do with this place," he said.

He never left Philadelphia.

* * *

Sitting in his office, a year-old wooden skybox overlooking the main ring, Roger Artigiani looks exhausted, especially for a middle-aged guy. Big bags sag below his eyes, creases line his scruffy cheeks, and his short, gelled blondish hair fades into gray. A blue polo shirt hangs from broad shoulders over a solid paunch. He wears light blue jeans. He's explaining how it all happened.

In 1996, Joe Hand, a man who invested in Joe Frazier's career in the 1960s and now runs a company that distributes pay-per-view fights, opened a boxing gym in Kensington, a northeast Philadelphia neighborhood. The gym held amateur tournaments, but Hand wanted a big venue in which to stage them. In 2004, he asked Artigiani whether he could hold a Golden Gloves show in the old warehouse. Artigiani said yes. When that worked out, Hand asked if they could bring on Russell Peltz and hold pro fights in the arena. Artigiani said yes. The three men went to work. They finagled parking for five hundred cars across the street, under I-95. They put in new bathrooms, new sound systems, new paint, new doorways, new stairways, and skyboxes. They dumped the high school–style bleachers in favor of folding chairs. As for the culture of the place, they drew on South Philly's past. Eras earlier, in 1952, promoter Jimmy Toppi Jr.—the same man who would later create the Blue Horizon—had bought the Alhambra movie theater at Twelfth and Morris. He had turned it into a skating rink and banquet hall, and in 1959, the owner of the nearby Passyunk Gym—where Mr. Pat trained kids—began staging fights at the Alhambra.[2] It was another of those hazy block jewels that existed primarily in the mind, a romantic club for those who put in a long week. It could hold 1,600 with standing room, and though the city leveled it for a parking lot only a few years later, it lingered in South Philly thoughts like an adolescent kiss.

Peltz decided to call it the New Alhambra. He installed a ring of only sixteen square feet (which is only legal in Pennsylvania), because the fighters should be there to fight, not to avoid each other (more commonly, fights are held in rings of eighteen, twenty, or twenty-two square feet). The commissioner hassled Peltz over the size and asked to measure it, but Peltz told him to leave it alone. "You'd have them fight in a closet," I once told him, "if it were legal."

On the first night of pro fights, in May 2004, the air conditioning failed. On the second, the air conditioning blew out and so did the lights. The ref had just finished reviewing the rules with the fighters in the locker room when it got dark. "There are so many different electrical panels—I didn't even know which one to go to," Artigiani said. Peltz had just been elected to the Hall of Fame. In the darkness, his wife, Linda, said to him, "You don't need to do this anymore if you don't want to." After somewhere between ten and twenty minutes, one of the lawyers from Stein and Silverman, the owner of the property, hit the electrical breaker, and the ring lit up again. By then, 30 percent of the crowd had left.

They fixed the building's systems. The New Alhambra built a following.

The regional Golden Gloves started holding its championship there, and one newspaper ad read, "Hey Dad, remember your first fight?" In March 2005, an Alhambra card was broadcast nationally for the first time on the Spanish channel Telefutura. A year later, ESPN2 held *Wednesday Night Fights* there. That night's show was a sellout.

A few months later, ESPN chose the Alhambra as venue of the year.

"Cookie-cutter TV camera angles and conformist courts and fields are the business of other sports," wrote commentator Joe Tessitore. "But in boxing, anything goes with the venues we visit. And perhaps more than any other sport, the feel and look of boxing on TV is greatly affected by the setting we are in. . . . I find it tough to pick a better venue than the New Alhambra in South Philly. It is packed with fans—real fight fans. They seem to have a rooting interest in each fight, even the four-round swing bouts. Hall of Fame promoter Russell Peltz lines the walls with black-and-white posters of legends. The whole atmosphere is like something out of an old-school boxing movie. The New Alhambra has taken the place of the Blue Horizon as the home of Philly boxing. It's a must-visit for every fight fan."

❋ ❋ ❋

Call it the new old scene.

Like the original, it consists of many gyms in many neighborhoods. Champs, Augie's, Shuler's, Frazier's, Front Street, Bozy's, Joey Eye's, Joe Hand's, Marian Anderson, Harrowgate, Rumblers, Upper Darby, Manayunk, Costello's, Martin Luther King. Most in the city don't know about them, though they might have seen Joe Frazier's, a brick place on North Broad next to a Hess Station. Amtrak trains whiz right by—the trains *used* to stop here—and from a window seat, you can make out "Millwork" in flaking white paint on the building's side. Yes, that's a gym. Frazier's gym.

Citywide, especially in the black community, institutions are asking older men to step up to help the kids. There is an overwhelming early turnout for the city's program to place ten thousand men on patrol as mentors and watchmen in bad neighborhoods. In October 2007, about that many volunteers—ten thousand—showed up on Temple's campus for an intro session. Whether they would follow through remains to be seen.

Many have long understood what the kids need. In 1947, Philly cops founded the nonprofit Police Athletic League to organize afterschool sports. This led to the creation of the famed Philadelphia PAL boxing program, which was recognized as the country's best. The Twenty-third district PAL, at Twenty-second and Columbia, bred an entire generation of boxers that included Joe Frazier, Gypsy Joe, Bennie Briscoe, Jimmy Young, and Boogaloo Watts. In the 1950s, PAL kids fought two three-round matches on a local Saturday morning TV show, *The Robin Roberts Sports Club*. In the 1964, the PAL was a refuge for fighters during the riots.

This refuge couldn't last. In 1986, the PAL looked for liability insurance and found only one firm willing to insure it. It signed up, despite the threefold increase in premiums and the firm's single demand: that the PAL close its boxing program.

"We all felt bad that we had to get rid of PAL boxing because it had a great name," recalls James McCabe, the now-retired Coopers & Lybrand partner who chaired the PAL in those years. "We had been told by many cities it was the best PAL in the country. Philadelphia is the home for many, many famous boxers."

In some way, McCabe did save the boxing program—but in a consolidated form and in a new location, the Athletic Recreation Center at Twenty-sixth and Master. In 2007, that gym remains the last vestige of the PAL world.

I visit it in late August 2007. My cab passes the Blue Horizon and turns left off Broad, onto Master. Going west, we pass a church and an empty concrete lot sprouting grass. Rubber tires dot the northern sidewalk like relics of an old obstacle course. We pass guys on a stoop, across from a boarded-up house. One wears a wool hat with NBA logos, another a Raiders cap. We pass two women sitting on a stoop next to a baby carriage. "You go from a decent place to ghetto," my cab driver says in a thick African accent. "Neighborhood change." At Twenty-sixth Street, we reach a decaying brick building adjacent to a field and a playground. This quote-unquote Athletic Recreation Center was known for supplying talent to the nearby Blue Horizon in the 1970s. Fred

Jenkins, Charlie Brown, and Jerome Jackson trained there. Jenkins had been a part of the Twenty-eighth and Oxford gang and had been arrested forty-three times and sent to reformatory. He got out after a year and a half at age fifteen with nothing to do. He convinced his friends to join him in the gym and the trio took nicknames: "Herk" (as in Herculean strength) Jenkins and "Silky" Jackson and "Choo Choo" Brown. They all turned pro: Jenkins got hurt and barely fought; Jackson didn't make it; and Brown won a world title but lost it right away. "I've been to the top, and I even took the city to the top by my being from here," Brown said. "It didn't last long."[3]

My cab drives off. "You watch your mouth!" barks a middle-aged man on the corner at a skinny boy straddling a bicycle. I walk through the Recreation Center playground. Two weeks earlier, a shootout here during a basketball tournament ensnared four, dropping a mustachioed seventeen-year-old next to a slide, his chocolate body stained in blood. The kid just lay there in his blue suede New Balances, gasping for air. Then his eyes rolled into the back of his head and he stopped heaving—killed, apparently, by a twenty-two-year-old gang rival at a tournament the cops had already been monitoring with undercover officers.[4]

The bicycle boy, perhaps twelve, wears a light blue T-shirt advertising bagels and narrow jeans ripped at the ankles as if they were bootcut. He's accompanied by an even younger boy—perhaps six or eight. Two other elders back up the shouter. "You are a young *man*!" rumbles one of them from the depth of his imposing, authoritative belly. A guy I pass in the playground, in a black Eagles jersey, turns to look. The child tries to protest, but the corner elders raise their voices even louder. I knock on the building door, a rusty metal piece with a narrow window caged in steel. A man splayed drunkenly over the field bleachers eyes me. I knock again. After what seems five minutes though is probably only fifteen seconds, a girl undoes two long sliding locks and opens up. But only a crack. "I'm here to interview Fred Jenkins," I say. She looks me up and down and squints. Then she turns to her right, to an office I can't see and says something about a guy here to see you. I hear a man shout something back, and the girl nods her head and lets me in.

"Shirts and shoes are required in the building," reads a sign on the inside of the door. I take a seat on a bench outside the office as the man inside talks on the phone about raising money to buy trophies. Suddenly the voice hushes. Footsteps. Then a man with a mustache appears before me. He carries a healthy paunch—and yet it seems just that: healthful somehow, as if he's storing food for a famine only he can see coming. He wears jeans and a T-shirt that drapes some places and clings to others. I apologize for interrupting his office hours. No, fifty-one-year-old Fred "Herk" Jenkins says. "I want you to watch this." From behind me, the bicycle boy strides into the office and takes a seat facing Jenkins's desk.

"Your voice and your attitude—you gotta change that," Jenkins says firmly. "I talk to people in the neighborhood about you. They might not get your name, but they know you. I'm attacking that attitude, trying to make you change. If they see the attitude you got, they gonna brush you off. The nicer you is, the more you get out here. When you playing with you homies, that's a nice thing, but when you see adults come by, change yo attitude." The boy sits there listening, his face frozen in either indifference or intimidation. Jenkins asks him whether he knows the consequences of his current path. The boy says he's gonna get locked up. They both stand up, and the boy walks out of the office. "How many times you curse me out?" Jenkins asks the boy, who's already halfway out the building.

"Never," the boy answers.

"I mean behind my back. Ten times?"

The boy turns to look at Jenkins for a moment, then exits.

* * *

We don't know what will happen to the skinny, perhaps-twelve-year-old boy in the light blue T-shirt—the one who has left Fred Jenkins's office.

He may turn out like another boy.

William Boggs was a junior middleweight from North Philly who beat all the local kids in the amateurs and was going to turn pro in the beginning of 2005 when he went with his stepdad and nephew to sign up the latter for the year's Golden Gloves, the country's premier amateur competition. While in line, they heard the boy in front of them boast to a friend that he was going to run through the 165-pound weight class. And if Boggs is in the division? the friend asked. "I'll run through him, too," the boy replied, not knowing Boggs was standing behind him.

Boggs took the boy's boast as a challenge, entered the tournament, and beat the kid in the first round.

"He had the natural ability to box," recalls Mike Plebani, his trainer.

Boggs turned pro, won his first fight with only his left hand, because his right was broken, and beat a forty-one-year-old in his second fight.

A group of kids his age grew jealous. According to his parents, Boggs hung out in one area and these kids in another, but they often saw each other at the barbershop (where Boggs got his prefight haircuts), which was in neutral territory. After Boggs's first fight, they held him up.

When his mother, Maria, told him to be careful, he tried to assuage her. "That's my friends," Boggs said. "I can't hang with my friends? Why? Cuz them fools acting stupid. Nah, them fools not doing nothing."

He was shot at near a Chinese restaurant on April 19, 2005. Two days later, on the same corner, he was shot at 4 p.m. A drive-by.

"I was away for the weekend," Plebani recalls. "And I got a phone call from the sister first, and she said that—they called him Manzy—she said, 'Manzy just got shot. On the way to the hospital.' And about five minutes later, the mother called me. 'They just killed my son.' That's how I was notified. He died on the way to the hospital."

Not long after, I visited the Boggs's house. It was a narrow place with a living room in front, a dining room and kitchen behind that, and then a small room behind the kitchen. That was Manzy's room. It hadn't been touched since his death. The stereo was still in the back, and the posters were still on the left wall, and the boxing gloves and jock strap hung from the right wall. His blue Adidas amateur jersey (amateurs wear shirts) was hanging over a pair of blue TITLE shorts and a newspaper clipping.

Some objects had been added. There were candles on the counter and a wreath and a plush Homer Simpson doll. There was a yellow pillow on the bed with the words "R.I.P. Manzy." There were two wooden boards leaning against the wall that had been covered in memorial notes from friends.

There was a Frito-Lay box in the back of the room.

* * *

In the mid-1990s, Joe Hand, who, as was said earlier, had been one of the founding members of Cloverlay, the business partnership that invested in Joe Frazier's burgeoning career after the 1964 Olympics, opened a gym in Kensington—a white, working-class neighborhood north of Center City where Rocky supposedly lived—on the charred grounds of an old envelope warehouse. He bought the building from the city for $1 and, upon renovating it, found dead dogs—victims of dogfights—in the basement and needles on the roof. Hand installed a twenty-station computer lab in his gym for the kids, so they could do homework, and asked for only a $40 yearly membership fee, which included insurance.

But "there were some structural damage in the other building" on the lot, recalls Pete Papaleo, a longtime friend of Hand who volunteered to supervise the gym. "Some inspectors inspected the building and said there might've been some structural damage."

So Hand moved his gym to the back of the newly renovated warehouse in South Philly, the one under the Interstate that had suddenly become a boxing arena. The one they called the New Alhambra.

"Just telling people what our rules and regulations were was a little tough at the beginning," Papaleo recalls. "But they got the hang of it afterward because we asked them not to come back if they didn't follow it. Even if a kid wasn't right at the beginning, when the trainer got done with them, they turned it around."

In 2004, two of the gym's fighters won titles at the National Golden Gloves in Kansas City, and the Pennsylvania state team won the team title for the fourth time in five years.

There were also tragedies.

In 2003, John Santiago, a twenty-three-year-old featherweight and three-time Golden Gloves champ, was burned alive in his house when someone walked in and doused it with gasoline. A neighbor told a reporter then, "There's nothing like the screams of death."[5]

Still, there was something cleaner and newer about this new gym. Papaleo vacuumed the place even while the boxers trained, and he sniffed about and sprayed Febreeze wherever he thought it was needed. "We knew that we wanted to be clean," the man known as Petey Pop says. "I dunno how the rest of it turned out, but we knew we wanted it to be clean."

The white paint, the movement of boxers from one station to another—the whole place feels like a nice kitchen. There's even a glass wall at the front to allow family members—who may not enter the floor—to watch their breadwinners train. One September day, a woman with a small girl stares intently through the glass. In the ring, a twenty-five-year-old southpaw amateur named Derrick Webster spars shirtless. He's six feet four inches and 165 pounds, a stretched sculpture of bones and muscle. A gothic tattoo extends over his elongated back: It reads "The Bank," with a hooded grim reaper and two dollar signs. The reaper's skull is just beneath his shoulder blades.[6] I ask the woman, Kesha, what her beau, Derrick, needs to improve. He has only been training for a year and a half, and he still needs to accumulate more amateur experience before he can become a pro and begin providing. Their daughter turns fourteen months today. "Mostly his uppercuts," she says. "Everything else he's good with."

On the right side of the gym hang a few heavy bags and a puffy target that juts from the wall to allow uppercut practice. To the left, two mirrors face a floor of mats, on which guys do crunches and whoosh the speed rope. They wrap their hands there, too.

There is a blue ring in the middle of the gym. The canvas is marked with a grainy *Daily News* logo. A row of bar stools lines the back of the ring—the peanut gallery. One day I sit there next to a stubbly man in a sweatshirt. He holds coffee from Dunkin' Donuts. When a fighter lands a good shot, we turn to each other and nod.

Each afternoon, starting at 4, the cars pull into the lot outside the New Alhambra's back entrance, which leads into the gym. The much-heralded twenty-one-year-old featherweight prospect arrives in a teal Kia Sorento mini SUV (it's his mom's). The heavyweight prospect—who made the Olympic team as an alternate after boxing only a year and ten months—rolls up in a white Cadillac.

The signs greet the entering fighters: "Prepare to win" and "Respect. Give it. Get it." Flags gently sway from the rafters—a random assortment of nations: the United States, Brazil, Russia, England, Spain. They walk through the floor to the dressing room, and everyone already there greets them with "hey" and a handshake. Petey Pop gives them a hearty hug-shake-smack on the back. He wears a fitted orange gingham shirt with a spread collar over black pants and a pair of canvas sneakers with rubber toes.

The fighters change into togs and take their positions.

The heavyweight prospect, "The Gentleman" Chazz Witherspoon, who went to St. Joe's on academic scholarship, jabs the heavy bag. The bag shakes and shimmies, rattling the steel chain from which it's suspended and the steel rafters from which the chain hangs. You can actually chart the impact move its way up the bag, through the chain and into the ceiling, where a white electricity wire quivers en route to a high-voltage lamp.

The fighters train for three minutes, and then a buzzer goes off and they rest. The gym gets quiet.

The gym has relatives of Philly's great fighters train there. Chazz Witherspoon, a cousin of former heavyweight champ Tim Witherspoon, trains there, as do the grandson and great-grandson of Joey Giardello, the Hall-of-Fame middleweight from South Philly who trained in the Passyunk Gym when Mr. Pat taught there in the 1960s. "It's like my *Cheers* in Philly," the grandson once told a filmmaker about the gym. "It's just a place where everybody can go."

One time, Chazz Witherspoon sparred with his middleweight cousin Derrick Webster, a lefty. The idea was for Witherspoon to work on balance against a southpaw and for Webster to toughen himself against a bigger opponent. As it turned out, Witherspoon couldn't keep his left foot to the outside of Webster's right, and his stability suffered. Webster, for his part, punched scared, wasting precious energy on anxiety alone. He was soaked in sweat.

"You fighting nervous," Chazz told him at the end of the round. He looked his cousin in the eye. "Just fight like you fighting."

Petey Pop watched, smiling widely while chewing on what looked to be a piece of paper or a bandage.

* * *

As a young boxer in the 1950s, Sweet Pea Adams used to go down to Pep's, Spider Kelly's, and Showboat to listen to all the jazz greats: Armstrong and Ellington, Coltrane and Miles, Thad Jones and Sonny Stitt, and Jimmy Smith and Lee Morgan. "All these guys—I used to go see 'em play because that would inspire me as a fighter, to see other entertainers," Sweet Pea says. "People who were in a different field but who were entertainers."

Philly gym wars are a mythological form of entertainment. There are so many stories about sparring sessions in gyms in the old days that turned into full-on battles, where neither fighter wanted to give, where pride and respect were on the line.

The *Inquirer* writer Clark DeLeon summed up Philly's gym ethos like this: "What profiteth a man to become champion of the entire world and still be a chump on his corner?"[7]

There was a price to be paid for this mentality. Some argue that Philly contenders so drained each other in the gym that they couldn't win the real fights. They were already very damaged.

You don't see gym wars like that in Joe Hand's Gym, but on occasion you see it get rough. One day, 15–1 Texan middleweight Brian Vera, fresh off his appearance on ESPN's *The Contender* series, walked in. He needed a sparring partner for his upcoming bout, so they threw in Dennis "The Assassin" Hasson, a kid from the Kensington section of the city who lives on the street Rocky supposedly did. Hasson landed several crisp Philly left hooks, drilling the outsider from bell to bell. Hasson was only an amateur at the time.

✶ ✶ ✶

There is a kid in Joe Hand's who should never have to wage war against his opponents. He is too technically skilled for that. He is a junior featherweight (or a super bantamweight; they're the same thing—122 pounds) and he is very quick.

The problem is that he likes waging wars.

"To me it doesn't make a difference," he says. "Sometimes gym wars even help you in a fight."

His girlfriend once told me of the time the Kid beat another in sparring to the point where he was smeared in his opponent's blood. The girlfriend protested his behavior. "But *he* trying to kill *me!*" the Kid replied.

The Kid turned pro when he was twenty years old. It was the first fight card of 2007, in the New Alhambra. He wore red gloves and white Adidas high-tops with three blue stripes down the side.

"I'm gonna knock him out," the Kid thought in the corner before the bell rang.

The bell rang.

The opponent jabbed five times, and each time the Kid eluded it, sliding his head to the side or gliding backward. The fifth time, the Kid coiled like a snake, lowering his right arm from its protective position in front of his face.

He pounced.

He threw a right hand that knocked back the opponent's head like a bobblehead.

The opponent jabbed and missed, retracting his left hand below his chest, nowhere near his face, which hung wide-open now. The Kid noticed the hole and threw another right.

"Oh," the crowd gasped.

The Kid continued with overhand punches and hooks and hooks to the body. The Kid hit his opponent wherever he saw a hole.

The Kid buried his head in his opponent's bellybutton. The Kid threw a five-punch combination that progressed upward from the body. The final blow snapped the opponent's left cheek.

"Whooa!" said a man in the crowd.

At 2:41 of the first round, the opponent collapsed.

The Kid had won by KO.

Teon Kennedy's career had begun.

7

THE YOUNG KIDS

"Which fighters currently coming up in Philly excite you?" I ask.
"There are two kids," Peltz says. "Teon Kennedy and Mike Jones."
—From my first interview with promoter Russell Peltz

The only thing real in life is sports and sex. Everything else is phony.
—Ernest Kennedy, Teon's father

By 2007, two years after I had first met Mr. Pat, I was out on my own.
A year or two earlier, he had dictated to me a list of fighters I should
look up on the Internet or try to interview, and I had faithfully put the
names down as best I could (I misspelled most of them). Now, he was a
little older, he seemed to have a little less money than before—and he
was already very poor—and I had become familiar with the sport and its
players. Familiar enough, anyway, to know which questions to ask
which people. What I wanted—what I felt I needed—were current
fighters who could grab the public—me, especially—and hold our attention the way the fighters Mr. Pat had listed once had.

It's true that Bernard Hopkins was still plying his trade (the longtime
middleweight champion had moved up to light-heavyweight nearly
twenty years after beginning his career). But youth is what captivates
us; potential captivates us. When I heard about Teon and Mike, I implored Mr. Pat to come down to the gym with me just to watch them
train. I offered to buy him a ticket to see them fight. Always it was a no.
It wasn't a matter of energy—he walked around his neighborhood still,
and we would've taken a car, and I would've been by his side.

There was something about the boxing world he feared. He could talk about it for hours, but actually going back to where it was being plied and enacted—that scared him. Most likely because it was part of that past of his with its myriad small tragedies and one very great one.

❈ ❈ ❈

In 2007, the city replaced its mayor, John Street, a man who was bugged by the FBI as part of a corruption investigation and whose brother was on trial for fraud and tax evasion, with Michael Nutter, a former city councilman who had tried to declare a "crime emergency" in the most violent areas of Philly and station more cops there and who, after being elected, recruited ten thousand citizens to help him spend a full day cleaning the city (somewhat symbolically, a discarded body was found).

Boxing insiders tabbed Teon Kennedy, a junior featherweight, and Mike Jones, a welterweight, both of whom were in their early twenties, as the new fighters.

Teon's career began almost the same way Jimmy Young's had: something was stolen from him. In Teon's case, it was a bike.

Soon after, at an amateur boxing tournament in which Teon was competing, Teon's dad, who was then his coach, pointed to his opponent. "That's the guy that stole your bike," Ernest Kennedy said. Teon KO'd his opponent.

But that wasn't exactly the beginning. It started before Teon was even born. Before he was ten or eleven and his old, Christian granny had a vision in which she saw him become the greatest of all time. Before he was four, and his dad was running laps in the morning heat around a local track and Teon decided to mimic him and he kept running and running and never stopped. Before even his first birthday, when he was served a cake with a boxing ring on top.

It started with his father, who grew up in the projects of Greensboro, North Carolina, with a single parent and began boxing at the age of twelve. Ernest Kennedy boxed as a kid and he boxed in the army in the late 1970s, and then, just when it seemed he had given it up, at the age of twenty-six, when he was working for the Department of Parks and Recreation back in North Carolina, he entered a local toughman contest in a rec center and won it. A trainer saw him and urged him to take up boxing again, and he did, fighting in the amateurs for a year before turning pro.

His pro career wasn't much. He was recruited by scouts for Joe Frazier's Gym and traveled to Philly, but he didn't like the matches Frazier set up for him and he eventually left for a different management group. He lost a couple of fights that could've been stepping-stones, and the highlight of his career was when he was featured on the undercard of a match featured on ABC's *Wide World of Sports*.

❋ ❋ ❋

Ernest Kennedy had a son, Teon, with his wife, Nettie, a girl from Fayette, Alabama, whom he had met while in the army. They all lived in the Strawberry Mansion section of Philadelphia. "All you could hear was gunshots or ambulance," Nettie recalls. "I was like, 'Oh, my God.' You never know when it's gonna come through the window."

Ernest had Teon take up boxing. He says it was to keep him off the streets, but a part of him probably wanted to make up for the way his own career had gone.

Every day, Ernest took Teon to a different gym and taught him to box. He might go to Champs one day, a gym in Northern Liberties the next, and then a place in South Philly. Ernest didn't want Teon to get used to any single coach because they all had recognized Teon's talent and they all wanted to train him exclusively.

Ernest was demanding. He wouldn't take Teon to the gym unless Teon ran two miles every other day. And if he didn't think Teon was working as hard as he possibly could during sparring, he'd scream, "You're not giving it up!"

Other times, a coach might tell Teon to try a certain move while sparring and for whatever reason, he wouldn't execute it. "Do it!" Ernest would scream. "Or we can get up outta here! You can go ahead and do it—it ain't gonna kill you!" Then the other coaches would yell at Ernest for his treatment of Teon. "Leave him alone!" they'd say. Sometimes they'd say, "We kickin' you out today."

"So what?" Ernest would shoot back. "You kickin' me out? I takin' my son with me."

"You can ask anybody," Teon says about his father's reputation after finishing his workout one day at Joe Hand's. We sit in the New Alhambra Arena part of the building, where behind us, semipro wrestlers practice moves for an upcoming show. They bounce from one side of the ropes to the other, then launch themselves into the air and slam into the canvas backward. The smack of their spines against the floor echoes across the empty warehouse. "I used to cry all the time," Teon says. "He tried to push me real hard because he's my dad. But then, that's why I started training with my other trainer."

✿ ✿ ✿

"He wouldn't let the coaches do what they wanted to do," Nettie remembers. "And they felt like he was interfering."

"I wouldn't criticize the coaches," Ernest says. "Just when he go against me. You don't tell the kid, 'Nah, nah, don't do what your dad said.' Because once you start saying that, he done lost all confidence in his dad. So I used to be like, 'Yo, man! What *are* you doing? Don't never say that again.' And I tried to explain to Teon why. Because you don't go home with him. You come home with me."

With his dad as his coach, Teon didn't win any amateur tournaments. So finally, after years of considering it, Ernest turned Teon over to another trainer—Al Fennell, who had guided "Bam Bam" Hines to a professional title. Now he had Teon. He led Teon to the national PAL championship in New Orleans at the Junior Olympic level of ninety pounds in a tournament packed with future pros. Ernest threw a party, because the victory meant USA Boxing would sponsor Teon in the future, and he'd no longer have to pay up to $3,000 a year to enter his kid in tournaments.

People started recognizing Teon because he'd throw punches on the way to the store or in the halls of middle school. He got into a couple street fights. He won most of them. Guys who picked on him were the ones who didn't realize he was a boxer. Once he was playing basketball in the playground, and a bigger guy shoved him and took his ball. Teon got mad and started throwing punches, just throwing punches everywhere. The guy fell, his nose started bleeding, and he apologized. He returned the ball to Teon, who was only fourteen.

There was one kid Teon couldn't beat, though. His name was Rau'shee Warren, and he was also a little flyweight, not much more than 100 pounds, and he came from Cincinnati. He and Teon would breeze through the tournament brackets until the final round, and then Rau'shee would beat Teon. It happened often enough that Teon's dad got to know Rau'shee's mom. Rau'shee would go on to make the Olympic team in 2004 and 2008—the first time someone had made two consecutive Olympic boxing teams in more than thirty years. Teon would lose to him in the 2005 national championship, and he'd later call it his worst moment in boxing.

After Teon's freshman year of high school, his trainer decided he should move to the U.S. Olympic Education Center in Marquette, Michigan, where the best young boxers in the country trained. The coach there was Al Mitchell, a former Philly fighter who had trained in the 1960s at the Twenty-third Police Athletic League, home to Gypsy Joe Harris and Joe Frazier and Bennie Briscoe and Jimmy Young.

Nettie was against the move. "I just didn't think he was ready," she says. But she sent him anyway, giving Teon's new coach temporary custody of her son (as all the boxers' parents did). Teon often skipped school and wound up failing several classes, but he impressed the trainers with his boxing skills.

Teon returned to Philadelphia the next year and continued ditching school. He'd leave home in the morning and hang with his friends. Eventually, the school told him he'd have to take night classes just to graduate in time. He did. A few years later he'd tell me his greatest regret was that he hadn't taken school seriously. And his parents would say missing school was the worst thing he had ever done—except for maybe the time he crashed his mom's car on the way to his job in New Jersey.

＊ ＊ ＊

"Teon [is a] pretty quiet guy, too," Mike Jones says, one frostbitten winter Sunday in his new house in northeast Philly. "I notice that about Teon. I know Teon [is] pretty much like I am. Pretty quiet dude."

Mike Jones is similar to Teon. He is three years older, but like Teon, he also has a sister eight years his senior, a military father, clashing parents, and a history of owning pit bulls.

Mike Jones sits on his couch, watching a Bruce Lee movie. At this point in his career, he is an undefeated prospect—a shade under six feet, yet able to slim down to the severe welterweight limit of 147 pounds. He wears white Adidas rubber-toed sneakers, blue jeans, a black polo shirt, and a brown hoodie sweatshirt that conceals his V-shaped torso, which tapers from broad shoulders to a tiny waist.

Mike wears his hood up today, though he's lying on his own couch, in his own den. It's a pretty good indication of who he is.

＊ ＊ ＊

Mike Jones grew up in Mount Airy, an integrated suburban middle-class neighborhood that lies just below Chestnut Hill, a neatly trimmed community, and just above Germantown, a violent ghetto.

Teon Kennedy and Mike Jones fight to build their records: Teon with technical skill, Mike with sheer power. John DiSanto, PhillyBoxingHistory.com.

From an early age, Mike had two directions before him, two paths he could take. And, as the hood indicates, he never really took either path, never really opened himself to the outside world at all. Instead, he grew ever more closed.

"I had a few friends on my block," he says, as he fixates on the television, ignoring his daughters' toys on the floor, the fake plastic kitchen and the fake plastic convertible. "It was pretty good neighborhood. Ehh, it was cool. Like I'm really a loner. I really don't hang out all the time."

Mike stammers and stutters as he speaks but not, it seems, for lack of confidence. He sounds like he's trying to hold onto his words, as if he understands, once released, they can never be recovered.

"You don't know how to talk," says Marisol, his smiley, fleshy girlfriend, as she enters the den. "You mumble all the time."

If you speak to Mike long enough, you find out he wasn't always so guarded. It developed gradually, during his Mount Airy childhood, sometime between his parents' divorce and his uncle's death. Before that, he was vibrant. As a baby, when Liza, his sister, would take his diaper off, he'd pee in her face. At the dinner table, he'd sit in a high chair and shove the table into Liza's belly and giggle as it crushed her. He'd hide behind doors and pop out to frighten her. He'd wrestle her but freak out if he got pinned. One time when he was nine and she seventeen, she got off from on top of him after wrestling, and he punched her in the stomach, buckling her knees. He was so wild, so spoiled, Liza began calling him "Prince Mike." He had video games— the Pac-Man joystick game, his sister recalls—and Fisher-Price roller skates that snapped onto his sneakers. He had a mini electric car. And a ping-pong table. And a pool table. And a trampoline in the basement.

His giddy grade-school peers slept over some nights, playing cards and watching movies. Mike once tied up one of them and forced him to mush like a dog. Liza kept watch for safety (though she often said, "I'm outta here"), and Mike's mom, Denise, put out a ton of junk food as a way of keeping the kids off the street with the allure of sugar.

Today, Mike says he was six when his parents split, but "I really don't even remember." And then there was the other hurt. He had an uncle on his mom's side named Wilbert who was only a decade older than he was, and until that time, Mike and Wilbert had attended Eagles practices together and boxed together. And then just as Mike's parents started yelling, Wilbert met a girl, settled down, and stopped coming around for Mike. "Then he would come around every blue moon," Mike's mom says. "As a matter of fact, I really got on my brother's case about that because I knew that that hurt my son."

Then Uncle Wilbert died suddenly.

"The relationship with my uncle, I think that had something to do with him shutting down," Liza says today. "People think a lot of stuff don't affect the children. The damn kids know! And they feel it just as much as the parents do. And then when my uncle died, it was crushing to him. I just remember seeing Mike at the funeral. He shed a tear or two, and he sat in the back seat on a bench by himself. He didn't want to be bothered. When you see somebody in that state, it's like, 'Do I approach him?'"

Somewhere in the chaos his sister became a mother, Mike became an uncle, and their relationship changed. She could say, "Mike, take the trash out," and he'd do it instead of saying, "Mommy didn't say so." He saw her now as an adult, and she saw him as a child, not the sibling who received all the toys and attention. She stopped going out and getting in trouble. They huddled together, as if for warmth. "I would go to his room to be with him," Liza says now, "just because he became so quiet."

Sometimes Mike would seat Liza's daughter in a chair next to him in his room and just watch TV silently with his baby niece. Then one day, the silent boy acted out. He was nine or ten, and he and two friends stole hats from the Cheltenham mall. Just shoved 'em into a big bag. And the store caught him and his mom whupped him with a belt.

"I dunno what made him do that," Denise Jones says today over a steaming mug at a bar and grill in Chestnut Hill. She looks just like Mike—the same beady, almost naive, eyes, the same raised cheek-bones, the same jutting chin. She wears a white tank top and a grey hoodie, though a sign on the restaurant window reads, "No Hoodies, No White Tees, No Timbs." A heart pendant hangs from her neck, and earrings that say "Denise" from her ears.

"I dunno what was going through his head at that time," she says. "I think maybe something was bothering him. Because it ain't that he needed the hats or really wanted the hats because Mike was a spoiled child."

"Do you think he wanted attention?"

"Oh, no. Mike always had attention. From me, anyway."

From me, anyway. It's a reminder that there's another side of the equation. And Mike's dad certainly should be mentioned, for his toughness played a part in Mike's shutting off. Like Teon's, Mike's father was a severe military man—a corrections officer and prison guard of many years who had boxed in the army. Mike's four paternal uncles were also in the service. The first time Mike Jr. tried to walk as a baby, he stood up for an hour in the archway of the apartment, unable to start moving. "You're gonna walk!" Mike Sr. shouted. "Stop that crying! You gonna be a man!"

"Mike!" Denise said to her husband. "That's enough."

But Mike Jr. walked that day while the family stood there. "You have a dad like that," Liza says, as we stretch out on the couch in her house, "that's the type of influence—*no*, you don't show emotion. His dad made him strong like that. . . . [Mike] was always *made* to be a boy's boy."

So the boy's boy grew quieter and quieter, absorbing life in silence. A lanky boy of average height—though ox strong—he did two hundred pushups (in sets) every night before bed. Like Teon, he played football. And like Teon, he was undersized for the sport. Then he became obsessed with basketball as he curled inward, away from other people. He'd go alone to a nearby court every afternoon and shoot and shoot. He'd shoot into the darkness, picturing himself in the NBA, and Liza had to search for him to bring him home, following the echo of the bouncing ball.

So sports was part of his change. And there was also his pit bull puppy, which was so small he brought it home in his pocket. He named it Chaos (Teon's was named Honey), though its gentleness was one of the few stable things in his life. The dog used to sit at the door in the late afternoon, knowing exactly when Mike would return from school. Mike even let it sleep in his bed, cradling the dog in one arm and the basketball in the other.

He got another pit bull, Nightmare, but before long, the two dogs were grown, and they escaped the house. So Mike got new ones: Scarface, Summer, Felony, and Ransom. And years later, Mike cried when he had to give them up, when he could no longer care for them. It was one of only three times his mom recalls him crying. And he got "Scarface" tattooed down his arm in memory of her. "I love 'em, man," Mike says today, watching Bruce Lee on the couch. "Since with me, I was a loner, I had dogs. They show you love unconditionally."

"It wasn't that he didn't have friends," adds Liza. "He had still those same friends. He [just] wasn't interested in doing the things they were doing."

Loner Mike *was* interested in basketball, and he devoted all of his time and energy to it until ninth grade, when he was cut from the jayvee team at Martin Luther King High. His mom urged him to stick with it, saying, "Jordan didn't make it the first time he tried out, and look at Jordan"—but Mike decided he "had to think of something else" and asked his father to take him to a boxing gym.

This was just one more way in which Mike failed to adjust well to disappointment, his sister says. He was a "sore loser" back when he'd claim his sister had cheated to win Monopoly, flipping over the board and scattering its pieces. And "when his parents broke up, when he didn't make the basketball team, he's a sore loser." Not that Liza blames Mike or criticizes him for it. She had her own problematic ways of dealing with it. She'd get into fights at school and run track for the team to take her mind off everything. But she didn't really *deal* with her family issues—"how things fell apart," in her words—until she went to counseling as an adult for three and a half years.

Healthy or not, boxing marked the completion of Mike's transformation into an introverted man who suffered in silence. "Yeah, I had a lot of anger man, inside," he mutters today, and only after I've pried for hours. "My mother and father, they wasn't together. I never really got along with my mom's boyfriend. I never got along with him. I wanted to get outta there. I wanted to hurt something. So boxing was the perfect sport for me."

"When my mom and his dad split," Liza adds, "I think that's when he started to be like in a shell a little bit, holding onto that. I don't think he ever got it out. . . . When he started boxing, he was letting out his aggression of all things he never expressed verbally."

All the things we never express verbally—could there be a better definition of boxing?

Mike dedicated himself to the fight game, bopping a speed bag in his room, which his mom had bought him and installed there, instead of in the basement. Liza heard it at two in the morning. "Mooooom! Make him stop!" she shrieked. At school, Mike remained silent, tumbling through his inner world. He studied computer repair, which is what his mom wanted him to go to college for and do professionally. But he also started training at Joe Frazier's Gym with an oldhead named Mr. Val, who was kind of like a father. Today, sitting on the couch with me one Sunday, Mike speaks of him in the same sentence as his deceased Grandma Ida.

Mr. Val taught the fundamentals well, but after Mike had learned those, Mr. Val became one-dimensional. He kept training Mike on punching power, on leveraging weight into punches. And Val *was* a master at that. Mike was even good at it, which is how he earned the nickname "Machine Gun." But after training for punching power for so long, he realized he needed to learn other things, like footwork. Many fighters in the gym (like the not-yet-deceased William "Manzy" Boggs) felt the same way—that they were all being bred to be Joe Frazier when in reality few of them were suited to his unique style. "It's very common," Mike says. "Everybody got to be fighting just like Joe Frazier, look like Joe Frazier, talk like Joe Frazier. It's crazy."

Mike knew he couldn't continue bull-rushing opponents. And he knew of another trainer who had done wonders with other fighters. Vaughn Jackson had taken boxer Rashiem Jefferson to *three* national Golden Gloves championships. He also had his own tragic past. Jackson's ten-year-old son had died from a freak vocal cord injury in 1998.

Mike approached Vaughn, and they joined up.

◦ ◦ ◦

The fighter has to bring his own natural talent and his own dedication and his own willingness to learn, but the trainer is always the last piece of the puzzle.

After leaving Michigan and after going through one more trainer whom his father dismissed, Teon finally hooked up with Smokin' Wade Hinnant, the trainer with whom he'd later win the 2004 National Golden Gloves. Wade had been a lightweight in the 1970s, when he trained at the Athletic Recreation Center at Twenty-sixth and Master. That's where Herk Jenkins, Silky Jackson, and Choo Choo Brown had trained, and it's where the very last PAL moved its program in the mid-1980s.

As a boy, Wade had moved with his family from North Carolina in 1967. "It was a shock," he says now, "because I had this vision as an eight-year-old kid coming to Philly—ice cream, lawns with white picket fences. I didn't see none of that. I saw some terrible neighborhoods.

Houses like Herman Munster's house. It was not what I anticipated at all. We got teased a lot coming up because we had that southern accent, particularly me, my sister, and my mom. People talk about your mom back then. It was a fighting time."

It was a fighting time, and he was in a foreign city, so Wade took up boxing, turning pro at sixteen. But of course, he was now a Philly guy, and his precocity turned in on itself, and he started having eye problems after only his second fight. He retired and became a roofer—until the game lured him back as a trainer in the 1990s.

His training methods are based on his own experiences in the ring, particularly his December 1978 loss to Bruce Curry (one of only two losses in his sixteen-fight career), who was such a feared puncher that Wade's trainers had him grow a beard to cushion his jaw. Curry charged Wade all night, leaving him no room to breathe. "What I think I like to do most," Wade says of his training, "is put a lot of mental pressure on them, force them to do things at a faster mental pace, to push them past the limits they put on themselves. When they feel they can't hit the bag another round, I push past that—not for another round, but maybe two or three more rounds. . . . In the ring that's how you're gonna feel when they don't give you time to breathe."

Teon immediately noticed the concentration Wade demanded. "He a hard worker," Teon says. "Know what I mean? If you doing something wrong, he gonna tell you. He don't hold nothing back."

It's hard to pinpoint the degree to which Wade's training improved Teon, who was gifted. But in the first few years after Teon joined up with Wade—from 2004 to 2007—Wade's pro fighters went unbeaten, including heavyweight Chazz Witherspoon, who was considered America's top prospect in the division; LaJuan Simon, who became U.S. middleweight champ; and a buzz saw junior middleweight named Latif Mundy. Clearly, Wade knew what he was doing.

So Teon joined up with Wade and won the Golden Gloves in 2004. Chazz, before turning pro, also won that year. Still, Wade thought Teon was special. "He's the only one I have that reminds me of myself," Wade said. "He's real quiet outside the ring, but I'm really, really excited about him, because he's the kind of kid that can fight at 118 to 130 and be highly competitive in that twelve-pound span and definitely carry the power all the way up to junior welterweight [140 pounds]."

✧ ✧ ✧

Teon was ranked fourth in the country among amateurs in his weight class in 2005. Mike was never ranked as an amateur, but his game of power punching was more suited to the professional ranks, and Vaughn was still trying to teach him the technical side of the game.

Teon and Mike were signed by the same pair of managers: Doc Nowicki and Jim Williams. Doc, a businessman who made money "invisible-mending" cars (a form of dent removal), and Jim, a boxing lifer who had begun his managing career in the late '60s, were an odd couple who had teamed up several years earlier to manage the careers of a bunch of scrappy fighters from Eastern Europe.

"We wanted to sign Mike up," Jim said, "because we think he's, in a mental area, unbelievable." It couldn't have hurt that Mike was able to fight at welterweight even though he was five feet, eleven inches and had a seventy-two-inch reach.

They were attracted to Teon for his natural ability. "He's almost like a beast in the gym," Doc said.

Both fighters were also signed by famed local promoter Russell Peltz.

Mike turned pro in 2005. He had suffered two serious injuries to his right hand while boxing, and though he still had a lot to learn, he couldn't fight for free as an amateur anymore. He didn't know how long he'd hold out. He was twenty-two.

Teon turned pro in 2007. He was twenty.

8

THE ALIVE

O pleasant exercise of hope and joy!
For mighty were the Auxiliars which then stood
Upon our side, we who were strong in Love!
Bliss was it in that dawn to be alive,
But to be young was very Heaven!
—William Wordsworth, *The Prelude*

It ain't easy to be out in front with a black Philadelphia fighter.
Everyone's watchin', waitin' for somethin' bad to happen.
—Sam Solomon, trainer[1]

In December 2008, on the day I was to leave college for winter break of my senior year, I called Mr. Pat and found out that he had pancreatic cancer and about a month to live. We had been out of touch for only a couple of months, not an unusual gap over the years, depending on how busy I was with work.

He sounded frail and pained on the phone, groaning when I asked whether I could come over. His caretaker said he couldn't take visitors. She said he was all skin and bones at this point. She told me what the doctors had said, in broad terms—that the cancer had been silently spreading within him for years, probably the last four, at least.

It had been spreading within him even as we met.

* * *

Boxing is not uniform—there is no overarching organization seeking what's best for the sport and its participants. There are just people, looking out for themselves.

In the 1950s, Frankie Carbo's gang at the International Boxing Club (of which Blinky Palermo was a main member) controlled all the fights and the TV broadcasts. Fighters bent to their will or lost everything. This is what the novel and movie *The Harder They Fall* was about. In the 1970s, Don King took over, distorting rankings and matching fighters based on his own interests—not the fighters' and not the fans', although when the fans' interests happened to coincide with his, he produced incredible events. King's "Rumble in the Jungle" will be cherished for years, even though King won't be.

Meanwhile, the concept of the "champion"—perhaps boxing's purest ideal—was diluted and then rendered meaningless by so-called sanctioning bodies, which began identifying their own, separate champions so that no one person could claim supremacy. These sanctioning bodies essentially forced fighters to pay them to have their "title" fights "sanctioned"—even though no real government had vested any authority in the sanctioning bodies to hand out titles and even though the titles themselves were disputed, since each body picked its own champ. If a fighter refused to pay the fee—even if he was clearly the weight class's dominant figure—the sanctioning bodies would strip him of his title belts and award them to someone else. Sometimes, even if a champion had done nothing wrong, a sanctioning body would strip him just so it could stage another title fight and demand even more sanctioning fees. Sometimes, a sanctioning body would name two champions or even three or four (one would be called a "champion in recess"; another would be a "champion emeritus"; yet another would be a "super champion" or an "interim champion"). To quote my father, who would shake his head each time the topic came up: "This is why it's not a sport." And he wasn't the only American who began feeling this way.

Since the bodies didn't agree with each other on champions (because the more champions there were, the more fees they could collect), the number of champions proliferated, and the very idea of the thing was lost. The public could no longer identify the best—which is how people attach themselves to any cultural meme, whether it be artistic or athletic—and so could no longer track the sport. And it grew even more difficult as the bodies themselves multiplied. Of the more recent ones, there were initially two—the World Boxing Association and the World Boxing Council. Then in 1983 the International Boxing Federation was established in New Jersey by a guy who would later resign for taking bribes to fix ratings. In 1988, the World Boxing Organization was founded, and it would later distinguish itself by moving a super middleweight up two slots in its rankings, from seventh place to fifth, months after he had died. ("We obviously missed the fact that Darrin was dead," the organization president said. "It is regrettable.")[2] If the International Boxing Organization takes off, there will be five groups telling the public whom to call "champ." Recently, *Ring Magazine* tried to resolve this by handing out its own official belt again, which in olden days had signified the public's champion, sanctioning bodies be damned. But then Oscar De La Hoya's promotional company, Golden Boy, bought the magazine, and its belts and rankings lost a bit of their authority.

This fiasco, the phenomenon of sanctioning bodies endlessly creating new titles, dates back to Jimmy Young's controversial loss to Ken Norton, when Ali refused to face the winner, and the WBA and WBC split on whom to call champ (the former backed Ali and the latter Norton).

"The proliferation of titles, to me, is one of the biggest problems in the sport," says promoter Russell Peltz. "Because people who go to football and basketball games, they know who the NBA champs are. But you ask them who the fighters are, they have no idea. You know, four champions in each division. I tell this to everybody: if at the end of the season, the Dodgers win the National League West, the Phillies win the National League East, you know, all these teams win their divisions but they never play each other—that's what boxing is. You got all these guys walking around saying they're champions. Nobody knows."

The business of boxing hasn't only been hurt by the people who run it. It has also suffered from shifting American tastes. It was once, alongside baseball and horseracing, one of the three sports Americans cared about. It was so popular that politicians tried to use the game to curry favor with the public. A city councilman in Philadelphia once held a press conference to announce that the third fight between Sugar Ray Robinson and Carmen Basilio would be held in Philadelphia, just in order to impress his constituents (the truth is, Basilio had never been informed of this development).

"Nowadays," says former *Philadelphia Daily News* editor and current boxing commentator Larry Merchant, "they do that when they think they can bring a football franchise to town."

The business of boxing was further damaged by the death of several fighters on national TV, the closing of neighborhood clubs, and the rise of casinos in Las Vegas and Atlantic City, which often held shows but handed out complimentary tickets to major gamblers and celebrities instead of building an audience of true fight fans.

Then there were promotional and television contracts. Fighters started signing pacts with specific companies and channels, prohibiting them from fighting on competing networks or on other promoters' cards. Each fighter was legally tied to a different, competing party.

"You can't make the big fights anymore," Peltz says. "Promotional contracts helped kill boxing. And network contracts. An HBO guy won't fight a Showtime guy. I can't get Kassim Ouma a fight with Cory Spinks because King wants options [the right to promote that fighter's future bouts] if we win the fight. And I don't want to do business with King under those circumstances."

Having long ago yielded to team sports, boxing is now said to face competition even from other fight-based sports. MMA, or mixed martial arts, sets two men in a cage and has them box, kick, and grapple with four-ounce, open-fingered gloves (eight ounces is the smallest allowed in boxing) until one collapses or submits (or until time expires and a decision is rendered). It has swept the eighteen-to-thirty-four demographic and recently overtaken boxing in ratings and revenue. In 2007, Ultimate Fighting Championship, the most popular MMA league, took in $223 million in pay-per-view. HBO's boxing PPV operation took in only $177 million—$120 million of which was from a single event.

The question of MMA's impact on boxing extends beyond HBO and Showtime ratings to sponsorships. Boxing still makes money pasting logos on the canvas and on fighters' trunks. Tecate, a Mexican beer, sponsors a Friday night boxing series on the Spanish channel Telefutura. If corporations shift their dollars to MMA for more exposure, boxing could lose yet another source of revenue.

But there was some good news as Teon turned pro in 2007 and Mike's career began to take off—America witnessed something of a boxing renaissance.

"Everybody agrees this was a comeback year for a beleaguered sport," *Sports Illustrated* wrote, "with top fighters committing to dangerous and, not so accidentally, entertaining fights."[3] What the magazine meant, of course, was not that fighters began placing themselves in physical danger, but that they were finally facing opponents fans wanted them to face, regardless of how difficult such opponents might prove to beat. "Know What's Better than a Big Fight in Vegas?" read the *ESPN Magazine* headline on Bill Simmons's last column of 2007. "Not Much."[4] And the column continued: "Despite the ongoing efforts of sleazy federations and sleazier promoters to undermine the sport's credibility, boxing has regained its footing with memorable battles."

Meanwhile, overseas, boxing was as popular as ever. In Wales, more than thirty thousand people attended a fight involving their beloved champ Joe Calzaghe. In Germany, three TV networks aired primetime boxing in millions of homes. Philly cruiserweight champ Steve Cunningham moved there to boost his career.[5] He's an unknown to Americans, but he said, "When we got off the plane, reporters were waiting, taking pictures. Walking through the market, people were asking me for autographs."[6] The Klitschko brothers, heavyweight champions both who hail from the Ukraine and fight out of Germany, held their fights in soccer stadiums filled with sixty thousand fans.

There were also signs that MMA wasn't quite the threat it had been perceived to be. A senior vice president at Showtime said 27 percent of MMA's male twenty-five-plus demographic was also watching Showtime's *Championship Boxing* series.[7] And Ultimate Fighting Championship's last event of 2007 took in $4,994,000 at the gate, but the top fighter on the card, Chuck Liddell, took home only a $500,000 payout (before tax), and the next highest-paid fighter got $160,000. Boxing's top events still paid combatants millions of dollars.

Still, it wasn't the best time to be starting a boxing career. But for Teon and Mike, it was too late.

* * *

Teon won his first match by knockout in two minutes and forty-one seconds on January 11, 2007. His opponent had entered with an 0–2 record. Teon wore shimmery blue trunks that read "RIP Vaughn T. Jackson"—a memorial to Mike's trainer Vaughn's deceased son, whom Teon knew from the amateur ranks.

His second fight was March 2 and was supposed to pose a slightly greater challenge. He faced flabby twenty-two-year-old Omar "El Torito" (Baby Bull) Reyes from Chicago, who entered with a 2–5 record.

"I knew Kennedy was a tough kid," Reyes's manager said, explaining why he made the match. "I think on that fight the price was right. . . . We were going in as a spoiler."

It was another quick bout. Forty-four seconds into the first round, Teon knocked Reyes across the ring with a right hand. Reyes, lying motionless, was counted out by the ref and then swarmed by paramedics. He was later taken to the hospital and kept overnight for observation and tests. Teon kept asking everyone, "Is he gonna be alright?"

At home, Teon's mom asked, "How did they say he was when they took him out?"

* * *

Mike turned pro December 16, 2005, against Jason Thompson, a 1–0 New Yorker who had reached his city's Golden Gloves finals months earlier, though Mike didn't know it (Doc and Jim didn't want to scare him; they just wanted to test his mettle).

Mike felt out Thompson in the first round to see what his opponent had and what he could do in response. Vaughn had instructed him to hide his power—not to throw any hard shots that would cause Thompson to go into a defensive shell. It was an odd strategy and one that would perhaps later give Mike some trouble. But for now, Thompson chased Mike and caught him with a good left hook. "He caught me right on my chin," Mike would recall. "It made me fight harder. It made me pick my hands up. I got less nervous. I knew I could take it."

After the round, Mike returned to the corner. "It's time to turn it up now," Vaughn said. "Let him feel your power."

In the second round, Mike noticed he could land a right hand over the top of Thompson's jab because Thompson wasn't pulling back his left fast enough. Mike threw it, it landed, and Thompson backed up into the ropes. Mike opened up and threw everything he had. He caught Thompson with an uppercut.

"A lot of that stuff, a lot of the punches, I don't even remember them," Mike would recall, "because it was off of instinct."

The referee stopped the fight and declared Mike the winner. A technical knockout. Promoter Russell Peltz received a bunch of calls from people in New York wanting to know who Mike Jones was.

Mike's second fight was in March 2006 against a 1–1 opponent. After the first round, Vaughn told Mike that the opponent was dipping away from Mike's right hand. "Bring him *into* the right hand," Vaughn said. "Hit him with a hook." Mike left the corner, threw a left hook to the body and then a hook to the head. The opponent staggered into Mike's straight right hand. The opponent's legs slid out from under him in an involuntary split. TKO at 2:30 of the second round.

"I was more comfortable being in the ring because it wasn't my first time," Mike said. "It felt a lot more comfortable."

He knocked out his third opponent in the first round. Again he left-hooked the guy into his right hand, which so completely thwacked him that it looked as if the guy had run into a plate of glass. The guy waited on his knee until the ref reached the count of ten and then rose. Mike knocked out his fourth opponent in the first round, too. This time he threw an old-school uppercut to the body. As the guy doubled over, Mike double jabbed and crushed him with the right. The opponent curled into a ball in the corner, just across the ring from where the last opponent had yielded.

Mike TKO'd his fifth opponent in the first round in less than two minutes. It was a tight left hook, twisted from the shoulder, and it landed flush on the opponent's jaw.

"OOOOH!" shouted the announcer for the local Comcast channel. "The left hand delivered! And that is a thunderous knockdown! The classic Philadelphia left hook!"

But Mike thought he could've fought better. "I shoulda jabbed more," he said. "Cut off the ring more."

"Mike Jones has TNT in both hands," one writer said after the match. "Although he has not been tested yet, he is definitely Philly approved!"

His sixth fight took place in Washington, four days after Teon's pro debut in the New Alhambra. Mike faced a guy with twenty-two fights on his record. He didn't know too much about him, other than that he was a dirty fighter. The opponent tried to head butt and hold Mike, but Mike didn't get too close and kept him at bay with a stiff jab, buzzing around him like a stubborn fly. When the opponent neared, Mike stepped back and countered. Mike slowed him with a good body shot, backed him into the ropes, and caught him with the old one-two. The opponent started sucking air. "I knew he was getting tired," Mike said.

TKO in three.

His seventh fight was back in Philly on the night Teon sent his second challenger to the hospital. Mike faced an opponent with forty fights but only eleven wins. Mike strolled around the ring. He knew he could counter his opponent's slow punches. He thought he'd score another first-round knockout. But the opponent stood up to some of his best shots, and Mike didn't end it until fifteen seconds into the second round, when he landed two left hooks to the head and then a straight right. The opponent flew against the ropes like food flung onto a wall.

Mike was 7–0, with seven knockouts.

* * *

Mike's life outside the ring was still unaffected by his success inside it. He still had to work a regular job—he drove a forklift at night at Home Depot—and his favorite thing to do was to spend time with the two daughters he had had with his longtime girlfriend, Myana and Alyza. He had been only twenty-one when the first was born—his girlfriend had still been in high school—but Mike was not an immature parent. He loved his daughters and spent every moment he could with them. Instead of hiring babysitters, he watched them. Instead of having his girlfriend cook their food and buy their clothes, he did. He wrestled and tumbled with them. He learned their tendencies and laughed. Myana, the older girl, was devious in the way that he had been as a kid. She once handed her sister a jump rope and told her to hold on. Then she tugged her sister down the stairs with the other end.

The only thing Mike banned in the house was candy.

Something about Mike had always been old anyway; he had always retreated from the world. He was probably one of the few young men in America who was not only ready for kids at a young age, but was greatly benefited by their presence. They opened him up to life. Made him joke again. He had the look of someone who would do anything for them.

This intense passion was reciprocated. At fights, Myana would shout, "Get 'em, Daddy!"

Mike's family watched all this with pride. But as much as they loved Mike's daughters, they had doubts about his girlfriend, who still, after six years of dating Mike, made a habit of going out on the town with her girlfriends and not leaving food for Mike or the girls.

"When [Mike] gets off of work, he goes jogging," said his mom, Denise. "Then he goes to the gym. Then he goes to the spa. Then when he comes home, [he's] tired. The only thing I disagree with Marisol is: *Please* have meals ready for my son. Because he takes care of his family. *Do* that. He needs that."

✿ ✿ ✿

Teon still made a habit of partying, too, though he also had a girlfriend. Unlike Mike, he was not a homebody. Though he still lived with his parents, he loved nothing more than spending time with his friends in the streets. So long as he had more than six weeks to go before his next fight, he felt free to go out and carouse. His parents started to worry about the girls he was hanging out with—especially as his renown as a boxer grew in the inner city.

"Being a boxer, you need to concentrate," his mom, Nettie, said. "You need to watch any girl you get involved with. Because you never know what they're out for."

One day Teon told his family that his girlfriend was pregnant.

"I was not happy at all," Nettie said. "Not happy."

"He done did it now," Ernest said. "I ain't gotta say nothing else. The only thing I've been talking to him really now about is boxing, since the girl been pregnant. I don't have to say anything else no more. I think the world gonna do it for me now."

✿ ✿ ✿

Teon's next fight was April 2007. He had a really nasty cold, and Wade had given him time off from training, but Teon had decided to go through with the fight. "This is my career," he reasoned. "This is what I want to do. So I got to push forward." The fight was in the Armory in Northeast Philadelphia, part of a show promoted by Dee Lee Fischer, a redheaded hairdresser who has been in the boxing business for years. She sat ringside in a white shawl. Mike Jones watched the match in a white T-shirt and long black shorts. Teon fought a tall boy from the Bronx. "Six foot tall," Doc would recall. "The kid had arms on him down to his knees almost. And when you fight a big kid like that, you can't fight on the outside. You gotta fight on the inside." Teon dropped him with a body shot in the second round but was too tired to finish him. The fight lasted the entire scheduled four rounds, the first time that had happened in Teon's career. He won a unanimous decision.

✿ ✿ ✿

Mike's eighth bout was against a 5–1 boxer in Las Vegas on the undercard of a big fight. The opponent was supposed to be able to take a really good punch. Mike felt out the opponent, being cautious, not throwing any major punches. Then he saw the opponent lower his head and cover it with his arms. "When they do that," Mike would recall, "I know to bring them up with an uppercut." Mike threw the uppercut and followed with a right hand.

TKO in the first.

Mike next fought a bit more than two months later, on July 20, 2007, in the New Alhambra. The bout was broadcast live on Telefutura, a Spanish channel, making it his first nationally televised match. It was also his first bout scheduled for eight rounds, though none of his previous fights had ever gone the distance.

His opponent was considered a step up. He was a brawler from Lancaster, Pennsylvania—a boxing adjunct of Philly—with a 10–4–1 record, and he had beaten guys with records of 13–0, 9–1, 10–3, and 14–5. The fight was an eliminator for the state welterweight title (a meaningless trinket, but one that still would have given Mike a title to his name). It had originally been for the vacant title itself, but the state required a ten-round fight, and Mike's managers were nervous about that length. All of the opponent's previous seven wins had come by stoppage—either KO, TKO, or retirement. Going into the match, critics called Mike one-dimensional. They said he had power, sure, but he couldn't move around the ring and he didn't know how to jab. "All the people that always talk crap about him—as soon as they see him fight, they jump on the bandwagon," his girlfriend said.

Mike heard that a lot of Alhambra patrons thought he was going to be KO'd. So he and Vaughn planned to jab the stuffing out of Doel Carrasquillo, who wore trunks with the Puerto Rican flag (aching Marisol's Puerto Rican heart). And that's exactly what Mike did. In the first and second, he pumped his left like a piston, jabbing smack into his opponent's nose. Carrasquillo tried to sneak in a right, but Mike evaded it and launched the left hook. "I don't think I've caught anyone with a real good clean overhand right yet," Mike said after. "In the pros, the punch has been the left hook." In the corner after the second round, Mike's opponent threw in the towel, retiring on his stool. The television announcers and Internet writers speculated that Mike had broken Carrasquillo's nose. But Mike's camp believed what they saw: that their fighter had again broken another man's will.

"Punchers are what make the boxing world go 'round," Russell Peltz said in a statement released to boxing websites. "They bring people in the door. I know it's early and I could be getting carried away, but when I look at Mike with his massive shoulders and back, I see turnstiles clicking. He looks like a young Thomas Hearns."

Mike signed a contract extension with his managers, Doc and Jim. It came with a bonus: a three-bedroom house in the Bridesburg section of the city, with reduced monthly payments subsidized by Doc. Mike filled the house with the kinds of toys he loved as a kid for his daughters: mini cars and plastic kitchenettes and a mini-trampoline for the basement. "Now he's progressing," Philly Keith, a local boxing blogger, said of Mike at the end of the sticky summer. "He's leaving Philadelphia, going out on more of a national end."

* * *

It was late August 2007, and there was a nice breeze, and you could almost smell the turning of the leaves. Peltz the promoter had signed a contract to promote fights at a new Indian casino resort on the New York side of Niagara Falls. He hauled up there his whole stable: the guys managed by Doc and Jim, Mike, Teon, and a rough twenty-one-year-old southpaw named Kaseem who was involved in the street life. For an opponent, Mike was assigned another tough Philly kid with a billy goat beard. Teon drew a kid from the Bronx.

They drove up in a van on Wednesday afternoon, August 29, 2007. Teon said leaving Philly didn't matter—he was going to fight the same fight he always did—and actually, being outside of the city with all its harmful attractions would help him focus more. Mike, who was still working the Home Depot night shift but got off for the fights, slept on the drive up.

The area around Buffalo is known as western New York. It is east of Rochester and Syracuse and as far west as you can go before hitting Lake Erie. That body of water flows north through an area known as the Tonawandas, diverging into two rivers, the East and West Niagara, around Goat Island, a broken-off crumb of land, where they split and spill forth in the famous waterfalls, like juice from a straw around a toddler's gap teeth.

The cab driver who conveyed me to my motel summed up the place. "Not much going on here," he said. "Just—what do they call it? Doing production research more or less. This is a stinko place. A lot of pollution here, guy. A lot of pollution. . . . There was industry here. Yeah, there was industry."

Downtown Niagara is laid out in a grid like Philly. The casino stands on the spot of the old convention center, which held the last boxing match in the area, a 2001 win by "Razor" Ruddock, who had been the victim of another controversial stoppage by referee Richard Steele, against a Don King fighter, years after Meldrick Taylor's. That fight had been a joke, pitting two washed-up guys against each other for the Canadian heavyweight title in an American venue. The majority of the action went down in the restroom, in fact, since the local newspaper editor was attacked by three men supposedly angry over antiunion coverage.[8] Months later, they began converting the convention center into a casino, hoping the newfound revenue would revitalize the area. Walking through the decrepit downtown, I saw it hadn't.

❀ ❀ ❀

It's odd. Boxing takes a man many places, and they usually bear no relation to his home. But Teon and Mike were sent to Niagara, which quite clearly resembled Philly. There was the slum. The boarded-up houses lining Niagara's Seventh and Eighth streets. With signs that read "auction" or "demolition" and collapsed roofs. Bulldogs who barked at passersby who scarcely noticed the small "beware of dog" signs. The graffiti that said "fuck you," and the lots that had been reduced to piles of rubble and rusty cranes.

A century ago, Niagara had created the first power station to use an alternating current. Edison helped create it and so did Tesla, Westinghouse, and J. P. Morgan. And then, just as manufacturers had built up Philly, they clustered in Niagara for its intelligent power: the Carborundum Company, for instance, which was led by the man who invented artificial graphite; and the Natural Food Company, which created shredded wheat and the Triscuit.

But as fast as industry came, it rushed out for the very same reasons Philly's did: high union wages and suburbanization and a co-opting of technologies. The downtown emptied, and the country looked away until a local mom realized her whole neighborhood was built on the waste of the city's chemical past—not recycled, but carelessly filled into

Love Canal to poison her children. Then the city created the USA Niagara Development Corporation in 2001 to attract tourists. And then Seneca Indians built a twenty-six-floor, 594-room resort in 2006, just around the time casinos were approved for the Philadelphia area as well.

❊ ❊ ❊

A couple nights before the fights, inside the events center on the casino's second floor, the ring already constructed, glowing in an otherwise dark room under the heat of nine spotlights, workers put the finishing touches on the whole setup. The room had a kind of nauseating, tumultuous silence until a hotel worker climbed into the ring. He bounced his back off the ropes and said, "You know, it's pretty big when you get in here." The other workers chuckled. Then an administrator in a tan suit and black shirt turned to two workers leaning on the ring's apron. "What's under here?" he asked. "Plywood, right?" The workers nodded.

❊ ❊ ❊

A floor below, not too much later, at the lobby bar, a fat bearded man spoke into a cell phone about staging fights at casinos, especially the new Venetian in Macau. "Concentrate on independent hotels like this one," he urged. A wrinkled old man with a prominent nose pulled up to the bar. "I coulda been something," he said. He ordered coffee and Sambuca, but it came out in a thick boxing accent, and the bartender thought he said coffee and Drambuie. A guy in cornrows turned to the older white men. He talked about fucking a female escort in a car. As long as his girlfriend doesn't find out, he said. They laughed.

At 10:40, Jim and Doc and I drank beers at the circular bar at the center of the casino. Doc told me of a featherweight prospect from Lancaster, Pennsylvania, who'd be the perfect challenge for Teon if only his manager would acquire the balls to make the match. "That's why they call him 'The Technician,'" Doc said, of Teon's reputation. "Because he does everything right."

Doc got up to gamble, and eventually he went to sleep, and so it was just Jim and me. Jim talked about the boxers he had managed who hadn't made it, either from drugs or crime, and the lone "success story" he had—a guy named Tyrone Taylor who went back to school and earned bachelor's and master's degrees. At the end of the night, once we were both wobbly, he said, "They don't think they're going to get old. You're gonna keep your figure like your fighting stomach? I kept mine till I was thirty-five. It's like, what happened there? My ripples are gone. I'd do like five sit-ups and it'd come back. Then it would go away, and it would take ten sit-ups and then like a dozen sit-ups. Nobody thinks they're gonna get old. Time gets everything. Time gets everybody. Have a good time while you can have it. The stuff I turned down, I would give my left nut to get back."

The next morning, Thursday, was the press conference. A few local reporters showed. The hotel manager crowded maids into the room to fill it. The president of the Seneca tribe said, "We don't want anyone to get hurt, but we know one person has to win." Mike and Teon were not the main attraction and were not seated on the dais. They were on chairs in the back. Mike listened to headphones, not looking up. Teon laughed, nervously swinging his legs from side to side under his chair. The third fighter in Jim and Doc's stable, the 154-pound southpaw named Kaseem, with a reputation for spending too much time in the street, got up, then sat down, then got up again. It almost seemed as if he was considering leaving.

In the back of the room, the guy in cornrows told the fat guy that he wasn't gonna get any tonight because he needed to rest for tomorrow's fights.

The next night Mike scored his usual knockout, and Teon took his customary decision. The most spectacular performance was put on by Teon's opponent, who kept charging Teon even though Teon kept punching him hard. The crowd cheered the opponent afterward for his effort.

Kaseem wasn't right—he was TKO'd by a boy nicknamed "Spider-man." After that, Kaseem stopped training, and Jim and Doc lost track of him.

Mike told me, "Going into the fight [Kaseem] was mental. No, I don't talk to him. Since he hasn't been in the gym I haven't talked to him at all. Nope. I heard nothing about Kaseem. He got a lot of talent, man. He let the personal life get to him. If it's not in your head to fight, then you're not gonna do good. If you don't got it all the way up top."

❊ ❊ ❊

"He got a lot of groupies already," Marisol gushes. Her voice carries pride, not worry. "I know he'll probably tease me, but he doesn't go out.

If he went out on the town, I'd be more worried. I trust *him*." Her voice changes tone. "I just don't trust *them*. He got a lot of them. I be hearing them. I be like, 'Oh, god.'"

Such is the life of the boxer's girlfriend. As Mike and Teon advance, everyone around them went along for the journey, willingly or not. It's an inevitable fact about most jobs that increased success leads to increased stability. The excitement of work's beginning fades into the routine of the office. With money comes bourgeois scheduling: dinner at this restaurant, lessons for the kids at that club.

In boxing, on the other hand, success breeds irregularity. The Philly boys entered Niagara, then another town, and then another. They traveled and trained, and their previous routines—of hitting the local gym, putting in a shift at Home Depot, sleeping—changed under new demands. Suddenly there were groupies and interviews with boxing websites and critics who voiced displeasure over the smallest mistakes.

Ours is a culture that deconstructs celebrities' lives. Its rising boxers are subject to this attention even as they remain unable to reap its benefits. They draw all the eyes without making any money like Internet ads we note and pass over. "It's not even the boxers," Mike said. "Anybody who's got any bit of any kind of fame—women are just attracted to them, especially the athletic ones. Football, basketball. They want a piece of something. What woman doesn't like an athletic guy?"

For Teon, life changed similarly. One night I asked to interview him at his house in the dangerous Strawberry Mansion neighborhood. Teon agreed but later insisted I meet him on a street corner where he picked me up in the Kia SUV his handlers had helped him get and took me to the front porch of his friend's house. He kept demurring when I asked to see his place. As for the new attention, the street life, the way so many boxers had been led astray before him, he said, "Sometimes I lose focus because girls be walking around. I try to holler at girls and stuff like that."

On the sidewalk just below us, Teon's buddies milled about, snickering and shoving each other. One raised his middle finger to a kid across the street. "I like going to the parties," Teon said. "That's about it. Most of the time I come over here and we chill outside. Have fun. Crack jokes."

This was one world for Teon as he moved ahead in boxing. Chilling outside, cracking jokes. It sounds like a cliché to speak of the street's allure, yet here the phrase was both apt and literal. Teon and I sat on a porch, and immediately below us in the street, a group of boys idled. They seem to care about him—they called out to him—but their very idleness was itself a threat.

I met Teon's girlfriend several months later behind the glass window of the spectator section of the gym. She was rocking their daughter—just born on December 27, 2007—to sleep in her arms. "I don't really go out," she told me, "so I don't really want him to go out." She wore a mustard-colored sweater and blue jeans, and she struggled to hold the baby and the diaper bag at once.

A few feet away was a woman whose ten-year-old son trained at the gym—a woman who had once dated Teon's trainer, Wade. She turned to us and said, "Them—they fathers—they don't change. We *mothers . . .*"

But Tati said Teon could change if he wanted. "He just stopped partying a lot—like recently," she said. "He decided to."

Teon's dad, Ernest, still noticed his son toeing around the house suspiciously, trying to avoid him sometimes, especially after going out. Having a kid *"should* change everything," Ernest said, "but I don't know what they do now. She got to give him the ultimatum."

Both fighters continued advancing, racking up wins against thirty-six-year-olds from Virginia and thirty-three-year-olds from North Carolina with records of 10–19–2. So the competition wasn't great, but again, they were doing what they were told. Then Mike got a headlining gig in November at the New Alhambra against a former title contender with a record of 36–7 and took him out in three rounds. It was his first signature win, and Peltz smiled in the dressing room after the fight, assured that Mike's rating would climb. It did. Boxrec.com, the site used by promoters to make matches, bumped Mike to forty-forth in the world out of 1,000 welterweights in its computerized rankings.

"I'd like to see if there's a way to squeeze in one more fight this year," Peltz said. "Somewhere. Anywhere. I don't know. He's certainly the hottest fighter in Philly right now."

But fortune, always involving herself in the fate of Philly boxers as though she was singularly obsessed with the game, planned a very different schedule for Mike. It turned out he had sustained another hand injury, this time in his left knuckle, and had to undergo surgery and rest for five months. It was just one more reminder—not that it was required in the first place—of the precariousness of the game in which a man's currency is his body, a body no less subject to the snapping and brittleness we observe generally in people and, in fact, given the beatings a boxer must take, one that's all the more so.

It was not the first lesson Mike has received in this regard, and it certainly wouldn't be the last, and since he really didn't have any control over it, the best he could do in the situation—what ultimately recommended him as a prospect to watch—was the way he responded. He spent the next several months learning how to jab with his healthy right hand. In other words, when he could no longer fight as an orthodox fighter, he taught himself how to fight southpaw.

"I keep a positive attitude," he said. "I'm gonna be a bigger problem when I come back."

* * *

As Teon and Mike moved onto a national stage, their city was attempting its own rise in the rankings. Some days it seemed obsessed with obtaining a better future. Other days the city moved dangerously back into the past, dredging up names and stories that reminded everyone of its darkest days.

There was Guy Sciolla, the former assistant district attorney who argued in room 243 of City Hall on July 11, 1979. It was a hearing on the defense's motion to suppress the oral and written statements Tyrone Patterson—Mr. Pat's son—had given cops the night of his crime. The statements in which he had admitted to stabbing his grandfather and taking his money, then driving around South Philly aimlessly. "Detective," Sciolla said to the man on the stand, in redirect examination, "did you ask this defendant if he was under the influence of any alcohol or drugs?"

"Yes, I did."

"And what was his response?"

"No."

Now, in April 2008, the fifty-eight-year-old lawyer was back in the news after a gang of kids from Simon Gratz High—the school Meldrick Taylor had attended and run track for—had attacked a thirty-six-year-old Starbucks manager in a subway station at Thirteenth Street, for no reason other than because they could, and the manager had suffered an asthma attack and died. "There's no prohibition to charging them [with murder] as long as there's sufficient evidence of an agreement to participate in a crime," Sciolla told the *Inquirer*. He wasn't involved in the case, but in his current job as a defense lawyer, as a man who had seen Pattersons stab grandfathers, he had perspective. He appeared in the news again later in the month, when he got a twenty-nine-year-old client acquitted on all counts. Police said they caught the client with two pounds of coke, a .45 semiautomatic, and $1,300 cash. Somehow, Sciolla had successfully argued that his client was a barber making a house call—even though the DA had pointed out that the guy didn't carry hair-cutting appliances.

These stories made it seem as though Philadelphia hadn't changed, so I called Sciolla to see if he remembered Tyrone. He didn't. But when I mused on the endless string of crimes, he said, "It's a rainbow city, brother," which I took to mean the city sees men and crimes of every stripe, though I'm not quite sure that was what he had intended.

Still, even the boxers noticed that the city was changing under Mayor Nutter. Bernard Hopkins, who had grown up a bad North Philly kid and had spent fifty-six months in prison beginning at age seventeen for strong-arm robbery before becoming the middleweight and light-heavyweight champion of the world, was now forty-three years old and living in a posh suburb in Delaware. But he saw changes in his hometown. "We got a new mayor," he said. "Things are turning around."[9]

He could've been referring to Mayor Nutter's environmental initiatives, anticrime measures, or his urgent pleading to Philadelphia's fathers to stay involved in their children's lives and to the children to stop the senseless crime.

But the funny thing about turning around is that it's a never-ending process. Let up for a moment and you might be right back where you started.

☼ ☼ ☼

Mike staggers into the corner, the same corner under which Vaughn sits watching helplessly. Sanders bruises Mike's ribs with a hook. Mike cranes his neck down, to see what's coming next. Sanders mills his left into Mike's gazing eyes, snapping his head to the side.

Mike flails his arms out, desperately trying to grab Sanders's shoulders and smother the punches. But as he sets his hands down, Sanders strafes him anew. His head spins. He can't clinch—probably because he has never had to before. Thirty seconds left. Punch after punch after punch. Mike's drowning in the corner, his eyes bulging wider, searching the room frantically as though looking for someone to swoop in and save him, like the eyes of a small boy lost in a big room who suddenly finds himself detached from his mother and, turning frantically, can't seem to spot her at all, only a sea of faces, of strangers odd and unfamiliar, uninviting faces, of people who do not care what happens to the boy, who don't feel a vested interest in the success or failure of his upbringing and thus will ignore him or worse.

✣ ✣ ✣

It started with a choice. Mike's injured left hand meant he wouldn't be able to jab until the end of February 2008. But after surgery in December 2007, he decided not to take a break, not to feel bad for himself, but to use the injury to his advantage. He got his trainer to teach him a southpaw stance, in which the boxer advances the right hand—Mike's healthy hand—to jab. Two days after surgery, he was back in the gym doing calisthenics. He refused to take weekends off.

Meanwhile, Peltz still couldn't find anyone decent willing to fight Teon. So he set up a match with a 1–4 kid out of Lancaster. A stay-busy match. Teon won all but a single round on the three scorecards, raising his record to 7–0. Now the pressure was on Peltz to find his boxers truly rewarding fights. Neither Mike nor Teon had gotten much national exposure. Luckily, the Seneca Indians were in a similar jam. They, too, were trying to raise their profile and they, too, were trying to revive an entire swath of a depressed city. And finally, they, too, believed boxing was the key.

So they contacted Peltz and gave him a few dates in March on which they could run a show. They made Peltz an offer with a caveat: He could stage a boxing show at one of their hotels so long as it was picked up for national broadcast by ESPN2's *Friday Night Fights*. Peltz liked the idea and decided to pitch Mike as a power puncher for the co-main event. Doc and Jim were thrilled at the prospect of putting their guy in front of the cameras. ESPN would "want something to say about who he'd be fighting," Doc told me. "But that wouldn't matter to us. We'd put him up against almost anybody now."

Peltz also wanted to feature Teon, but there wouldn't be a way to fit him on a two- or three-card show on ESPN. So Peltz made Teon the co-main event of his March 7, 2008, card at the Alhambra. That show would be televised by *Solo Boxeo Tecate* on Telefutura—not as prestigious a program as *Friday Night Fights*, but one heavily viewed by the nation's growing Hispanic fan base. It would be Teon's first nationally televised bout.

As Peltz searched for opponents, Mike began his recovery. His stitches were removed at the end of December 2007. The doctor was going to prescribe physical therapy, but then he looked at Mike's hand. "Christ, Mike!" The doctor said. "You're balling up your hand already. I don't think there's anything a therapist is gonna do that you're not already doing."

At the gym, Mike was also back to doing 100 to 150 push-ups. The doctor cleared him to swim, so he restarted his swimming routine with wrist weights, ankle weights, and waist belts. He shadowboxed and tuned his footwork. A few weeks later, as soon as the doctor allowed it, he resumed full-contact punching. Still, there wasn't an opponent yet, just names being tossed out by Mike's crew—guys they could envision Mike beating, guys they wanted to see lose. Potential victims.

Francisco Bojado was one. He was twenty-four with a record of eighteen solid wins against only three losses, two of which had been close split decisions. He had been a member of Mexico's 2000 Olympic team and was trained and managed by the best. A win over him would catapult Mike into the top of the rankings.

Andre Berto was another. The twenty-four-year-old North American champ, a former Olympian on the verge of his first world title shot, Berto had knocked out seventeen of his twenty opponents, including Miguel Figueroa, the Camden welterweight whom Doc and Jim had once managed. That loss, or more accurately what followed it, had prompted Doc's current desire to face Berto again. After the match, Doc and Jim were just trying to ascertain whether their boy Miguel was physically alright. Lou DiBella, Berto's promoter, walked over. "You know, Doc," he said. "Your guy has huge balls."

"I wanna show Lou that there's someone out there better than his guy," Doc said in January 2008. "I think we got someone coming up in the shadows here who can do that."

Mike began to emerge from the shadows when ESPN picked up Peltz's card for March 28. It would be at the Seneca Allegany Casino, the other major resort run by the tribe, an hour and a half south of Buffalo. The opponent would be Gilbert Venegas, a tough guy from Illinois who had recently drawn with a world-rated contender. On the Telefutura card, Teon's opponent would be Castulo Gonzalez, a thirty-year-old Guatemalan with a 9–4 record and a win over one of Doc and Jim's other featherweights. It would be Teon's first test against an opponent with a winning record, and it would be his first bout scheduled for eight rounds.

Ernest decided he would attend, which was unusual, because this would be a step up for his son. He told me Teon would get a "blank check" from a manager if he could win the next two fights because his three-year deal would be ending. Apparently, Teon hadn't told him about the new contract he had just signed with Doc and Jim for three *more* years. That deal wouldn't expire until August 24, 2010. "I would've told him no," Ernest said, crestfallen, when he heard about the new contract.

But Teon hadn't asked. He just kept returning to the gym, as his dad had taught him to do, day after day after day. On one particularly windy and snowy afternoon, the place overflowed with kids; some had to train in the adjacent Alhambra arena for lack of room. There Vaughn wrapped Mike's hands with tape and gauze. Vaughn wore a burnt orange thermal shirt from Old Navy. Doc and Jim leaned over, watching intently. They didn't always come to observe their guys train, but lately, they'd been staring at Mike's hands in the same way that owners of horses fixate on their animals' powerful legs.

Latif Mundy, another of their boxers, walked in wearing a bright orange reflective vest. He was flecked with cement. "How's the wife and baby?" Doc asked.

"Good," Latif said. "I got 'em here."

"I know how it is," Doc said.

A little boy ran around the perimeter of the New Alhambra jumping rope. He stopped at Petey Pop, the gym supervisor. "I just saw the bat with barbed wire," he said. "Um, is there gonna be a wrestling match or something?"

"Yeah, probably this weekend," Petey Pop said. "They always have something like that here. Why? Is that something you like?"

Inside the gym's ring, Teon shadowboxed. The timer beeped the start of an imaginary round. His feet glided like air hockey pucks.

Thirty seconds remained in the round when Teon quit the ring, moving to hit the heavy bag under Wade's watch. Back in the other ring, in the arena proper, Vaughn mowed down Mike with the medicine ball. Mike wore a baggy black T-shirt and beige track pants. He wore heavily padded eighteen-ounce training gloves (eight or ten ounce is standard for actual bouts) on both hands. And he didn't hesitate to throw his left, formerly injured hand—he was back to jabbing with it already. When the round ended, he lay on the canvas, hooking his feet under the ring's bottom rope to do sit-ups. Then he "worked the pads": Vaughn would hold two thick mitts in front of him and he'd jab them three times, then throw a straight right and a left hook.

Mike's hands looked fast. His forehead gleamed with sweat as each punch snapped like a rubber band. Vaughn and Mike worked on the overhand right, making sure Mike bent his knees and threw forward his imposing shoulders. Then it was back to the medicine ball.

"Vaughn!" Doc shouted from below the ring. "His shoe's untied."

"Alright," Vaughn said, ignoring him and continuing to plow ahead with the medicine ball. Mike pounded the ball at first, then slapped it, pitter-patter, when he lost steam.

"Keep that pace!" Vaughn yelled. "Pick it up now! Pick it up now!"

Doc leaned on the apron with his chin on his hand, staring up. The imaginary round ended.

"We didn't work on no southpaw, V," Mike said to Vaughn.

"Southpaw? You want to work on that more?"

The trainee called for *more* work. So Vaughn showed him how to step out of the pocket from a southpaw stance and throw an overhand left to the opponent's midsection. Mike was not as quick as a southpaw. He hesitated just the tiniest fraction of a second before each punch. But when he did swing, it was with great authority and a smile, because the thing that most encouraged Mike was the extra work, the self-imposed excess that—as the clichés correctly have it—separated the weaker-minded contenders from the more incorrigible, ultimately masochistic, champions.

"AH!" Mike screamed. "AH! AH! AH!"

With each punch it sounded like he was responding to a Band-Aid being forcibly yanked from his skin, which unintentionally took with it a great, painful clump of hair.

When everyone packed it in for the day, Vaughn whispered something in Doc's ear. Doc slipped him a $20. I asked Vaughn whether he thought Mike would ever give up—in a fight or in his career. "Never!" Mike interjected before anyone else could answer.

The same couldn't be said for his opponent. In the weeks leading up to their televised bout, Gilbert Venegas couldn't be found. He wasn't reporting to his gym, and his management hadn't heard from him. We would find out later he had gone on a drinking bender. But Peltz scrambled and managed to land an even better opponent: Germaine "Silky" Sanders, also out of Illinois, with a 27–5 record. Sanders would be turning thirty-eight on the day of the fight, but in his case, the experience would help. He had developed a style based on sliding across the floor and well-timed counterpunching. "He fight just like his name," Vaughn said. "*Silky.*"

Winter gusted by fast, and soon it was March, sunny and foreboding.

* * *

"*Y se nota la velocidad y la certeza de Teon Kennedy, un producto de Filadelfia. . . . Que el público . . . estar atrás de él cien por cien.*"

"And note the velocity and certainty of Teon Kennedy," the announcer says on the Telefutura broadcast. "The public is behind him 100 percent."

March 7. The camera zooms into Teon's corner. Teon looks left, perhaps at someone in the first row of seats. He wears a shiny blue Everlast jacket that zips up into a hood. The hood wraps tightly around his head, twisting with each jerk of his neck. It adheres like a reaper's cowl. He rocks back and forth to the beat of the music like an addict after his first puff, withdrawing inside himself, into the rhythm of a different world. He blinks. Doesn't smile or frown. He purses his lips together. His pupils expand as if taking in everything and nothing. The camera tries to pierce their glossy surface, but they only reflect the light back into the camera. Teon has already made the change, has already shifted his every bodily accessory into a tool of the trade, the boxer's practice from the time he enters the ring. He has shut off one aspect of the senses to concentrate another: He looks beyond the ring but doesn't see. He bobs and weaves to his own rhythm (and soon, that of his opponent, his partner), but though the cramped room fills with more than a thousand other selves, he senses only his own. He listens but hears only the grunts of muscle memory. Screams of the crowd fade into the purest white.

He bobs from side to side. Randy Hinnant, who helps his brother, Wade, train Teon, adjusts Teon's left glove—it's light blue with a red logo. Teon slides his body weight from one side to another, pulling back

the gloves as if they're controls and he is the marionette. "Bailando"—
dancing—is how the announcers describe it.

In the other corner, Castulo Gonzalez hops in his red Everlast robe
with a white shawl. His goatee appears freshly trimmed, and his hair is
all gone except for a Mohawk straight down the middle. He and his
cornermen all look the same: clean-shaven with a soul patch under the
bottom lip and a chiseled lower jaw. One of them raises his right arm
and pumps a fist. Gonzalez shadowboxes, ending in a crisp left hook.

Back in Teon's corner, Wade speaks to him, and Teon sways side to
side. Doc the manager balls his left hand into a fist and rests it on the
top rope.

Opposite corner. Gonzalez licks his lips with just the tip of his
tongue. One of his cornermen yells into the camera.

The ringside announcers send it up to the tuxedoed, bow-tied emcee, Lupe Contreras, "para la presentación de las pugilistas."

"Desde el New Alhambra Arena," Contreras begins, "damas y cabal-
leros prepárense para sentir el poder de Solo Boxeo Tecate.

"De Puerto San Jose . . . Castulo 'El Poderoso' Gonzalez!"

"BOOO!" the crowd yells.

"En la esquina azul . . ." The standing room guys begin clapping. The
sitting guys begin barking. The swell rises. "Four of his victories coming
by way of knockout. . . ." Teon bends low, bounds off his left leg, then
off the right. He slides his hood back, revealing his eyes. He bounces
side to side. Street rhythm, ascending. Randy lowers the hood to Teon's
shoulders. "Yeah!" rises the crowd. Contagion. "Representing *North
Philadelphia, Pennsylvania . . .*"

"YEAAHHHHHHHHH!" the crowd wails into the rafters, shrieking
the fever of loss and pride, reality and symbol. Howling a pain sublimat-
ed, into a boy, with a nice smile, a nicer punch, just a boy, but for a
moment more—suspension of disbelief. Remember: Teon's shorts now
and always have borne the letters "RIP." Teon bows to the crowd and at
the bottom of this motion, starts rolling his gloves in a whipping cycle.
Slow, then fast, then faster, twirling them up toward the ceiling like
clothes in a washing machine's spin cycle. The crowd claps and claps.
"Teon 'The Techniciaaaaaaaaaaaaaaaaaaaan' Kennedy!"

Teon waves to the crowd. And if you've been following him and his
people for sixteen months, you may go cold and bumpy when you see it,
knowing that all they have, beyond threadbare reality, is symbol and

storytelling—the ability to fabricate narrative in the absence of factory. Boxing won't change anything really, and the beauty of the match will be reality's unimportance. All that matters will occur inside the ropes.

∗ ∗ ∗

Sweet Pea Adams once told me, reflecting back on his aborted career, "Sometimes you lose, but you win." The flip side can also be true. Sometimes you win, but you lose.

Teon landed several good combinations in the fight against Castulo Gonzalez, which he ultimately won by a unanimous decision, taking six of the eight rounds on two scorecards and five on another. He threw a few beautiful uppercuts and also defended himself cleverly, wrapping his arms around himself in a kind of turtle shell so that most of the incoming punches deflected off his shoulders or elbows. The announcers compared the style to that of Floyd Mayweather, Teon's idol.

"He looked really good in the first round," Peltz told me. "I thought I was getting ready to see one of those breakout performances with the perfect foil in there with him."

But as the fight progressed, Teon's performance showed distressing hints of what could come. He looked sluggish in the middle rounds and was caught by a few hard punches, one of which opened a gash over his left eye. While his superior skills were never in doubt, he let himself be outworked by the hustling, charging Hispanic fighter who never stopped throwing, while Teon occasionally took breaks. And then there was his most disturbing tendency—to pause against the ropes at certain points and trade punches with the Hispanic fighter—the *puncher*—instead of boxing and moving, instead of using his slickness and speed. It was, for this wary Philadelphian fan, too reminiscent of a boy-man named Meldrick who had had too much heart.

In Teon's next fight, four months later, in July, he'd dispel these worries, at least temporarily, knocking out in less than two rounds one of the best prospects from Washington, D.C., a 10–0 super bantamweight named Thomas "KO" Snow. It would be Teon's first professional bout at super bantamweight, 122 pounds—his camp believed he could make the weight easily and, in so doing, carry greater power in the ring relative to his smaller opponents—after moving down from featherweight, or 126. It was, all in all, a masterful performance, not even accounting for the drop in weight.

But what happened that night against Castulo Gonzalez in March in Teon's national television debut had to be accounted for by Teon's people, because it contained too many allusions to other fighters' stories—stories that ended badly—than could reasonably be ignored. There was something about that March night. And it presented Teon's handlers with a choice. They could, of course, repress the memory of it altogether, or try to, and simply hope it wouldn't be repeated, that such hints were illusory and wouldn't show themselves again, or they could face the fight head-on, doing everything in their power to prevent its recurrence.

Peltz, for one, chose to talk about the fight openly, telling me that Teon was plain out of shape and recalling how he had arrived at the arena an hour late.

"He wasn't disciplined outside the gym," Peltz said. "I don't know if he parties—he doesn't impress me much as a party-type guy, but who knows? Maybe when he's around me in the gym he's a different person. Maybe he wasn't running as much as he should."

"He wasn't the Spartan liver that Mike Jones was. And even Mike faltered a little. . . ."

Three weeks later, March 28, 2007, it *was* finally Mike's turn, his opportunity on the biggest possible stage for a prospect who hadn't yet become a star coveted by HBO or Showtime—*Friday Night Fights* on ESPN2. It was at an Indian casino an hour and a half south of Buffalo, far from Philadelphia, at the foot of a snowy mountain under a dense fog that had rolled in by Friday, shrouding the entire casino and the trees surrounding it in a grey blur. There was something magical about the way little flakes kept falling outside, while inside men stripped down to nothing to work and sweat under the heated spotlights.

There had been little preamble to the show, despite its taking place on national television, and despite the fact that another of Peltz's boxers, a former world champion, had also been slotted on the card. It was as though this little hamlet tucked away in the hills of a remote region was part of a different world, a supernatural little area secluded from all the terrible, real-life concerns that usually occupied Philadelphians' lives.

The day before, at the sparsely attended press conference, Mike had come in late in an orange sweatshirt and his usual accessory: headphones. He was gently nodding his head to the music that only he could hear even while ascending the stairs to the dais—the first time Mike was invited to the front of such a conference—before he remembered himself and in his gawky, sweet way, yanked the buds out of his ears and asked Peltz, "Where should I sit?"

Mike's opponent, Germaine "Silky" Sanders, once again lived up to his nickname, as Vaughn, Mike's trainer, had promised me he would. Sanders arrived to the press conference wearing a black suit, a silver shirt, and a silver tie. Even his interviews had the sort of silkiness and finesse the good boxers employ:

"Can I ask you a few questions?" I asked.

"That depends on what they are," he said.

Later I asked what he was going to do to minimize or negate Mike's strength advantage.

"Not get hit," he said.

That night, on the eve of the fight, I joined Mike and his entourage—Vaughn, the trainer; and Doc and Jim, the comanagers—in the hotel's fitness room. Mike, quiet, ran forward and backward on a treadmill while watching a replay of an old heavyweight fight on television. Jim and Doc sat on stationary bicycles, but neither was really peddling—though Doc could be said to have moved a bit more than Jim—and I got the clear impression that they were there not to oversee Mike's work, or to ensure he was behaving before the fight, or to prevent him from ingesting anything harmful, but because they didn't know what else to do. In the lead-up to the fight, when everyone is silent and nervous and hopeful, there was no place for Mike's crew to go, nothing for them to do, other than to stay with Mike, huddle with him, and commiserate, silently, over the shared agony of the seemingly endless wait.

Vaughn, the trainer, was looser, more jovial. Perhaps it was because he had the most confidence in Mike of everyone in the room, having prepared the fighter for this moment, having already tested the limits of his ability and endurance. Vaughn, a paunchy but strong man, joked that he needed to work off the shrimp he had eaten for dinner—Doc footed the bill—so he lifted weights and did crunches on the floor, until Doc, looking on with a frown, said, "You're gonna be sore tomorrow. You better not get hurt. We need you." About this point, a little boy walked into the room. "Is that Mike Jones?" he asked.

And soon it was time to fight.

❊ ❊ ❊

It started with a choice. Mike had hurt his hand and could've nixed the entire bout and decided he wasn't ready yet, that he hadn't had sufficient time to prepare after healing. In fact, he *hadn't* had as much sparring before this fight as he was accustomed to, and as playful as his trainer Vaughn was, this seemed to be a real concern.

On ESPN, however, Mike is now being touted as the prospect Philadelphia has been proudly cultivating for three years. "All shoulders," Brian Kenny says to describe Mike's body. "Big things expected for Mike Jones."

Mike wears white trunks with black trim—basic—and true to form, Silky Sanders, thirty-eight years old and from the notorious Cabrini Green housing projects of Chicago, wears elephant print trunks with pockets in the back.

Mike hops in his corner; Doc claps; Mike pounds one of his gloves against his chest, then raises it in the air.

On ESPN, Teddy Atlas says Sanders needs to set up counters—little traps—on the outside, with left hooks. For Jones, the key will be "to go to the body of the thirty-eight-year-old to negate his ring savvy."

The first round: Mike is hesitant, whether because he's wary of Sanders's skills or once again using Vaughn Jackson's highly unconventional—and maybe even counterproductive—strategy of "hiding power." Mike lands a right to the body and snaps a hard jab into Sanders's face.

"He could be a world-class fighter," Kenny says.

"I love his dimensions, the body on him," Atlas responds. "I like his pure talent. Fast hands. Good puncher."

Sanders pops Mike with two jabs.

Mike "doesn't want to rush into anything," Teddy says. "He wants to see what [Sanders] has."

Mike raises his gloves in front of his face, peering for holes in his opponent's defense. He triple jabs Sanders but barely touches him, then lunges for Sanders's body with a right hand but can't land flush.

"The question is," Atlas says, "is the prospect Jones a step up? I think he is."

With fifty seconds left, Mike wings a left hook from his waist that smashes Sanders's face, then throws a right to the body and another left hook—a three-punch combo. Sanders bounces away, circling clockwise.

Mike throws a right uppercut into Sanders's body and a double left hook to his shoulder. As the bell rings, Mike lands a few jabs, and Sanders returns a few weak shots.

All in all, a relatively quiet first round, but one giving Mike little reason to doubt himself and perhaps a small, but significant, feeling of confidence.

The second round begins with a surprise for Mike. If he was taking it easy in the first round, waiting to see what Sanders has, what his skill level is, what he can and can't get away with, apparently so was Sanders. For ten seconds into the second round, Sanders sneaks a jab, under Mike's guard, to his sternum and follows it with an overhand right to the jaw—a very old-school move designed to hurt the fighter low and force him to drop his hands and expose his face. Mission accomplished. Instead of slipping the second punch to the side, Mike makes the amateur mistake of pulling straight back. He launches a left counter, but it's too late—Sanders has already vacated the area. *Silky.*

Sanders is crouching now, looking for angles, appearing more offensive minded. Mike's arms flail uselessly—pumping double jabs into Sanders's raised gloves, a tight defense.

Sanders stretches to reach Mike with his left jab, and Mike leaps back and to his right, leaving Sanders falling forward on air—a nice defensive maneuver from Mike.

The two fighters clinch, and Mike flings his left hook seemingly out of nowhere into Sanders's chin. Sanders looks shocked—he hadn't thought, in such a smothered position, that Jones could extend his arm and hook for such power, but he has, and Sanders has flown back a few feet.

"Oooh," the crowd gasps. The ref steps in and warns Mike to raise his punches above the belt. The crowd boos. Mike throws a hook-uppercut-hook combo, but Sanders blocks most of it with his gloves.

"He comes up with a wicked hook to the head," Brian Kenny says.

"Dangerous combination," Atlas says. "Speed with power."

"Sanders making him miss," Kenny says, "by just a hair."

Mike seems to be gaining momentum, picking up speed. He throws a double left jab, then a hook, and then a right. It rocks Sanders back, toward the canvas, an inch. But a valuable inch. So far, Mike has landed nineteen of his fifty-six shots, while Sanders has landed only four of fifteen.

Mike seems calm and attentive to detail and not at all hurried or harried or overcome by the moment. And just then, when he seems about to settle into one of those grooves that can change a fight, that give a man ownership over the proceedings, Sanders, using another silky, Ali-esque move, launches a first punch that's not the conventional jab but rather a straight right hand. He leads with his power. And it lands, flush, right into Mike's oblivious face.

Ding-ding.

"Mike Jones is being tested," Brian Kenny says. "What we wanted to see in this fight."

Russell Peltz, the promoter, screams from his ringside seat. "C'mon, Mike! You're throwing one at a time!"

Round three: Mike sprints from his corner at the bell, eager to atone, at the very least in the judges' minds, for the blows he took at the end of the previous stanza. But his eagerness isn't equaled in accuracy—he double jabs, but neither comes close to landing. There's a sense that the tide is turning. With 2:13 left in the round, Mike has landed only two more punches since the stats were last tabulated—to Sanders's six.

And here he comes: Sanders shoots a jab between Mike's raised gloves. Sanders crouches really low, trying to wade in under Mike's seventy-two-inch arms. Sanders jabs, uppercuts to the body, and then turns the punches over into hooks to the head. Mike bum-rushes him to retaliate, but it's a foolish rush, not one underpinned with any planning, just aggression, and again, silky Sanders takes a step back and nails Mike with a long overhand right, a punch that lands on Mike's skull with an echoing thud. Sanders notices the damage—he leaps forward to capitalize on it, hitting Mike with an uppercut, then a hook as Mike staggers backward—a movement Mike has never involuntarily made in the professional ring since turning pro three years earlier. Worse, Mike isn't properly defending himself in the retreat—once again he's pulling straight back, once again his hands are too low. Sanders pops another jab and whips his arms into Mike's cut abdomen. It looks as if Mike, having never been put on the defensive in a fight, has no idea how that role works—the star who never learned the role of second-fiddle. Again Mike tries to compensate for these received blows with unthinking aggression. He counters with a comet of a left hook—a scything left hook, but it's too big a punch, too wide, too premeditated, and Sanders merely ducks. Easy-breezy. And now Mike is falling off-balance because his large punch, far from landing, has carried him forward into nothing but air.

Finally, with one minute to go, Mike launches his greatest weapon—a weapon he almost invariably keeps tucked away in his arsenal during fights for the simple reason that it requires so much room and space to enact that it's almost impossible to get off in the midst of a heated volley. It's his long, arching overhand right—the monster punch—the one that catapults forward, that travels 180 degrees.

Yet Sanders ducks it, watching it whiz by his face like a bullet in *The Matrix*.

On the TV: "Sanders just able to stay out of the danger zone."

Twenty seconds to go: Sanders tries to press his advantage. He leans in to throw yet another lead right hand. But as he bends on his knees to get leverage, Mike pivots in under Sanders's guard and torques his own right hand right into Sanders's gut. Sanders grimaces—looks queasy.

On TV: "Good body shot!"

Ding-ding.

Between rounds, Vaughn, calm but determined, looks Mike in the eyes. "Alright, Mike. Time to step it up."

On TV, Teddy Atlas has Sanders winning the fight two rounds to one, because the veteran is "using some of that ring savvy."

And maybe Sanders hears him from his corner because when he comes out for the fourth, he's bobbing and weaving and popping hard jabs into Mike's face at unexpected moments—a jarring, unpredictable, violent pitter-patter.

And yet Mike really does believe—having never lost—that these roadblocks, however unfamiliar, are only that. Little blocks on the way to his victory. He still has his power, and if he can land the monster punch, even just one, this fight will turn around immediately. And then he does—maybe not the hardest shot, but his first clean overhand right, his first clean left hook, and, at the round's final bell, two break-your-nose jabs.

Teddy Atlas now has the fight a 2–2 tie.

And that's how it goes in the fifth—the fight is a back-and-forth affair. Mike is no doubt stronger, faster, and an all-around greater monster waiting to unleash. But if he's waiting to unleash, if he's contained, then he's effectively no better than Sanders, whose movement in and out of the pocket, whose constant turning, whose pure technical boxing ability—sliding away from Mike's power, under his punches, around them, returning fire always with quick little shots, cute bursts of punk—renders him even with the prospect, still alive, and quite possibly dangerous. Mike throws a hard one, Silky slips it, and the next thing you know Silky's glove is all up in Mike's face, his cheeks rippling backward.

"Sanders nailed Jones with that hook," Brian Kenny says.

"Using a simple formula," adds Atlas, "move a little bit in and out, keep Jones off balance."

Sanders snaps jabs, Jones returns his own, and Sanders's face begins turning red, as if blush were being applied to it. Mike lands two sizzling jabs—his long arm has a whipping effect when it suddenly appears, almost out of nowhere, to lash Sanders's cheeks.

"All night long with those jabs," Peltz yells from his seat. "All night."

"A little abrasion under the right eye of Sanders," Atlas notes. And it's indicative of the round's ultimate damage—the back and forth has yielded better, harder results for Mike, who has landed twenty-eight punches in the round to Sanders's ten.

Ding-ding.

In the corner, Sanders's trainer says, "Listen, stay busy when you're in front of him. Stay busy, and you won't ever get hit. He's tiring down now. You can see it."

Teddy Atlas now has it three rounds to two—or 48–47 on the ten-point must scoring system—for Jones.

Round six is Mike Jones's time. Teddy Atlas now has him winning, and everyone in the arena can sense his eminent advantages—in power, speed, and, most importantly in this brutal, unforgiving game, youth.

Mike launches the monster—what Kenny calls "a long, wicked right hand"—into Sanders's mug with blazing speed. Sanders continues to roll Mike's punches and even begins popping him with his own jab, but Sanders is huffing and grunting. With forty-seven seconds to go, Mike snaps a hard jab followed by yet another blinding right. This is the punch. Mike knows it. Peltz knows it. The TV audience knows it. *This* is the punch.

Sanders's knees buckle, dropping his body a few inches closer to the canvas. But no further. No further?

No further.

Unlike all of Mike's previous opponents, Sanders doesn't fall from his lowered position but instead rises, leveraging his crouch into a lashing left hook. "Oooh!" the crowd coos as Mike staggers six feet across the ring. "And there's the counter left hook!" Teddy Atlas yells.

Sanders backs Mike into a corner, against the post under which Vaughn, Mike's trainer, helplessly sits, watching his charge, only inches from being able to step in, but unable to. Sanders shatters Mike's left side with a hook to the body. He claws into Mike's ribs. He's like a ravenous man ripping into animal flesh. Mike looks down at Sanders with an apprehensive look, as if all he wants to know is what form the punishment will take next. But just then Sanders flails his left into Mike's gazing eyes, catching him looking, momentarily blinding him, jolting Mike's head to one side. Sanders thrashes Mike wildly now, trying to put him down for good. Mike stretches his arms to grasp Sanders's shoulders, to hold on and smother the punches. Thirty seconds left. Mike pushes down on the back of Sanders's neck. The ref moves in to separate them. Twenty seconds left.

Mike throws a perfunctory jab at Sanders's gloves. He can almost see the light now. Sanders returns the same—he is tired from all those punches. Fifteen seconds. Mike, reaching for that bell at the end of the round, throws a big right—a Hail Mary punch. Sanders sidesteps it and slaps Mike on the back of his head. Five seconds. Mike moves in, Sanders bends down, Mike hits Sanders on the small of his back—an illegal area, although Sanders is the one who offered him his back. The crowd boos Mike. The bell rings. Mike has survived. But he has also been exposed.

The rest of the fight proceeds as perhaps it should have been expected to from the start. Time and again Sanders uses his style to turn Mike around, to make him miss and then make him pay, but in the end, Mike lands the harder, more substantive shots; and though there's some nervousness about the judges' cards, there also seems to be some certainty about the result—and how little it matters. Because this was never supposed to be the ultimate fight for Mike. It was a stepping-stone before a national audience whose like or dislike of the fighter would determine his popularity, which would determine his attractiveness to HBO and Showtime. And Mike, though undoubtedly the promising, powerful one, has unwittingly fallen into the role of hapless villain in this fight. He's the one being turned and spun and out-moved by a

slick, clever thirty-eight-year-old—on the thirty-eight-year-old's birthday. He's the one being booed. The one who can't seem to transition
seamlessly between offense and defense, who has to stop one in order
to begin the other. "He's gotta learn how to intertwine both," Atlas says
during the seventh round. And in the eighth, when Mike comes out
rumbling, throwing hard shots, unsure of the judges' scorecards but
certain he needs to win over the fans, the audience actually starts cheering for him, hollering even. Maybe that's what Mike has on his side—
what he does in the eighth round, the round where he lets it all hang
loose, landing two hooks, a right, a left, and then another right. When
Sanders starts to gasp and Mike clubs him with yet another big left hook
with a minute left and the muscles in Mike's body bulge and he grits his
teeth and he throws every last bit of energy into his punches. When
Sanders grabs for Mike's waist just to hold on and keep from fainting,
and Mike wriggles out of the hold and Sanders wilts to the canvas,
though the ref calls it a slip and not a knockdown. Maybe that's the
takeaway from the fight—not his defensive lapses or his lack of continu-
ity or his having been occasionally outthought, but the sheer exuber-
ance of the uppercut he lands with ten seconds to go. And on national
TV, Germaine "Silky" Sanders's face is covered in pinkish lumps and
mounds and his processed hair sticks straight up like Alfalfa's.

Maybe.

❋ ❋ ❋

When the final bell rings, Peltz asks one of the ringside writers how
he has scored it. He flashes six fingers and then two and mouths the
word "Mike."

During the commercial break before the decision, Sanders jumps
onto the ropes on all four sides of the ring, soliciting big cheers from the
crowd. Then he runs to my side of the ring. "Hey, Russell!" he shouts at
Peltz. "Pretty good for a thirty-eight-year-old, huh?"

Mike sees the crowd cheering his opponent. He scrunches his face,
as if worried that the crowd has a say in judging the winner. He raises
his arms to promote his cause. But weakly, without full extension and
not for very long. He looks down at his shoes, not at the people. They
barely clap.

Sanders does tell Jim, Mike's manager: "Excellent fighter, baby."

Sanders's trainer complains about the wait. He says something about
a "Pennsylvania" or "Philadelphia decision," but I can't quite hear. In

reality, the announcer is waiting for ESPN to cue him through his beige earpiece, which looks like a hearing aid attached to a telephone cord.

The final numbers: Mike landed 210 of 628 punches and Sanders landed 100 out of 273. Teddy Atlas scored it 77–75 for Mike.

And then the ring announcer Mike Williams grabs the microphone.

"After eight rounds of action, we go to the judges' scorecards. Julie Lederman, Ed Weisfeld, and Eddie Scunzio all score the bout exactly the same at 78–74 for the winner by unanimous decision and still undefeated . . . Mike Jones!"

The ESPN cameras try to zero in on Mike's face, but he avoids the lens, looking dismayed.

✿ ✿ ✿

In the dressing room afterward, Peltz visits Mike, and when he leaves, I enter. The dressing room is no more than a corner of the hotel conference room. Mike slumps in a chair in the middle of the room, sucking an orange. To the side, Doc and Jim pack up. "Pretty good for a guy with no sparring," I say, offering him my hand. He takes it limply and barely looks up. "That's what I was just telling him," Vaughn says, like a father trying to rouse his son. Mike doesn't budge. I say something to Vaughn about scraping off rust for a couple rounds, about it being a big step up. He doesn't say much. I nod at Doc and Jim, and Doc raises his hand to me and half-smiles. He, a manager, appears pleased. I walk to the door and turn back.

The winner sits hunched over his orange, still sucking it dry. He looks utterly, forebodingly, disconsolate.

✿ ✿ ✿

I was walking through a store in Philadelphia's 30th Street Station in January of 2009 when I received the call from one of his children. Mr. Pat had passed away a few days earlier. As per his wishes, he had been immediately cremated, and no service had been held.

We had all known this moment was coming. I had already felt the punch to the gut, had already cried, had already said what I knew would be my final words to him. All that remained, in that moment, was this sense that a period of my own life had just ended. And then I got on the train I was scheduled to take, from Philadelphia back to New York.

EPILOGUE

It was a sunny spring day. The ceremony was held in a catering hall in a kind of no-man's-land in Philadelphia—an area in the northern part of the city filled with big empty lots and big warehouses and big-box stores. The ceremony felt a little like the wedding of a hometown kid—some working-class guy who never left Philly, who was marrying his high school sweetheart, and whose friends were the same friends he had had as a boy. It was that kind of place. The ceiling was lit with blue mood lights; the bar served beer.

It was the 2008 ceremony for the Pennsylvania Boxing Hall of Fame, and Meldrick Taylor was being inducted.

The tables were filled with all the characters who are associated with the local fight game: Russell Peltz, the promoter; John DiSanto, the enthusiast behind PhillyBoxingHistory.com; and tons of fighters, old and new. The old ones were easily distinguished as such. Their faces were creased, their shoulders slumped, and some even seemed bedraggled. Matthew Saad Muhammad, the man previously known as Matthew Franklin, the fighter who was left to die on the highway as a child, and rescued by nuns, and taught the pugilistic game by Mr. Pat many decades earlier in a barebones gym, walked around the ceremony in a daze, his tattered white button-down shirt stained by what appeared to be wine. Several years later, I would find out he was suffering from amyotrophic lateral sclerosis—likely related to his past brawling—and soon after, he would suffer a stroke and pass away.

But there was regality in Saad Muhammad's mein that day. Like all the fighters there, he wasn't secluded from the fans by a group of handlers, and he didn't think of himself as anything other than a fan in a way. Yes, this ceremony was not only about letting a new group of heroes into the imaginary hall that had been created for them, but also about once again bringing the fighters together with the aficionados who had given their bruising meaning, whose raised voices and strong applause had ennobled the struggle between the ropes as something more than an animalistic death match. Romano's Catering Hall in North Philly was filled that day with as many fight fans as fighters, and they talked and mingled, and even the boxers who seemed bent by time or loss or poverty were as happy and bright faced to recall the past as the most effervescent up-and-comers.

I didn't get to speak to Saad Muhammad, but I did talk to some of Mr. Pat's other old charges. Buster Drayton, the 1980s 154-pound champ, who had begun his career, like so many others, under Mr. Pat's tutelage before leaving for a more prominent coach, recalled Mr. Pat as a solid teacher of fundamentals. "Yeah, I remember Pat," he said. "He always used to yell, 'Don't sit on the ropes!'" I told him Mr. Pat would probably love to hear from him, and he said he would give him a call, but I don't think he did before the end.

Tim Witherspoon was there. The former heavyweight champion, whose lawsuit against Don King over money withheld from him was a landmark in the struggle to uproot King from the heavyweight division and rid it of his influence, sat at a table and took comments from fans. I approached him and told him I thought he had beaten Larry Holmes in their title fight in the early '80s. He looked me up and down and laughed and said I was too young to have seen that fight, and I told him I had watched it on video and that it didn't matter how old I was. I remembered all the same.

But the highlight, of course, the reason we were all there, was the fighters being honored. We wanted to bestow a further recognition on the men whose work had moved us so many years earlier. Harold Johnson, one of the greatest light-heavyweights of all time, who had been a champion and a link in the Philly tradition in the 1950s and '60s, was honored for his lifetime achievement. He looked like an old man at times during the events—his eyes sometimes seemed closed—but he was nattily attired, and at times, he sprang to life like the bell was about to ring on his very first fight. In the men's room, which I happened to use at the same time as he did, he was full of humor. He tried to leave at the same time as someone else, then pulled back and opened the door for this fan. "Thank you," the guy said. "Congratulations on the award."

"I got five girls waiting for me downstairs," Harold Johnson said.

The fan asked him to sign a red boxing glove. He signed "Harold" and then said that was all he could do. The fan's friend pulled out another glove that Johnson had signed five years earlier and showed it to him. Johnson scribbled his last name now, copying his own signature.

"Perfect," the fan said.

When they announced Johnson to the crowd in the ballroom, he stood up from his chair—against the advice of everyone at his table—and began shadowboxing vigorously. The crowd erupted. He would not go gently.

Meldrick Taylor was nearly the last man to take the podium. He, too, was well dressed, wearing a green velvet sport coat that brought out the rich chocolaty complexion of his skin. The dreadlocks he had worn during his last fights in small arenas before hundreds of fans in the middle of nowhere were shaved off, and his head was a polished dome. He had a Band-Aid across the top of his scalp, but no one asked why. Primarily, the impression you got of him was of a still strong man who had put on a bit of weight after his playing days. His face was a bit bloated—it faded into his shirt collar—and his torso and arms really filled out the jacket. Since approaching his family for my chapter on him—and being told, in response to a letter I had sent and several phone calls—that he would not speak to me, I had not made any additional efforts in the intervening year and a half to talk to him. I wanted now to explain to him that I was the guy who had called and that I was not out to demonize him and that I just wanted to tell his story.

Before I could do that, though, I was taken in by the whirligig of his life. I walked over to his table, and a man who had something of an off-putting salesmanship about him introduced himself to me as Meldrick's new agent. He told me they had met six months earlier after he had been told Meldrick was on drugs and he had gone to investigate it for himself. He had decided that Meldrick was clean and that he should help him finally justify his career to the world. He told me about a new book Meldrick had written without a ghostwriter—*Two Seconds from Glory*. I tried to tell him that I, too, had written about Meldrick, but it was lost in the man's sales pitch. I turned away and hurriedly told Meldrick how heartbreaking his life had been to me, how much his career saddened me, how hard I rooted for him. He thanked me for all that in the slurry gibberish that is his only form of expression now. I didn't want to ask him to repeat himself, and the truth is, the medium really was the message when he spoke, and the slurring was all I needed to hear to understand. I asked him to pose for a picture with me—I didn't have a camera, but I gave someone my cell phone to use—and I still have that picture, grainy and dark as it is, of me standing over this short, chubby man with a Band-Aid on his head and his fists raised.

The only words anyone could really make out of his acceptance speech were "two seconds."

A fan approached Meldrick in an untucked shirt and a wrinkled tux and offered him a business card for a management company and asked whether he'd sign a boxing glove with his name. He then slipped Meldrick $100. Meldrick, bewildered, thought the guy wanted the bill signed and put the point of the Sharpie on it. No, the guy said. The bill is for you. Meldrick smiled and nodded and put the bill in the inside left pocket of his jacket.

I only heard him speak clearly and assuredly once. I asked him, "What do you think about at an event like this?"

He said, "Family."

I asked him, "Does it make you want to go back and box again?"

And he said, "I used to. . . . I'm past that stage."

He said he currently works as a personal trainer.

＊ ＊ ＊

Many of the city's great boxing venues closed. Joe Frazier's Gym, on North Broad Street by an Amtrak station that is rarely used now, was shuttered in April 2008, forty years after opening. Frazier had trained there himself during his career, and more recently, a boy named Mike Jones had been brought there by his father to learn the fight game. Of course, Mike had left for other trainers and other gyms as he had started to rise, because he had felt Frazier was teaching him a one-dimensional pounding style to which he wasn't suited. "I try to help the young guys and they keep walking away," Frazier told the *New York Post* that month. He had just had a major surgery on his spine and had been living meagerly in the back of the gym. There were reports that he was in bad financial straits; his gym had been sued by the city for not paying its taxes. He died three and a half years later of liver cancer at the age of sixty-seven. His gym was by then a furniture and bedding outlet store.

The Blue Horizon didn't make it, either. Vernoca Michael owed taxes on the former Moose lodge that *Ring Magazine* had named the best place in the world to watch a fight. The renovations she had long planned had never quite materialized, and the public monies she had counted on had never been provided. Its last fight was June 4, 2010. The city plans to turn it into a hotel and restaurant.

The New Alhambra, the warehouse-turned-arena in South Philly, just below I-95, quickly lost its luster. Russell Peltz and Joe Hand didn't see eye-to-eye with the arena's new management team; and in 2009, Peltz moved his fights back to the Blue Horizon, where he had first promoted a show thirty years earlier. But the Blue Horizon kept running afoul of the city's Licenses and Inspections committee and it had its tax woes, and Peltz moved most of his bouts to local casinos in the suburbs and Atlantic City, where he now operates. The New Alhambra's name was changed several times—to the Arena and the Asylum. A few fights are held there now each year, but almost none is significant for Philly, and the excitement about the place has entirely dissipated.

The Joe Hand Boxing Gym, where Teon and Mike trained while their careers took off, moved out of the New Alhambra/Arena in South Philly to a site in Northern Liberties—a neighborhood where many old warehouses have been repurposed into lofts and sleek offices, becoming Philly's first hipster enclave. Peter Papaleo—the man known as Petey Pop—continued to manage the gym there as he had since it opened until he died in March of 2013 at the age of sixty-eight. The headline of his newspaper obituary read, "Everybody's best friend."[1]

* * *

Russell Peltz, the promoter who had kept Philly boxing alive from the late 1960s, when he staged his first fight at the Blue Horizon as a twenty-two-year-old Temple grad, and the man who had believed in Teon and Mike enough to sign them to their first promotional contracts forty years later, the man who had taken the torch from the great promoters before him, who had carried on the tradition of Mugsy Taylor and Johny Burns, finally mentored and trained his own successor—the next in line for the Philly fight throne. Her name was Brittany Rogers, but her nickname, propagated through the e-mails she sent out to local aficionados on the state of the fight game, was "Bam." A blonde whom one website said "looks like a Hollywood starlet," she had approached Peltz while still a senior at Temple to intern at his office, having had a special passion for the fight game since her father had installed a punching bag in the house when she was thirteen. Peltz saw a lot of himself in her—in her precociousness and knowledge and even her Temple background. She seemed right for him in a way that other people hadn't. So he took her on as an intern in 2011, and from that point on, she could be seen around the ring on fight night making sure all the fighters were properly taken care of, the tickets were distributed, the officials were in place. On September 30, 2011, she staged the very first promotional card of her own. It was at the Armory in Northeast Philadelphia, where Teon had once fought sluggishly while sick, and the main event featured a fighter she had become friends with in the fight world. He won easily, and she donated some of the money she made to charity. Her next "BAM on Boxing" e-mail ended with her saying, "This was just the beginning. I want people to know that I am here to stay!"

* * *

Teon Kennedy beat someone to death in the ring, and Mike Jones became famous. Those are the short stories. The longer stories are more complicated—and more similar than that summary would lead you to believe.

The truth about Teon was that, as his career progressed, he became more and more like Meldrick Taylor. He never had Meldrick's speed, but his skill he had in spades—hence his nickname, "The Technician"— and yet just as Meldrick had been prone to abandon his skill and enter into exchanges with opponents, brawl with them, make it about heart and grit and a city's pride, well, Teon did just the same. He fought a series of tough but technically limited Hispanic fighters whom he could have jabbed and turned his way to solid decisions but instead, time and again, squared up to them, leaned into their bellies, and threw powerhouse rights and lefts that left him open to counters. He kept winning, running up his record to 13–0–1 (the one draw alone speaks to Teon's unnecessary brawling), but his face after each fight was a bloody and bruised mess—the welts on his cheeks like the shiny sphere of a bowling ball—and you just knew something awful, something passing horrid, would happen. And it did.

On November 20, 2009, he fought Francisco "Paco" Rodriguez, yet another game Hispanic fighter, this one from Chicago. The bout was in the Blue Horizon, where Russell Peltz was temporarily promoting fights after having left the New Alhambra.

Six years earlier, Teon and Rodriguez had fought a tough bout in the amateurs, and Rodriguez had been handed the decision. Since that time, Rodriguez had only improved. He had won a National Golden Gloves title, just like Teon had, and he had run his record to 14–2, with eight knockouts. The matchup was one in which Teon absolutely could not afford to engage any more than he had to—one in which war would erupt if he attacked straightforwardly.

That's what happened.

Not at first, not really. Teon played the counterpuncher, waiting for Rodriguez to lunge forward and then launching quick shots to stun his opponent. Rodriguez received a precautionary eight count in the first round after seeming to fall. Later, Rodriguez pounded Teon's body and busted up his right eye. This return fire—Rodriguez's relentless pursuit of Teon, his unwillingness to give any ground at all, no matter the punishment—is what precipitated the colossal, brutal exchanges in rounds seven and eight.

His opponent had decided that he would not relent, that he would not go down without a tremendous fight; and Teon, far from deciding to elude this sally and spare himself the pain, nodded and essentially said game on, and for the next three rounds, they traded ferocious, hellacious punches. In the tenth, the ref stopped the fight—saving Rodriguez from the sure punishment that would ensue in the following two rounds—and then it was over, and Teon was handed the TKO victory. He looked spent of every last bit of energy and will. Like after Ali–Frazier III, the Thrilla in Manilla, when Ali, though victorious, seemed almost like the loser himself, collapsing in his corner, the victor here was a drained and seemingly broken man. That was Teon. The loser, Rodriguez, though, was in even more dire shape. He actually did collapse and was strapped to a stretcher, which was carried to an ambulance, which brought him to the hospital, where he spent two days in a coma before succumbing to the blunt force brain trauma he had suffered and dying.

Hours before Rodriguez died, Teon and his handlers visited him in the hospital.

The death, as boxing deaths do, brought a new round of attention from the press, which otherwise would've taken no notice of the fight or of Teon, whose psychological well-being, in the wake of this unintentional killing, was solicited, whose welfare was brooded over, whose future seemed scary and cloudy and full of ghosts. The press also told the amazing story of Rodriguez and his family's ultimate generosity, after all of the deceased fighter's organs were donated to sick individuals around the country. His death, through these donations, really did save many people, and the whole arrangement was bizarre and somewhat redemptive and ultimately beautiful, if also ultimately tragic.

But boxing had so long ago ceased to occupy a prime spot in the American consciousness that once the pieces on ESPN's website were moved to the bottom of the page and once Teon had resumed fighting again, the story lost its legs and was forgotten. As for Teon, he insisted to his management team and to the press that he was fine, that this was what boxing could possibly be about and although he felt bad, he didn't focus on the outcome but the process. It was probably the truth. Teon had always been a quiet, inexpressive, almost meditatively calm man. And a bit of a street tough.

Against Alejandro Lopez, another tough Hispanic, another man who Teon should've used skills to defeat, Teon finally lost on August 13, 2011. Observers of the fight couldn't understand what they were seeing. This was not a case of Teon choosing the wrong tactics, of manning up and being too Philly for his own good. This was a case of fatigue, of exhaustion, of emptiness. The Teon we saw on the canvas that night was not the Teon we had fawned over when he debuted in 2007, nor the Teon whose ferocity had sent a man prematurely to his grave. This was an "after" Teon, a spent Teon, a Teon whose wars had caught up with him and lent his muscles the kind of rust and torpor most commonly associated with heavyweights in their sixties. This was Teon in 2011. He was only twenty-five.

But there is more to Teon's story. He was tired out then not only by his wars in the ring, but likely, too, by his exposure to those outside of them in the Philly street world. On May 30, 2011, a fellow twenty-four year old accused Teon of shooting him multiple times with a small caliber gun during a fight. Teon was charged with attempted murder, aggravated assault, conspiracy to commit murder, carrying firearms in public, possession of an instrument of crime, simple assault, and reck-

less endangerment of another person. His boxing handlers said it was all
a mistake—a street thing—that the victim was accusing Teon even
though he knew someone else had done it. But Teon spent two weeks
in jail on very high bail before being released, before Dante Wideman
of North Philadelphia changed his story and said someone else had
done it. "He was present," Teon's attorney said of the shooting, "but he
was not the shooter."

* * *

Mike Jones became famous, yes, but not in a way that would suggest
his end was so divergent from Teon's or any other Philly boxer's. He
kept rising in the ranks, but Russell Peltz, his promoter, was frozen out
from the big fights by the bigger promoters; and so, against his word—
he had always sworn he would keep Mike all to himself—he finally sold
a stake in the fighter to Bob Arum's Top Rank promotional company,
which had deals with channels like HBO and Showtime and could finally give Mike some exposure on a bigger stage. Mike's main fight on
HBO was on the undercard of a pay-per-view match against Jesus Soto-
Karass, yet another solid if unspectacular, come-forward, brawling Hispanic fighter (notice the trend here; the old-school black fighters Philly
had so long produced were now a rarity) who was supposed to be a
stepping-stone for Mike on his way to bouts against the top welterweights in the world (the Andre Bertos, the Tim Bradleys, the Victor
Ortizes). He was ranked as the top contender for the title by some
sanctioning bodies—not that their word meant anything, really—but
the real rise in public consciousness came from the fan chatter on the
Internet, which was heated and hyperbolic and polarized. Some said
Mike was the second coming of Thomas Hearns—that he was the next
long, freakishly athletic welterweight who'd dominate the division and
KO all comers—and some said that he was callow and flawed and
overhyped. The truth is, they were probably both right. Mike was indeed incredibly strong and tall and dedicated (his routine consisted not
only of boxing workouts but also of swimming exercises and nonstop
strength training), and the power he wielded in his hands was enough to
take out the very best fighter in the world. But he had issues marshaling
that power and being a boxer, which takes more than just athleticism.
His punches were wide and looping and took a long time to reach their
targets. He was easy pickings for a fighter with a straight counterpunch
that could be shot between his wide arms. He also seemed to need a lot

of room to throw his punches—he was unable to shorten them in order to fight in close—and he had absolutely no fluidity: he could not transition easily from offense to defense or vice versa, so as soon as his opponent began throwing punches, he went into something of a shell (he *was* good at picking off punches with his gloves) and couldn't return fire until his opponent tired out.

✽ ✽ ✽

ESPN debuted a new set for its *Friday Night Fights* series in 2012. Behind the anchor's desk was a row of photos of former fighters. Mysteriously—though fittingly—one face stood out from the rest. It was the face hovering above the anchor each time the camera turned to him. He had been in large part forgotten, but due to the work of a driven fan—perhaps someone who understood what had happened to the boxer after the cameras had been turned off, after the checks stopped coming, when he was left to his punch-drunk self to roam the streets of Philadelphia in search of food and shelter—he was now young and snarling again and shown on every screen tuned to the broadcast in the country. He was, in fact, now the face of the country's most prominent weekly boxing show.

It was Jimmy Young.

✽ ✽ ✽

Mike and Teon finally fought for world titles in Las Vegas on June 9, 2012, on the undercard of a Manny Pacquiao fight at the MGM Grand. Manny Pacquiao would lose his title that night in a decision that instantly would be deemed controversial and suspicious and that yielded—even in the mainstream media—the renewed proclamation that boxing was officially dead. But before all that, before most of the glitterati had entered the arena at the MGM Grand, when inside were only the diehards, and Doc and Jim, the old Philly managers, and Russell Peltz, the only old Philly promoter, Teon and Mike entered the ring in the first two bouts of the televised pay-per-view card.

It had been a crazy weekend in Vegas. The Electric Daisy Carnival, a dance music festival held on the infield of Vegas's speedway, had attracted thousands of glow stick–wearing, neon tube sock–bedecked twenty-somethings. There were, of course, the party drugs. The roads leading out to the speedway were blocked with three hours' worth of bumper-to-bumper traffic. On the strip itself, there were the tourists

and the athletes. Inside the Cosmopolitan, Lakers center Andrew By-
num could be seen leaning his massive frame over a craps table that
came up to his thighs, rolling dice. In the MGM, the computer system
temporarily shut down, and guests waited three hours to check in—a
snafu the hotel would rectify later by offering guests a free night.

It was a total free-for-all in the best Vegas tradition. And at its center, in a place where they needed quiet before their greatest moments,
there were Mike and Teon.

The Philly people came down. And privately, the cognoscenti worried. Worried because Teon's brawling would leave him ripe to be
picked apart by the highly skilled Cuban fighter he'd be facing: Guillermo Rigondeaux, a junior featherweight boxer who had amassed a 395–8
record in his native country before defecting and turning pro (Cuba
bans professional sports). Nicknamed "The Jackal," Rigondeaux was
known for his perfectly balanced southpaw stance, a stance from which
he could knock a man down with just a twist of his body, a reflex. When
Dan Rafael, the ESPN boxing writer, first found out about the match,
he texted Russell Peltz: "Poor Teon." The Philly people thought Teon
was in for it, too, unless he could return to his old technical style—and
even then, it might not be enough. Privately, there were concerns that
his trainer, Smokin' Wade Hinnant, wasn't calculating or knowledge-
able enough to teach Teon what he needed.

Mike was supposed to win. He was facing the aging Randall Bailey, a
thirty-seven-year-old power puncher whose best days had come in the
140-pound division ten years earlier, when he had held a world title.
Now he was facing the much-larger Mike for a welterweight title. They
say power is the last thing a fighter loses, so Mike would still need to be
wary of that one big punch. But if he could stick and move, could land
combinations from a distance, he wouldn't have a problem, the Philly
crowd thought—though here, too, there were reservations. Privately,
Mike's supporters wondered just how good he could be—how much of
a better game he'd have—if he were training with a more accomplished
teacher—someone like Na'azim Richardson, who had worked with Bernard Hopkins and Shane Mosley and had learned his craft from the
even more legendary Philly trainer Bouie Fisher.

Maybe it was supposed to happen this way. Teon fought the perfect
fight—he didn't come to brawl, didn't leave himself open, didn't swing
wide. But his opponent was just too good. Rigo, as they called him,

found every hole with quick punches and knocked Teon down once in rounds one, four, and five, and twice in round two. After the first knockdown, his supporters in the arena's upper deck screamed, "Use your jab, T!" and "Take your time!" After the second knockdown, they shouted, "Put it together, T! Pick your spots!" None of the punches badly hurt Teon—he snapped back up after all of them, alert, but with the resigned look of a man who knows he's simply being outclassed. The ref waved off the fight in the fifth round—it was too much of a mismatch to continue. It was an odd, sad truth.

Teon finally fought the smart, skillful, technical fight that he was supposed to—that he was known for—and it simply wasn't good enough. There was someone better.

Mike fought the fight he was supposed to also. He tried to load up on his punches, especially the left hook he had used to knock out so many fighters at the start of his career. But he also had the terrible habit of stepping away from Bailey each time he had an advantage, as if he wasn't sure what to do next, as if he had to think in the ring. The well-trained fighter, the inveterate one, acts on reflex, but Mike still looked unsure, hesitant, not in retreat, because he was winning the whole fight, scoring with outside shots, doing minor damage (though so little that the crowd booed vociferously after each round) but in uncertainty. And you had to wonder how someone so prodigiously gifted—with his height of six feet and wingspan of seventy-two inches, a veritable specimen for the 147-pound division—could make so little use of his talents. You wanted to blame his trainer, his initial upbringing in Joe Frazier's Gym, anything to explain this boring, ugly fight he was staging. But Mike was winning, at least. He at least had that.

Until the eleventh round, when, after having scored a flash knockdown at the end of the previous frame, Randall Bailey launched a patented uppercut, having noticed Mike leaning forward, and sent our boy, the father of two, the welterweight with the broad shoulders who had spent countless hours building to this very moment, sprawling half-conscious to the canvas. It was a vicious knockout. And it was over.

Neither Mike nor Teon would retire from the game after these fights. They may yet win titles; they may redeem themselves in the sport; they may build all over again to the big moment and this time seize it. You don't have to like boxing to root for them. They're not the sport. They're just people. If and when Mike and Teon reappear in the spotlight, I'll be watching.

But in a sport with increasingly fewer TV appearances, fewer stars, and almost no room for the almost-champion—the Philly fighter—they seemed, on that glittery night, consigned, too appropriately, to the periphery of a game to which they had devoted their lives but that had never—not once—guaranteed them anything in return.

❂ ❂ ❂

In the month following his title fight, Mike Jones stopped corresponding with his managers and with his copromoter Russell Peltz, the men who had conveyed him through the tough world of Philly club boxing and onto the Vegas stage on which he had been knocked out. Though Peltz's contract ostensibly called for him to remain Jones's promoter through at least 2015, Jones brought in a lawyer to review the contract—a lawyer who requested Peltz speak only with him and not with his fighter. The fighter himself, who had picked up a too-tough style in Joe Frazier's gym and had never thereafter attained real boxing fluidity, left his trainers in Philadelphia and started working out in Las Vegas with Floyd Mayweather Sr., the outspoken former trainer of and father of Floyd Mayweather Jr., the world's most technical fighter, and the man Teon had first wanted to emulate when he turned professional.

Meanwhile, a Philly fighter who had arguably flown under the radar—a 23–0 junior welterweight who, unlike Mike and Teon, had not come up through the Philly club system exclusively, but in venues all over the country under a big national promoter, Danny "Swift" Garcia—knocked out British champion Amir Khan in a major upset on HBO. Khan, a 7–1 favorite, had all the advantages of superior natural talent, greater support from boxing's movers and shakers, including the TV execs, and a more highly touted team of trainers and managers. And he strafed Garcia with one precision shot after another for two straight rounds in a fight Garcia had taken on short notice. But none of that mattered when Garcia, with one reflexive overturning of his left arm, knocked Khan down with a hook in the third round and pummeled him in the fourth until the ref wouldn't let it continue.

Afterward, Garcia, all of twenty-four years old, explained his victory to the media. "I'm a Philadelphia fighter in the truest sense," he said. "I never quit. I give blood, sweat, and tears inside the ring and I'm never going to stop working."

Philadelphia finally had its champion—though not necessarily in the person it had been eyeing from the beginning. But in a way it had always been like that—in recent decades, middleweight Bernard Hopkins and cruiserweight Steve Cunningham had boxed brilliantly before garnering the attention they deserved: the fighters the city had its eyes on weren't the ones who turned out. Maybe because the city had their eyes on them.

But that was all a month later anyway, and Danny "Swift" Garcia's story is only beginning.

❊ ❊ ❊

In the harsh Vegas sun on the morning after, the man who beat Teon Kennedy for the world title, small thirty-one-year-old Guillermo Rigondeaux, all of five feet four inches and 122 pounds, the man who had fled Cuba for a shot at a world title, loaded into a shuttle van for the ride to the airport. He was with his trainer and a few others, but his was a small, decidedly low-key group, and the only sign of their success the previous night was the great big grins on their faces. Rigo, especially, with his high, round cheeks, had an especially endearing smile. He was dressed in Gucci. The driver of the shuttle, as she pulled out of the driveway of the hotel, asked the bus occupants, "Did everyone enjoy the fights?" More smiles from Rigo's group, and sitting in the front row, I asked them who they would like to fight next.

The only photo I have of Mr. Pat—a photocopied scrap of paper showing him with a 1976 amateur boxing team from Harrowgate Gym. Mr. Pat is the trainer on the far right, in the second row, his hands on a young boxer's shoulders, his head partly covered by the paper folding in on itself. Courtesy of William Patterson (Mr. Pat).

✿ ✿ ✿

So in the end, what were Mr. Pat and I, this man who appeared as I began college and was gone by the end? Were we friends? Of course, in a way. I think we both felt appreciated by the other even if there was almost always some sort of gap between us. Mr. Pat used to say, "This kid, he must not have any friends on campus if he keeps visiting me." And then, just as I'd begin to protest, he'd set the hours on my visits, tell me when I should come and when he'd be busy (he claimed to entertain ladies in his apartment at night, and from the way women greeted him on the street, I didn't doubt it). We watched some TV together—we shared a love for *The Simpsons*—but as always, we weren't coming at the subject from the same place. Watching an episode where Homer gives up alcohol, Mr. Pat muttered that the barflies in Moe's Tavern were "drunks," with the disgusted look of a reformed addict.

There were small gifts. He let me take his entire collection of boxing newspaper clippings and photos (albeit in two separate piles, not all at once) to the university library for photocopying. I gave him a landline phone I wasn't using, an extra computer mouse when his broke (he played games on an old PC), and a book ranking the top 100 boxers for his birthday (he disagreed with the book's putting Sugar Ray Robinson ahead of Joe Louis, because to him, Joe Louis's pure fundamentals, his 1-2, were the essence of boxing).

Was he a mentor? He had led his life, and I was beginning one, but I don't know that his lessons had any bearing on what I was planning to do. His affairs, his family history of violence, his drinking—I never felt I learned from him how to live (or how not to), and I'm not sure he wouldn't have gone back and made the same mistakes again himself. And that was just as well. His gift was opening me up to the wider Philly boxing world, unveiling an entire community I never would have noticed at all. He set in motion my trips to promoters' offices and boxers' gyms. The world he introduced me to was to be found outside his apartment. And I think he agreed. He was never totally comfortable with the idea of my making him a character.

There were promises we made to each other. I told him I was going to invite him to my wedding one day, and he said he wouldn't have something to wear, and I told him not to worry, I'd make sure he did. He said he'd take me up on that. That was an exchange we had outside his brownstone, literally as I was walking away from the front steps. We needed that physical distance—most of the personal things we said to each other were said outside, not in his small, dark living room.

Mr. Pat gave me of his time. There's drama in time—it's the only thing that imparts drama. Knowing you only have an hour here or there, twelve rounds in which to win a fight, a single life span to do what you set out to do. Friend, mentor, someone whose life intersected with mine—the title doesn't mean anything. Those moments of intersection—that's what counts. They happened, and this was the result. And that's all I can say about it. And it's enough.

NOTES

I used notes when the information seemed to require citation—that is, when it wasn't a direct product of an interview I had personally conducted or when it was so obscure and out of the public record that more clarification and proof were required.

The remainder of the facts and stories in this book—the uncited majority—derives from my interviews and viewing of fights. The bouts that occurred before I was born I watched on DVD or DVR multiple times. I watched the fights in multiple speeds—several times at full speed and also at quarter speed and half speed. The idea was to see everything—not just the punches thrown at any moment, but the planning that was going into the next punch and the one after that.

I conducted interviews with the following players in the boxing world:

Boxers—Bud Anderson, Bobby Watts, Rogers Mtagwa, Chazz Witherspoon, Craig Houk, Dick Turner, Henry Milligan, Fred Jenkins, Jeff Chandler, Johnny Knight, Kenny Kidd, Joe Christy, Kitten Hayward, Mike Jones, Teon Kennedy, Germaine Sanders, Pito Cardona, Randy Neumann, Willie Torres, Charlie Sgrillo, Ernest Kennedy, Sid Adams, George Benton, and Tyrone Taylor.

Trainers—Bobby Watts, Mr. Pat, Wade Hinnant, Al Mitchell, Joey Eye, Mike Plebani, Charlie Sgrillo, Sid Adams, and George Benton.

Managers—Jim Deoria, Doc Nowicki, Jim Williams, Andy Morris, Frank Gelb, and Bret Hallenbeck.

Promoters—Russell Peltz, Don Elbaum, Lou Lucchese, and Vernoca Michael.

Club owners and gym managers—Pete Papaleo, Vernoca Michael, and Roger Artigiani.

Judges and referees—Carol Polis and Richard Steele.

Boxing PR—Bill Caplan.

Boxing writers and reporters—Bill Lyon, Larry Merchant, Tom Cushman, Tom Callahan, Thomas Hauser, Tris Dixon, Keith Mack, Bernard Fernandez, Gerald Early, Marcus Hayes, and Mark Kram Jr.

Boxing historians—Chuck Hasson and John DiSanto.

In addition to these primary players, I also interviewed the family members of current and past fighters, including the relatives of William "Manzy" Boggs, a promising junior middleweight who was gunned down in a drive-by shooting at the age of nineteen in 2006. They were willing to share his story after such a tragic loss—an incredibly generous gesture that I must acknowledge.

For general boxing information, I read several autobiographies—of Larry Holmes, George Foreman, Sugar Ray Robinson—as well as boxing reportage and creative nonfiction. *Only in America* by Jack Newfield is an incredible investigation into the way Don King ran his so-called business. *The Hardest Sport* by Hugh McIlvanney, a collection of the British writer's boxing columns, is my personal favorite boxing read. *The Boxing Companion*, edited by Denzil Batchelor, is a wonderful collection of boxing pieces by American and British writers. Gerald Early's brilliant *The Culture of Bruising* speaks of boxing in cultural terms in a unique way, as does Joyce Carol Oates's *On Boxing*.

For information on the city's history, I owe a debt to *Getting Work: Philadelphia, 1840–1950* by Walter Licht; W. E. B. Du Bois's *The Philadelphia Negro*; *Philadelphia: A 300-Year History*, the massive, wonderful history of the city published in 1982; *Philadelphia: Neighborhoods, Division, and Conflict in a Postindustrial City*, published by Temple University; *The Peoples of Philadelphia*, edited by Allen Davis and Mark Haller; and *Code of the Street*, by Elijah Anderson, who was a professor at Penn during my time there.

For background information on the possible mind-set of fighters, I consulted Ernest Becker's *The Denial of Death*, which attributes all human endeavor to a deep-seated need to deny mortality and overcome it.

I relied on old newspaper articles from the *Philadelphia Inquirer* and *Daily News*, which I obtained from microfiche and also photocopies—historian Chuck Hasson has photocopied hundreds, if not thousands, of old newspaper articles on boxing in Philadelphia.

I also used the digital archives of the *New York Times* and *Harper's* to find older articles, since their digital—and searchable—collections extend back more than one hundred years. There were a smattering of articles from other publications—the defunct *Philadelphia Bulletin* and the *Ring Magazine* were very helpful, for instance.

I'll always be indebted to the fight writers who sat ringside each card, in a den of smoke, pounding out lyrical reports on deadline. Without them, so many stories would have been lost.

INTRODUCTION

1. Richard Sandomir, *New York Times*, May 16, 2000.
2. Rich Hofmann, *Philadelphia Daily News*, January 8, 2008.
3. "Gentle Arts Claim Philadelphia Jack," *New York Times*, December 24, 1931.
4. Joe Lapointe, *New York Times*, July 13, 2005.
5. Denzil Batchelor, *Boxing Companion* (London: Eyre & Spottiswoode, 1964), 20.
6. "Dalmores in Boxing Bout," *New York Times*, March 18, 1909.
7. Jack Cavanaugh, *Tunney: Boxing's Brainiest Champ and His Upset of the Great Jack Dempsey* (New York: Random House, 2006), 76.
8. Tracy Callis, Chuck Hasson, and Mike Delisa, *Philadelphia's Boxing Heritage: 1876–1976* (Charleston, SC: Arcadia, 2002), 9.
9. Jack McKinney, *Philadelphia Daily News*, "Johnny Bang-Bang," October 1961, the week before Alford's fight with Clarence Dews on October 16.

I. THE YOUNG

1. A common theme: Muhammad Ali supposedly began boxing after his bicycle was taken, on the recommendation of a police officer. Ali, though, belonged to the Louisville middle class, while Young belonged to the burgeoning North Philly ghetto. Young wouldn't overlook this difference years later, upon challenging Ali.

2. Says former world bantamweight champ Jeff Chandler: "I had fought three or four times in the Blue Horizon at a young age. That's one of the toughest places to fight because it's so small, and everyone's right on top of each other. They're so close watching you when you fight. They got a balcony hanging right over the top of the ring. So you got people watching from the bottom of the floor and people from the top watching over you. So if you can't fight, they know it. You get caught. If you can fight, they know it."

3. Dave Anderson, *New York Times*, April 29, 1976.

4. For years, this fight was misreported as a first-round KO, probably because of an error in an early wire story.

5. Says Don Elbaum, who managed Shavers then, "She was a pretty good judge."

6. According to a friend, Young believed that Diana Ross was still in The Supremes, and he badly wanted to meet her. But he considered himself so battered, so embarrassed, that he refused to leave the dressing room after the fight and risk having her see him in that state.

7. This was a common nickname for Young in London, where he made many fans and spurred one reporter to write: "Young has talent and was a good winner. There will rarely be better!" (Edward F. Dolan and Richard B. Lyttle, *Jimmy Young, Heavyweight Challenger*, 37).

8. Young's manager at the time, Frank Gelb, says, "He was a defensive fighter and not a popular fighter. One of the big arguments I had with Russell Peltz when I would take certain fights to him: 'Would you promote and I'll manage?' I think if you take a look at Jimmy's record we *had* to travel. Russell Peltz turned him down. He didn't want any parts of him. He wasn't an exciting fighter."

9. Shavers's manager Don Elbaum says, "It was a fight right down the middle, and I thought Earnie won by one round, and I don't want to say it was biased. I was his adviser, so certainly I was biased. Jimmy was one of the slickest heavyweights around."

10. According to the FBI.

11. I declined their "offer."

12. Bill Lyon, *Philadelphia Inquirer*, April 29, 1976.

13. Lyon, *Philadelphia Inquirer*.

14. Tris Dixon, *Boxing News*, August 15, 2003.

15. This game of seduction mirrors the inner-city game played by adolescent boys, where "to the young man the woman becomes, in the most profound sense, a sexual object," according to Elijah Anderson's *Code of the Streets.* "Her body and mind are the object of a sexual game, to be won for his personal aggrandizement. Status goes to the winner, and sex is prized as a testament not of love but of control over another human being. The goal of

sexual conquests is to make a fool of the young woman." It's worth noting here Earnie Shavers's regrets: "I was young and foolish, and I let Don mistreat me."

16. "I sat there and listened to him, knowing where he was heading because of the people he was with," recalls Russell Peltz. "But I didn't say anything. And they, they just robbed him blind. It was terrible."

17. To quote the brilliant Hugh McIlvanney, King is "a hawk in peacock's feathers."

18. Jack Newfield, *Only in America: The Life and Crimes of Don King* (New York: William Morrow, 1995), 31.

19. It was then–*New York Post* columnist Larry Merchant who began calling him "Ali Baby" in 1967 "to suggest that he wasn't the grim religious fanatic he frequently was pictured as."

20. This from Hugh McIlvanney's "Requiem for the Heavyweights," first published in 1975 by Britain's *Guardian* and one of the most beautiful, elegiac essays ever written on this silly, vicious, poignant sport. The cited paragraph in its entirety: "The morning's work in the Philippines had drained him as none of his previous 50 fights—not even his two defeats, the first epic with Frazier and the night Ken Norton broke his jaw—had drained him. No champion in history has ever had access to a greater storeroom of physical and spiritual reserves, but Frazier seemed to have emptied it, to have forced Ali to lift the floorboards and scrape the very foundations of his nature for the last traces of strength. Ali's subsequent assertion that he wanted to retire as early as the tenth round was familiar hyperbole, but there was an aching honesty about a later admission: 'I felt like quittin' at the end of the fourteenth, well, not like quittin' but like I didn't want to go no more.' On the way back to the dressing room his face had the greyness of terminal exhaustion and he moved as if the marrow of his bones had been replaced by mercury."

21. Ibid.

22. Years later, not unlike Young, Koranicki would wind up punchy and bipolar and living with his brother John. One day, John's kids would come home from school to find Koranicki OD'd on the floor. The man who once took on James "Quick" Tillis and Gerrie Coetzee has been in and out of psychiatric hospitals ever since.

23. America was also looking to retake boxing from Nixon's co-opting hands, which penned this line about meeting Russian Premier Nikita Khrushchev: "I felt like a fighter wearing sixteen-ounce gloves and bound by Marquis of Queensberry rules, up against a bare-knuckle slugger who had gouged, kneed, and kicked."

24. This is according to Howard Cosell, who sat ringside. On videotapes, it sounds like "Keep movin'."

25. The bout was scored on the five-point must system, meaning that the winner of each round received five points and, since there were no knockdowns or point deductions, the loser received four.

26. A note on my description of Young–Ali: At least one newspaper reporter later questioned ABC's coverage of the fight, saying that the channel—that is, Howard Cosell—must have skewed the action because most writers at ringside had Ali winning, whereas most people watching on television thought Young dominated. In general, I'd almost always side with the writers, since they had seen enough in their day to tease out the nuances of boxers' interplay. However, in this instance, I believe those watching television, through the power of a zoomed-in lens, saw the fight with greater clarity and precision. I say this having watched tape of the fight multiple times, often at 1/6th real time, in order to grasp each motion exactly. And in many instances, I saw both fighters miss punches or barely graze each other on shots the writers and Cosell had deemed powerful. In most cases, though, it was Ali missing by inches on exchanges that seemed damaging in real time. For instance, in round eleven, Ali missed with a right and Young then ducked into the ropes. I watched this multiple times to ensure that Ali had actually missed. But Cosell said on air, "A good right lead by Ali! It's probably his best blow of the night."

27. Bill Lyon, *Philadelphia Inquirer*, May 1, 1976.

28. Michael Katz, *New York Times*, June 17, 1976.

29. Bill Lyon, *Philadelphia Inquirer*, March 17, 1977.

30. Dave Anderson, *New York Times*, March 17, 1977.

31. Anderson, *New York Times*.

32. Dave Anderson, *New York Times*, March 18, 1977.

33. All further unattributed announcer quotes come from Sheridan.

34. Thirty years later in his autobiography, *By George*, Foreman would write that Don King influenced him to go easy on Young early in order to prolong the bout. He'd say he had the chance to KO Young in the third and chose not to, and that in the seventh, "instead of delivering the crowning blow, I wondered whether Don King would be satisfied with a seven-round bout." Perhaps some indecision factored into Foreman's failure and Young's escape. But retrospect is a tricky thing, memories a hazy game, and the film explains itself: Young did escape. Foreman couldn't finish. And whatever reasons one can proffer remain moot: the fight stands. And only Young left the ring a winner.

35. Dave Anderson, *New York Times*, May 12, 1977.

36. Dave Anderson, *New York Times*, March 19, 1977.

37. Pat Putnam of *Sports Illustrated* called it "fifteen rounds of unremitting action, with each man alternately rising to or retreating from the occasion."

38. Referee Carlos Padilla would become notorious a few years later for separating clinching fighters too soon, thus precluding the legitimate and important tactic of infighting. In 1980, middleweight Vito Antuofermo lost his undisputed title after a bout in which Padilla prevented him from working inside. And three months later, infighter Roberto Duran tried to prevent Padilla from working his bout against Sugar Ray Leonard.

39. Leonard Koppett, *New York Times*, November 6, 1977.

40. John Cheever, *The Stories of John Cheever* (New York: Vintage Books, 2000), 603.

41. Dave Anderson, *New York Times*, November 7, 1977.

42. Pat Putnam, *Sports Illustrated*, November 14, 1977.

43. Later, they'd match Ocasio with Holmes, and Ocasio would lose by TKO in the seventh.

44. Nat Carnes, *Associated Press*, January 28, 1979.

45. Respectively, these are the figures Young gave to British reporter Tris Dixon for an August 15, 2003, *Boxing News* interview and to two fans, Tom Jess and Tom Space.

46. On page 208 of Jack Newfield's *Only in America*, Dokes says, "I was using blow steady since 1982. . . . Don King hurt me. One time I went to Cleveland to ask Don for some money when I was in a jam with the IRS. He said he didn't have any money and I started to cry. I loved that man. I looked up to him like he was my daddy. I even tried to comb my hair so I could look like him. And he had this big mansion, and millions of dollars, and he wouldn't help me out just a little. I became suicidal, close to a nervous breakdown. And I was still doing drugs all the time."

47. The children's book is odd, at the very least. Jimmy Young was no longer a contender, let alone a champion, at the time, so he made for an unusual children's book subject. More unusual: the writers go out of their way to include the allegations of mob ties and to argue strenuously that they aren't true. Why? Why not write about a boxer with actual promise? I have a hunch that there were external forces at work here. We're in the realm of children's literature, I know, and yet, would you put it past any of these characters? Thirty years later, though, it's a hard crime to pin on anyone.

48. Michael Katz, *New York Times*, May 3, 1982.

49. Dave Anderson, *New York Times*, February 11, 1978.

50. Marc Duvoisin, *Philadelphia Inquirer*, January 6, 1986.

51. George Anastasia, *Philadelphia Inquirer*, January 16, 1986.

52. Marcus Hayes, *Philadelphia Daily News*, January 22, 1996.

53. Gayle Ronan Sims, *Philadelphia Inquirer*, February 23, 2005.

2. THE WORKERS

1. Steven Conn, *Metropolitan Philadelphia: Living with the Presence of the Past* (Philadelphia: University of Pennsylvania Press, 2006), 72.

2. Russell F. Weigley, ed., *Philadelphia: A 300-Year History* (New York: W. W. Norton, 1982), 467.

3. Jack Cavanaugh, *Tunney: Boxing's Brainiest Champ and His Upset of the Great Jack Dempsey* (New York: Random House, 2006), 268.

4. Cavanaugh, *Tunney*, 281.

5. Cavanaugh, *Tunney*, 103.

6. Carlo Rotella, *Good with Their Hands: Boxers, Bluesmen, and Other Characters from the Rust Belt* (Berkeley: University of California Press, 2002), 44.

7. Joe T. Darden, ed., *Philadelphia: Neighborhoods, Division, and Conflict in a Postindustrial City* (Philadelphia: Temple University Press, 1991), 6.

8. A. J. Liebling, *The Sweet Science* (Westport, CT: Greenwood Press, 1973), 218.

9. Says Bobby "Boogaloo" Watts of the move: "Uh well, the country living and living in the north—much different. A lot more activities and things that were happening in the cities—a lot of corner guys. And that was one of the reasons that pushed me to the gym because, you know, you had jitterbugs on the corner and all that, and they push you to learn how to go fight, something like that, so you can hold your own. . . . I wasn't expecting jitterbugs hanging on the corner. And you walk two, three blocks up, and you're in different territory and getting chased home from school and all. That was the big difference. I didn't know it was like gangs."

10. Jack McKinney, *Philadelphia Daily News*, November 20, 1959.

11. Upon entering the International Boxing Hall of Fame, George Benton said, "I was lucky enough. My father, being a black man, couldn't get into the unions, so he would support us doing odd jobs. He told me, 'No matter what you do, don't be a thief or a crook. Find a job and stick with it.'"

12. Bernard Fernandez, *Philadelphia Daily News*, February 13, 2007.

13. Tracy Callis, Chuck Hasson, and Mike Delisa, *Philadelphia's Boxing Heritage: 1876–1976* (Charleston, SC: Arcadia, 2002), 60.

14. A great story of wartime industry: according to his recent obituary, Giosa's colleagues hung a punching bag and sewed a robe with the RCA logo. Every time the plant shipped out more war equipment, they had Giosa hit the bag "for luck" and ring a bell.

15. This is how Miller later described the setting of Willy Loman's flashbacks.

16. Weigley, *Philadelphia: A 300-Year History* , 596.

17. *New York Times*, September 23, 1928.

18. *New York Times*, February 15, 1925.

19. *New York Times*, September 3, 1928.

20. Darden, *Philadelphia: Neighborhoods, Division, and Conflict in a Post-industrial City*, 103.

21. Darden, *Philadelphia: Neighborhoods, Division, and Conflict in a Post-industrial City*, 31.

22. Chuck Hasson, *International Boxing Digest*, November/December 1998.

23. Jack Fried, *Philadelphia Sports Writers Banquet Program*, 1954.

24. Arthur Daley, *New York Times Magazine*, January 31, 1954.

25. Charles Einstein, *Harper's Magazine*, August 1956.

26. Philadelphia was known for producing splendid left-hookers, and Charley Scott was known as an exceptional specimen of such. Larry Merchant wrote a piece for the *Daily News* about the Philly boy's education: "They would give him a rattle in his crib," he recalled writing. "And teach him the left hook from that point on."

27. *Time*, September 4, 1964.

28. Mark Kram, *Sports Illustrated*, June 19, 1967.

29. Nathaniel Burt, *Harper's Magazine*, September 1964.

30. S. Kirson Weinberg and Henry Arond, "The Occupational Culture of the Boxer," *American Journal of Sociology* 57 (March 1952), 462.

31. South Philly's Rizzo served two terms in the '70s. He spoke mostly of cracking down on crime, which was usually code for cracking down on the perceived misbehavior of North Philly blacks. In this era of dangerous streets, the message met a receptive audience. Rizzo died of a heart attack while running for a third term in 1991, but Philadelphians will always remember him for his cantankerous vivacity. "Creep—get out of here!" he once barked to a local TV correspondent near his home. "Show what kind of a man you are! You're less than a man! You're a crumbum! I want to fight you because you're a crumb-creep-lush-coward! I know a lush when I see one—and you are a lush!"

32. The Black Mafia was an organized crime group founded in 1968 that worked gambling rackets and the illegal drug trade and was responsible for many murders. Its '80s offshoot, the Junior Black Mafia, trafficked in crack.

33. John R. Tunis, *New York Times Magazine*, November 6, 1949.

34. Zach Berman, *Philadelphia Inquirer*, January 16, 2008.

35. Tom Cushman, *Philadelphia Daily News*, May 20, 1969.

36. Current promoter and Atlantic City hairdresser Diane "Dee Lee" Fischer has a similar story, having suffered the 1982 loss of her sixteen-year-old daughter, Dawn, in a car accident and the dissolution of three marriages.

37. Peltz doesn't remember asking to work with Lucchese, but Lucchese recalled the period thoroughly.

38. Gene Courtney, *Philadelphia Inquirer*, November 16, 1971.

3. THE KID

1. Bernard Fernandez, *Philadelphia Daily News*, January 31, 1994.

2. Stan Hochman, *Knight-Ridder News Service*, March 31, 1990.

3. Bernard Fernandez, *Philadelphia Daily News*, October 30, 1992.

4. Fernandez, *Philadelphia Daily News*.

5. The losses also prompted *Daily News* writer Bernard Fernandez to say Taylor was no longer the fighter he once was. So Taylor stopped speaking to Fernandez, until two lawyers set up a reconciliation meeting. "I'm a Philadelphia fighter," Taylor began. "You're a Philadelphia writer. You should be writing more good things about me." "You fight 'em good, I'll write 'em good," Fernandez said. "You fight 'em bad, I'll write 'em bad."

6. Bernard Fernandez, *Philadelphia Inquirer*, May 7, 1993.

7. Tim Kawakami, *Los Angeles Times*, January 30, 1994.

8. At this point, after Taylor lost to Darren Maciunski following the Kidd fight in 1996, Don Elbaum urged Taylor to retire and refused to promote him further. Elbaum says he only helped Taylor because the fighter had been "fucked out of a million dollars" and was broke. Of his time promoting Taylor, he adds, "I have many discussions—I'll even say arguments—with commissioners and boxing people. You know, many fighters just don't have any place else to go when their days are over. Incredibly, I can understand that the only thing they can do is fight. I can understand that, and I have arguments with commissioners. I say, if the fighter can completely pass the physical, no one has the right to tell him he can't fight. I may not want to see him fight. I know they're doing this to protect you, but they have no place else to go. What you do, you do. There's no money put away for anyone. There's no unions.

"I've done this. Did it hurt me? Let me tell you what I did. I got people down my back on this. I'm glad he went to me because I did all I could to look out for him. I was not going to put him in over his head. I was looking to get him one major payday. There were a couple people I turned down because I thought he'd get destroyed. I didn't even tell him about them."

9. Dave Racher, *Philadelphia Daily News*, June 21, 2000.

10. Gene Courtney, *Philadelphia Inquirer*, November 12, 1975.

11. Joyce Carol Oates, *On Boxing* (New York: Harper Perennial, 2006), 70.

12. About this phenomenon, promoter Don Elbaum says, "You know something, I got a problem. Is he like he was prior to the first Chavez fight? No. I

have not talked to him in a year. I didn't notice the gait. Somewhat I noticed the slowness of the speech. This man gets so ripped apart because of the situation. I get so mad when someone calls a fighter 'punch-drunk.' It's like calling a black 'nigger' or a Jew 'kike.' It just bugs me so much. I understand the coming back, and I get big arguments on this. *What are they gonna do?* Are they gonna do it on the street? Start robbing? What else do they have? You just have to make sure they're matched correctly. As long as they can pass their physical."

13. Pierce Egan, *Boxiana* (London: G. Virtue, 1829), 145.

4. THE DEAD

1. The glut of pharma companies in Philly perhaps presages the area's reemergence as a "global city." Sociologist Saskia Sassen writes that one overlooked feature of the dispersal of firms' operations in the age of globalization is those firms' consequent needs for headquarters of overseers in cities with a concentration of professionals. She adds that such cities allow innovators to interact and coordinate services most efficiently, and one sees this in the agglomeration of pharmaceuticals in Philly. In November 2007, for instance, the heads of GlaxoSmithKline and Merck cut a deal that seemingly benefited both: Merck sold the rights to its statin drug Mevacor to Glaxo. Merck had once made a ton of money off the drug, but it was poised to go over the counter, an area in which Merck doesn't specialize. Glaxo, though, has made a point of targeting the over-the-counter market. So Merck got money for research, and Glaxo got another drug. Seemingly a win-win, though the FDA ultimately denied Mevacor's over-the-counter bid.

Philly still has a long way to go before it reenters the world's business elite.

2. Tracy Callis, Chuck Hasson, and Mike Delisa, *Philadelphia's Boxing Heritage: 1876–1976* (Charleston, SC: Arcadia, 2002), 10.

3. *New York Times*, March 21, 1897.

4. *New York Times*, March 21, 1897.

5. *New York Times*, December 24, 1900.

6. Callis, Hasson, and Delisa, *Philadelphia's Boxing Heritage*, 30.

7. *New York Times*, December 24, 1905.

8. *New York Times*, January 20, 1908.

9. *New York Times*, April 20, 1910.

10. *New York Times*, August 14, 1910.

11. *New York Times*, August 21, 1910.

12. *New York Times*, March 18, 1916.

13. *New York Times*, April 1, 1930.

14. Chuck Hasson, *International Boxing Digest*, November/December 1998.

15. Mark Kram, *Sports Illustrated*, March 10, 1969.

16. Murray Dubin, *Philadelphia Inquirer*, November 29 and December 5, 1977.

17. Vince Kasper, *Philadelphia Daily News*, March 21, 1986.

18. Thomas J. Gibbons, *Philadelphia Inquirer*, August 14, 1988.

19. Dan Gelston, Associated Press, February 19, 2005.

20. Pierce Egan, *Boxiana* (London: G. Virtue, 1829), 5–6.

5. THE WORKSITES

1. Stephen Noyes Winslow, *Biographies of Successful Philadelphia Merchants* (Philadelphia: James K. Simon, 1864), 178.

2. Ron Avery, *Philadelphia Daily News*, January 9, 1995.

3. Tom Cushman, *Philadelphia Daily News*.

4. When I told one local boxing fixture about my four-hour interview with Michael, he said, "That's all? You're lucky!"

5. Frank Rubino, *Philadelphia Weekly*, November 12, 2003.

6. Bernard Fernandez, *Philadelphia Daily News*, March 27, 2003.

7. Eye changes the precise wording of this with each retelling.

8. This is how writer Bernard Fernandez once described him: "Don Elbaum was telling a great story, which is how most of Elbaum's stories turn out. And if the truth occasionally gets in the way before the big finish, hey, how many great stories always stick to the straight and narrow?"

9. If the building had absorbed the surrounding row house architecture, it would benefit at least from being *of* the neighborhood instead of merely *in* it. But the building seems designed to quell emotion—that mercurial force that can breed love and violence. And the school hovers on the block as an imposition, as alien to its surroundings as homework to gangs. The school's effort to negate this effect, a mural on the wall facing Broad Street, depresses all the more for its strained and saccharine composition. For the obvious impossibility of its success, its failure at keeping it real.

10. The School District of Philadelphia provides these figures, which are for the 2006–2007 academic year. Across the city, an average of 74.4 percent of students receive free or reduced-price lunches.

11. Michael Decourcy Hines, *New York Times*, April 6, 1993.

12. John F. Morrison, *Philadelphia Daily News*, August 25, 1983.

13. Mark Kram, *Ghosts of Manila* (New York: HarperCollins, 2001), 29. Gypsy Joe Harris should've been the champion produced by the Arena. Kram

called him "a point-building, skittering electron that released a volume of leather from any angle." The reason he so excited crowds at the Arena, the reason his style was so unique was because he had been blinded in one eye as a teenager by a brick thrown at his face. He had to fight the way he did in order to survive—until the commission barred him from fighting after seemingly overlooking his blindness for a full decade. Yeah, Gypsy *was* the '60s, just as the workman light-heavyweight Harold Johnson from Manayunk in the northwest part of the city *was* the '50s. And it was in the Arena that the greatest mystery of Johnson's career unfolded. It was '55, and the number-one ranked Johnson was preparing to fight a young Cuban on TV. But after the weigh-in at the downtown Finance Building, Johnson wandered a hallway while his trainer made small talk with others (the following version of events follows Johnson's account to police detective Thomas Boyce). A swarthy-looking man with short, curly black hair appeared, carrying a paper bag and eating an orange. He sidled up to Johnson and began talking to him as if Johnson knew him. "Here," he said. "Have an orange. They're good for you." And Johnson ate it in his locker room that night, and turning to his trainer, said, "This is bitter. As bitter as you are." Later, after the second round, Johnson collapsed on his stool, and the crowd at the Arena screamed in confusion, and the doctor told the ref to end it. Johnson's dilated pupils suggested a drugging, and tests revealed traces of barbiturate in Johnson's urine from either Nembutal or Seconal. To this day no one really knows what happened.

14. Mark Bowden, *Doctor Dealer* (New York: Grove Press, 2001), 156.

15. Bowden, *Doctor Dealer*, 176.

16. This is what the man told cops initially, though he later claimed to be innocent and said the cops forced his confession under duress. He was convicted of risking a catastrophe and recklessly endangering others but not arson.

17. One of these was called Mammy's and featured a logo of an overweight black woman with a handkerchief tied around her head, her mountainous bosom heaving over her apron. It wasn't quite politically correct.

18. Tendler's manager, Phil Glassman, also owned a half-interest in the Arena in the '30s.

19. Sugar Ray Robinson with Dave Anderson, *Sugar Ray* (New York: Da Capo Press, 1994), 102–5.

20. Albert H. Morehead, *New York Times*, June 24, 1961.

21. Harold J. Wiegand, *Phildelphia Inquirer*, May 30, 1983.

22. Russell Sullivan, *Rocky Marciano: The Rock of His Times* (Champaign: University of Illinois Press, 2002), 38.

23. A. J. Liebling, *The Sweet Science* (Westport: Greenwood Press, 1973), 93.

24. Liebling, *The Sweet Science*, 92.

6. THE NEW OLD SCENE

1. Don Steinberg, *Philadelphia Inquirer*, November 17, 2006.

2. One could tell an insider of those days from a poseur by his pronunciation. The black boxing crowd called the place the "A-la-HAM-bri-a."

3. Benjamin Herold, *Philadelphia CityPaper*, September 16-22, 2004.

4. Dwight Ott, *Philadelphia Inquirer*, August 17, 2007.

5. Barbara Laker, *Philadelphia Daily News*, March 1, 2004.

6. A different message than that of middleweight Joe Christy's tattoos, which read, "Bad Boy," "Philly Style," and "SWP," which stands for Southwest Philly.

7. Clark DeLeon, *Philadelphia Inquirer*, February 6, 1989.

8. THE ALIVE

1. Mark Kram, *Sports Illustrated*, March 18, 1968.

2. Tim Graham, *ESPN.com*, February 20, 2001.

3. "Heavies Stay Lite," *Sports Illustrated*, December 31, 2007.

4. Bill Simmons, *ESPN the Magazine*, December 31, 2007.

5. Cunningham described fighting on the road better than I ever could: "I have Philadelphia with me every time I beat my opponents. I went to Germany; Philly was with me. I went to Poland twice; Philly was with me. I went to South Africa, and Philly was with me. It's in my heart. It's something in the air out here. I'm breathing that air in deep."

6. Don Steinberg, *Philadelphia Inquirer*, January 21, 2008.

7. John Ourand, *Street & Smith's SportsBusiness Journal*, August 20–26, 2007.

8. David Staba, *Niagara Falls Reporter*, August 28, 2007.

9. Bernard Fernandez, *Philadelphia Daily News*, April 4, 2008.

EPILOGUE

1. John Morrison, *Philadelphia Daily News*, March 20, 2013.

BIBLIOGRAPHY

Anderson, Dave. *In the Corner: Great Boxing Trainers Talk about Their Art*. New York: Morrow, 1991.

Anderson, Elijah. *Code of the Street: Decency, Violence, and the Moral Life of the Inner City*. New York: W. W. Norton, 2000.

Avery, Ron. *A Concise History of Philadelphia*. Philadelphia: Otis Books, 1999.

Batchelor, Denzil. *The Boxing Companion*. London: Eyre & Spottiswoode, 1964.

Becker, Ernest. *The Denial of Death*. New York: Free Press, 1973.

Bissinger, H. G. *A Prayer for the City*. New York: Vintage Books, 1999.

Bluestone, Barry, and Bennett Harrison. *The Deindustrialization of America: Plant Closings, Community Abandonment, and the Dismantling of Basic Industries*. New York: Basic Books, 1982.

Bowden, Mark. *Doctor Dealer*. New York: Grove Press, 2001.

Callis, Tracy, Chuck Hasson, and Mike DeLisa. *Philadelphia's Boxing Heritage: 1876–1976*. Charleston, SC: Arcadia, 2002.

Cavanaugh, Jack, and Gene Tunney. *Tunney: Boxing's Brainiest Champ and His Upset of the Great Jack Dempsey*. New York: Random House, 2006.

Conn, Steven. *Metropolitan Philadelphia: Living with the Presence of the Past*. Philadelphia: University of Pennsylvania Press, 2006.

Darden, Joe. *Philadelphia: Neighborhoods, Division, and Conflict in a Postindustrial City*. Philadelphia: Temple University Press, 1993.

Davis, Allen Freeman, and Mark H. Haller. *The Peoples of Philadelphia: A History of Ethnic Groups and Lower-Class Life, 1790–1940*. Philadelphia: Temple University Press, 1973.

Dolan, Edward F., and Richard B. Lyttle. *Jimmy Young, Heavyweight Challenger*. Garden City, NY: Doubleday, 1979.

Dubin, Murray. *South Philadelphia: Mummers, Memories, and the Melrose Diner*. Philadelphia: Temple University Press, 1996.

Du Bois, W. E. B. *The Negro*. Philadelphia: University of Pennsylvania Press, 2001.

Early, Gerald. *The Culture of Bruising: Essays on Prizefighting, Literature, and Modern American Culture*. Hopewell, NJ: Ecco Press, 1994.

Egan, Pierce. *Boxiana, or, Sketches of Ancient & Modern Pugilism*. London: George Virtue, 1829.

Foreman, George, and Joel Engel. *By George: The Autobiography of George Foreman*. New York: Villard Books, 1995.

Giacomo, Donna J. *Italians of Philadelphia*. Charleston, SC: Arcadia, 2007.

Heller, Peter. *"In This Corner—!": Forty-two World Champions Tell Their Stories*. New York: Da Capo Press, 1994.

Holmes, Larry, and Phil Berger. *Larry Holmes: Against the Odds*. New York: St. Martin's Press, 1998.

Iatarola, Louis M., and Lynn Iatarola. *Lower Northeast Philadelphia*. Charleston, SC: Arcadia, 2005.

Kram, Mark. *Ghosts of Manila: The Fateful Blood Feud between Muhammad Ali and Joe Frazier*. New York: HarperCollins, 2001.

Licht, Walter. *Getting Work: Philadelphia, 1840–1950*. Cambridge, MA: Harvard University Press, 1992.

Liebling, A. J. *The Sweet Science*. Westport, CT: Greenwood Press, 1973.

Lommasson, Jim. *Shadow Boxers: Sweat, Sacrifice & the Will to Survive in American Boxing Gyms*. Milford, NJ: Stone Creek, 2005.

Mauger, Edward Arthur. *Philadelphia Then & Now*. San Diego: Thunder Bay Press, 2002.

McIlvanney, Hugh. *The Hardest Game: McIlvanney on Boxing*. Chicago: Contemporary Books, 2001.

Merchant, Larry. *Ringside Seat at the Circus*. New York: Holt, Rinehart and Winston, 1976.

Molock, Anthony. *Gypsy Joe Harris: Son of Philadelphia*. Bloomington, IN: AuthorHouse, 2006.

Newfield, Jack. *Only in America: The Life and Crimes of Don King*. New York: William Morrow, 1995.

Norton, Ken, Marshall Terrill, and Mike Fitzgerald. *Going the Distance*. Champaign, IL: Sports Publishing, 2000.

Oates, Joyce Carol. *On Boxing*. New York: Harper Perennial, 2006.

Robinson, Sugar Ray, and Dave Anderson. *Sugar Ray: The Sugar Ray Robinson Story*. New York: Da Capo Press, 1994.

Rotella, Carlo. *Good with Their Hands: Boxers, Bluesmen, and Other Characters from the Rust Belt*. Berkeley: University of California Press, 2002.

Sawyer, Tom. *Noble Art: An Artistic & Literary Celebration of the Old English Prize-Ring*. London: Unwin Hyman, 1989.

Schulberg, Budd. *Ringside: A Treasury of Boxing Reportage*. Chicago: Ivan R. Dee, 2006.

Skaler, Robert Morris. *Philadelphia's Broad Street: South and North*. Charleston, SC: Arcadia, 2003.

Sullivan, Russell. *Rocky Marciano: The Rock of His Times*. Urbana: University of Illinois Press, 2002.

Teitelman, Edward, and Richard W. Longstreth. *Architecture in Philadelphia: A Guide*. Cambridge, MA: MIT Press, 1974.

Warner, Sam Bass. *The Private City: Philadelphia in Three Periods of Its Growth*. Philadelphia: University of Pennsylvania Press, 1987.

Weigley, Russell Frank, Nicholas B. Wainwright, and Edwin Wolf. *Philadelphia: A 300-Year History*. New York: W. W. Norton, 1982.

Winslow, Stephen Noyes. *Biographies of Successful Philadelphia Merchants*. Philadelphia: J. K. Simon, 1864.

INDEX